D0199283

DAILY LIFE OF THE AZTECS

DAILY LIFE OF
THE AZTECS

ON THE EVE OF
THE SPANISH CONQUEST

Jacques Soustelle

TRANSLATED FROM THE FRENCH BY
Patrick O'Brian

STANFORD UNIVERSITY PRESS
STANFORD, CALIFORNIA

Originally published as
*La vie quotidienne des aztèques à la veille
de la conquête espagnole*
(Paris: Hachette, 1955)

Stanford University Press
Stanford, California
English translation © 1961 by George Weidenfeld & Nicolson Ltd
Originating publisher: George Weidenfeld & Nicolson Ltd, London
First published in the United States by
The Macmillan Company, 1962
Paperback edition first published in 1970 by Stanford University Press
Printed in the United States of America
ISBN 0-8047-0721-9
LC 77-110282
Last figure below indicates year of this printing:
90 89 88 87 86 85

'For as long as the world shall endure, the honour and the glory of Mexico-Tenochtitlan must never be forgotten.'

Chimalpahin Quauhtlehuanitzin

CONTENTS

CHARLES GREEN

Lake Zumpango

Lake Xaltocan

Teulayucan

Tepotzotlan

Cuahtitlan

Teotihuacan

Chiconauhtla

Acolman

Tepexpan

Ecatepec

Lake

Tenayuca
El Arbolillo
Ticoman
Zacatenco

Texoco

Azcapotzalco
Coyotlatelco
Tlacopone
Tepeyac

Texcoco

Chapingo
Huexotla

Tlaltelolco
MEXICO –
TENOCHTITLAN

Coatlinchan

Chapultepec

Acachinanco

Ixtapalapa

Coyoacan

Tetelpan
Tizapan
Copilco
Churubusco
Culhuacan

Cuilcuilco

Lake
Xochimilco
Xochimilco

Tlahuac

Chalco

Lake Chalco

Tulyahualco

Mixquic

Tetelco

Ayotzingo
Tlalmanalco

Tenongo

VALLEY of MEXICO
and neighbouring cities

– – – – – – – *Hernan Cortes' route*

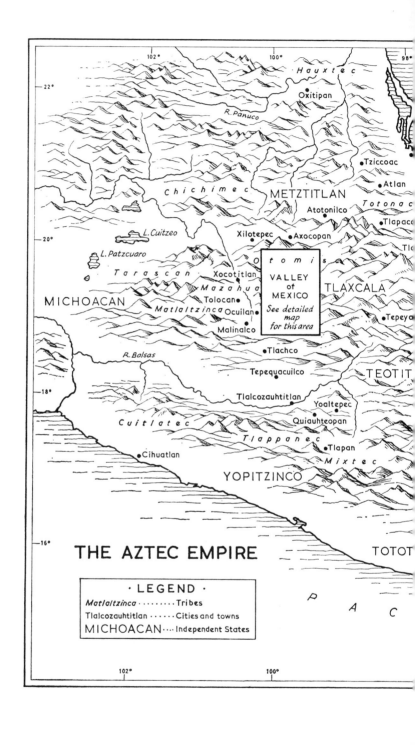

THE AZTEC EMPIRE

· LEGEND ·
Matlaltzinca · · · · · · · · · Tribes
Tlalcozauhtitlan · · · · · · Cities and towns
MICHOACAN · · · · Independent States

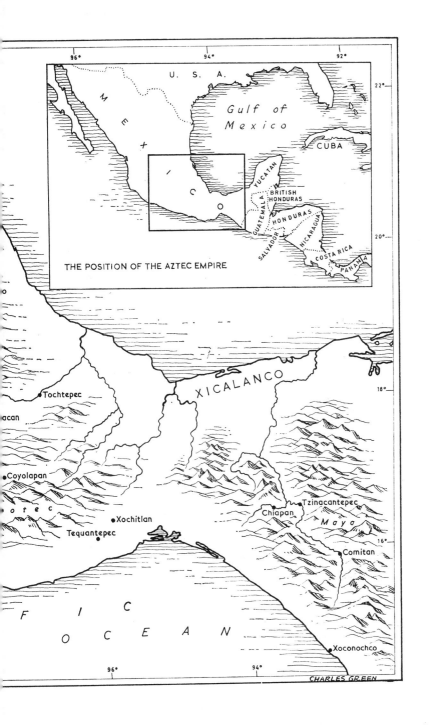

THE POSITION OF THE AZTEC EMPIRE

Tochtepec

acan

Coyolapan

o t e c

Xochitlan

Tequantepec

XICALANCO

Tzinacantepec

Chiapan

M a y a

Comitan

Xoconochco

F I C

O C E A N

CHARLES GREEN

INTRODUCTION

WE MUST first define the subject of this book in space and time, for during the two or three thousand years before our era and up until the fateful year of the European invasion (1519, or one – reed according to the native calendar) many varied civilisations followed one another in the huge expanse of Mexico, rising each in turn like the waves of the sea, and like the waves, falling in ruin.

The subject of this book, then, is the life of the Mexicans – the *Mexica*,[1] as they said themselves – at the beginning of the sixteenth century. The great feast of the New Fire, the 'binding of the years', took place at the end of each native 'century' of fifty-two years; and the last was in the year 1507, during the reign of Motecuhzoma II Xocoyotzin ('the younger'). The Mexican civilisation was then in the full vigour of its rise and of its youth. Scarcely a hundred years had passed since Itzcoatl (1428–1440), the first of the great rulers, had founded the league of the three cities, of which Mexico-Tenochtitlan had become the capital. And it was in this city, on the shores and even on the water of a lake in the hollow of the central valley, seven thousand five hundred feet high and overlooked by snow-capped volcanoes, that the Aztec power was built up – a power which became, within a few decades, the most extensive domination that that part of the world had ever known.

At that time, in 1507, nobody, from the arid steppes of the north to the burning jungles of the isthmus, from the coast of the Gulf of Mexico to the shore of the Pacific, could have believed that this enormous empire, its culture, its art, its gods, were to go down a few years later in a historic cataclysm that makes even the fall of Constantinople seem comparatively mild. In Mexico nobody knew that a white-skinned race from another world already had a footing in the islands of the western sea, and had had it since 1492. Twenty-seven years were to elapse between the first voyage of Columbus and the landing of Hernan Cortés upon the continent – a quarter of a century's respite during which the two worlds lived side by side in mutual ignorance, with no more than an arm of the sea between them.

> *Les peuples tout enfants à peine se découvrent*
> *Par-dessus les buissons nés pendant leur sommeil.*

These lines of de Vigny come to mind when we think of this strange marking time in history. In Europe the modern world was beginning to break out of its enclosing mould: in this same 1507, when the Mexicans once more 'bound the years', lighting the new fire on the summit of the Uixachtecatl, Luther was ordained priest. One year before Leonardo da Vinci had painted the Gioconda, and Bramante had begun Saint Peter's at Rome. France was engaged in her great Italian wars; and in Florence, Niccoló Machiavelli was the secretary of state for the militia. Spain had beaten the Moors of Granada and so had won back the last of her conquered territory; and an irresistible expansion urged the Spanish caravels, soldiers and missionaries towards the newly-discovered lands. But so far the wave had not carried them beyond the islands – Cuba, the Bahamas, Haïti. The coast of the mainland had only just been touched, at Honduras and Darien: not a single white man yet knew that beyond the Strait of Yucatán and the Gulf of Mexico lay huge countries, with their crowded cities, their wars, their states and their temples.

In Mexico there was the same ignorance: no notion that fate was already standing at the door. The emperor continued the methodical organisation of the territories subjected to the *Mexica*, the ruling nation. One by one the last free cities fell; and the distant villages of the tropics bowed to the rule of the high central plain. It is true that some little states kept their independence, particularly the aristocratic republic of Tlaxcala, a besieged enclave in the middle of the empire, cut off from all trade and from any kind of outlet; but the *xochiyaoyotl*, the flowery war, was essential in the very heart of the Mexican peace, for the service of the gods and the glory of the sun.

A few years later and the veil which hid the one world from the other was to be torn away. They would confront one another, steel blades against swords of obsidian, guns against arrows and spear-throwers, iron helmets against feather head-dresses. Palaces, pyramids, raised causeways across the lakes, stone statues and turquoise masks, processions blazing with jewels and plumes, priests, kings, sacred books, all this was to melt and vanish like a dream. Just before it disappears, let us try to catch the iridescent image, the splendour and the shadows of a world already doomed.

These late-comers to the central plateau, the *Mexica*, or Aztecs, as they were sometimes called in memory of Atzlán, the mythical starting-point of their wanderings, never thought of themselves as anything but the heirs of the brilliant civilisations that had preceded them. Their knowledge of the past went back no more than a few hundred years: for them the pyramids of Teotihuacán, which we date from the sixth century, were built by the gods at the beginning of the world, at the same time that they created the sun and the moon. For them all the highly-civilised arts, sculpture, architecture, engraving, feather-mosaic work, the invention of the calendar, were due to the former inhabitants of Tula, the Toltecs, who reached the height of their civilisation in the tenth and eleventh centuries.

The Mexicans placed Tula and its king-god Quetzalcoatl, the Plumed Serpent, in a remote and fabulous past: it was Quetzalcoatl and the Toltecs who had found out the arts and sciences that Mexico had possessed since then. But the black magic of Tezcatlipoca, the dark god of the night sky, had triumphed, and the shining Quetzalcoatl, exiled from Mexico, had set out over the Atlantic, 'the heavenly water'; or according to other traditions, had burned himself upon a pyre.

In the chaos that followed the fall of Tula, the wandering tribes of the north, who were known by the general name of *Chichimeca*, the equivalent of the Greek 'barbarians', came into the central plateau in successive waves; and at this point legend and history join. In the twelfth century began a great movement that brought the migrating nations southward one after another, nations of hunters and warriors, houseless and knowing nothing of agriculture or weaving.

These tribes, coming into contact with what was left of the Toltec civilisation and with the settled farming inhabitants who had stayed after the collapse of Tula, very soon set up villages and towns and adopted the way of life of their predecessors. They abandoned their rustic dialects in favour of the classical Nahuatl of the Mexicans: they built cities, Colhuacán, Atzcapotzalco, Texcoco, in which the upper classes led a highly civilised existence; and these cities fought for supremacy in the valley, each in turn winning it from the others. It was in this world, so reminiscent of Renaissance Italy, full of battles, plots and astonishing reverses, that a poor, unwelcome, humiliated tribe managed to acquire a few little swampy islands in the lake from their powerful neighbours. The *Mexica* founded their capital, a wretched village of reed huts, around the temple of Uitzilopochtli, the jealous and unyielding god who had guided them during a hundred and fifty years of migration. All about them stretched marshes, with no arable land, no timber or stone for building; the dry land was all owned by the established cities, and they rigidly held on to their fields, woods and quarries. It was in 1325 that these wanderers first settled in the dismal place that they were allowed – a place, however, in which they had seen the sign that their god had promised them, an eagle poised upon a cactus, eating a serpent. Another fifty years had to go by before they could arrive at a satisfactory organisation and name their first sovereign, Acamapichtli; and even then the Mexican state was still so weak and its destiny so unsure that they were obliged to accept the overlordship of Atzcapotzalco in order to survive, and they were not able to shake it off until 1428.

Nobody could have seen an embryonic empire in these humble beginnings: nobody, except the 'god-bearers', the warrior-priests who had been the attendants of the image of Uitzilopochtli during the migration, who interpreted his oracles to the people and who had faith in his promise of eventual domination. It was they who formed the primary nucleus of that ruling class which, in less than two hundred years, was to carry the *Mexica* to the height of their imperial power.

xvi

By the early days of the sixteenth century nothing remained of this poor and lowly start except the *chinampas* on the edges of the city, the ingenious floating gardens that were left over from the time when the landless Mexicans had been obliged to make their own earth by piling the mud from the bottom of the lake on to wicker-work rafts. Mexico-Tenochtitlan, the New World's Venice, proudly reared its embankments and its pyramids above the waters: to a score of nations,[2] the name of its emperor, Motecuhzoma, stood for magnificence and power. The wealth of the provinces flowed in: luxury continually increased. Since the fabulous days of Tula, no Indian of Mexico had beheld such marvels.

We know the Mexico of the time of the first coming of the Europeans by many sets of records that can be compared and combined. Archaeological research has yielded a great deal in the valley of Mexico, and one can scarcely open a trench without finding something from Aztec times or earlier. There have been abundant discoveries of ritual and domestic pottery, tools, arms and sculpture: yet as the Mexicans usually burned their dead instead of burying them like the Zapotecs, for example, or the Mixtecs, in this case we do not have the almost inexhaustible fund of utensils, clothes and jewels which the graves supply elsewhere. Furthermore, not a single ancient monument has survived in Mexico City itself, because of the systematic destruction of the town by the Spaniards during the siege of 1521 and after it. So paradoxically we are far better acquainted with the architecture of the distant Mayas, back in the seventh century, than with that of the sixteenth-century Mexicans. The temples and pyramids of Palenque or of Yaxchilán, lost in the jungle of Chiapas, have survived the attack of the weather and the vegetation for more than a thousand years, while those of Mexico have gone down before the destructive will of man.

But the period with which we are concerned is distinguished from all others by the wealth of its written documentation. The Mexicans were interested in themselves and in their history; they were tireless speech-makers and great lovers of verse; they were curious about the manners and productions of other nations. And above all they were preoccupied by the future, and so they paid the greatest attention to omens and portents. Thus an immense quantity of books came into being, written according to a pictographic system that was at once figurative and phonetic,[3] and treating of history, history combined with mythology, geographical description, ritual and divination. The Mexican civilisation knew books: it also knew red tape and piles of official paper. The Aztec empire was of a legalistic humour, and every dispute, every law-case, brought about the accumulation of files: for example, if two villages fell out over their arable land, they supported their testimony with maps and genealogical trees to prove that some given family had rights in the fields in question.

Much of this written record also was deliberately destroyed after the Spanish conquest. Many of the books had to do with religion or magic: Bishop Zumárraga had them seized and burnt, together, no doubt, with others of an entirely secular nature, such as histories, or the like. Fortunately a good many works escaped the fire; and in addition the Indians soon came to see the advantages of the alphabetic writing that the Europeans had brought, compared with the obscure and complex system that they had used hitherto. Basing themselves upon the old pictographic manuscripts (some of them undoubtedly preserved by noble families in spite of the prohibition) they drew up chronicles, sometimes in the Mexican language but in European letters, sometimes in Spanish – chronicles of an immense value, such as the Annals of Cuauhtitlán, the historical books of Chimalpahin Quauhtlehuanitzin, Tezozomoc and Ixtlilxochitl, which are literally crammed with the most exact information about the life of the ancient Mexicans.

Finally, the Spaniards themselves have left us some very important documents. The first wave of invaders, men as uncultivated as they were courageous, nevertheless had as its leader a statesman, Hernan Cortés, and in its ranks a born writer, a man who could both see and tell what he had seen, Bernal Díaz del Castillo. The first European testimony upon what was then a totally unknown world is provided by the letters of Cortés to Charles V and by the recollections that Bernal Díaz dictated in his old age, before he died. Cortés' testimony is more elaborate; Díaz' is spontaneous, amusing, tragic. It is true that neither of them attempted to see and understand objectively; their eyes were chiefly fixed upon fortifications and weapons, wealth and gold. They knew nothing of the native language, which they mangle shockingly whenever they quote a word. They were sincerely disgusted by the Mexican religion, which, as they saw it, was a damnable and revolting mumbo-jumbo of devil-worship. But for all that their evidence retains great value as a record, for through their eyes we see something that was never to be seen by man again.

After the soldiers, the missionaries. The most illustrious of them, Father Bernardino de Sahagún, reached Mexico in 1529. He learnt Nahuatl, and writing in that language under the dictation of Indian nobles and with the help of Indian scribes for the illustration of his manuscript, Sahagún wrote the admirable and monumental book entitled *A General History of the Affairs of New Spain*. He devoted the whole of his life to this work; and it earned him the distrust of the authorities, who took away his papers on two occasions, in 1571 and 1577. Having said farewell to 'his children the Indians'⁴ he died in Mexico in 1590, without having had the satisfaction of seeing the smallest fragment of his book published. Other ecclesiastics, although they did not equal Sahagún, also left respectable works, particularly Motolinía.

In addition to these books of the first importance one should mention the frequently anonymous sixteenth-century Descriptions and Accounts that were written by priests, civil servants or lawyers: although they must often be used with some reserve (a feeling for exactitude not always being the primary characteristic of their authors) they are nevertheless a mine of information. There are also the many native pictographic records which were made after the conquest, such as the *Codex of* 1576, and legal papers, for the litigious turn of both the Indians and the Spaniards had full scope in countless suits over land and taxes;[5] and these are rich in valuable facts.

In short, there is an abundant literature upon the subject, and it allows us to see this last phase of the Mexican civilisation with a vision which, although many unanswered questions leave it imperfect, is nevertheless detailed, vivid and lively.

To avoid both anachronism and confusion we must limit ourselves not only in time but also in space. It is primarily urban life that we are going to describe, the life of the city-dwellers of Mexico-Tenochtitlan. Yet there was an obvious cultural unity between this city and some of its neighbours, particularly Texcoco, on the dry land of the shore of the great lake, and so there is no objection to our using the historical sources available for Texcoco, any more than there is for taking some details of our description from Xochimilco, Chalco, Cuauhtitlán or others. Indeed, everything leads one to believe that life was much the same throughout the valley of Mexico, at least in the towns.

But one cannot leave out all mention of the empire, whose existence, products, political activity and religious ideas had so strong an effect upon the capital itself. The empire began in the fifteenth century as a triple alliance, a three-headed league which joined the city-states of Mexico, Texcoco and Tlacopan (now Tacuba): this league came into being as a consequence of the wars that had destroyed the supremacy of Atzcapotzalco. The original nature of the triple alliance was soon corrupted, however: first Tlacopan and then Texcoco itself found their privileges and their independence growing less and less under the unyielding pressure of the Mexicans. By the beginning of the sixteenth century, although the 'kings' of Tlacopan and Texcoco were still in theory the associates of the Mexican emperor, in fact their association had, to a very large extent, nothing more than an honorary character. The Aztec sovereign intervened in the succession of both dynasties to such a degree that to all intents and purposes he appointed dependents of his own, who were in fact imperial officials: when Cortés entered Mexico he was received by Motecuhzoma,

attended by the two kings and certain appointed governors[6] – an indication of how nearly the status of the kings
had been brought to that of civil servants. Theoretically
the taxes from the provinces were still divided between the
three ruling cities according to the original scale (two-fifths
to Mexico and Texcoco, one-fifth to Tlacopan) but there is
reason to think that in fact the emperor of Tenochtitlan
shared out the taxes more or less as he chose. In all likelihood,
the league was on its way to becoming a single-headed state.

At the end of the reign of Motecuhzoma II, the empire
consisted of thirty-eight tributary provinces;[7] and to these
must be added the little states, of uncertain status, that
stood along the road of the caravans and the armies between
Oaxaca and the southern limits of Xoconochco. It reached
both oceans; the Pacific at Cihuatlán and the Atlantic for
the whole length of the coast of the Gulf from Tochpan to
Tochtepec.[8] In the west its neighbours were the civilised
Tarascas of Michoacán;[9] in the north the hunting nomads,
the *Chichimeca*; and in the north-east the Huaxtecs, a
separated branch of the Maya family. In the south-east the
independent but allied province of Xicalanco formed a kind
of buffer-state between the Mexicans of the centre and the
Mayas of Yucatán. A certain number of lordships or of
tribal confederations had remained independent of Mexico,
either enclosed within the empire or lying on its frontiers:
this was the case with the Nahuatl republic of Tlaxcala on
the central plateau, the lordship of Metztitlán (also Nahuatl)
in the sierras of the north-east, the little Yopi state on the
Pacific coast, and the *Chinanteca* highlanders who lived
then, as they do today, in the impenetrable massif between
the coastal plain and the valleys of Oaxaca.

The provinces themselves were much more fiscal than
political entities. A civil servant, the *calpixqui*, lived in each
provincial capital, charged with the collection of the taxes:
his duties and his powers were limited to this. There were
no governors appointed by the central authority except in
the fortified towns on the frontiers or in the recently subjected lands, as, for example, at Oztoman, opposite the
Tarascan country; at Zozolan in the Mixtec territory; at

Oaxaca; or at Xoconochco on the Mayan border – some fifteen or twenty towns in all. Everywhere else 'province' meant no more than a financial frame within which the incorporated cities lived under widely varying political régimes. Some kept their own chiefs on condition that they paid tribute; others were more severely colonised, and they had new chiefs appointed by Mexico. In every case, each city kept its political and administrative autonomy, with the one condition that it paid its tax, supplied its military contingent and submitted its law-suits to Mexico or Texcoco as the final court of appeal. There was, therefore, no true centralisation: what we call the Aztec empire was in fact a somewhat lax confederation of city-states with widely differing political organisations. Up to the end, Mexican political thought had no conception of anything beyond the city (*altepetl*): the fundamental unit was the autonomous city; it could be allied to others or subjected to another, but nevertheless it remained the essential unit of political structure. The empire was a mosaic of cities.

The existence of the empire, and its condition, had necessarily a great influence upon the ruling city and the manner of life in it. Either by way of tribute or by trade the produce of all the provinces flowed into Mexico, especially tropical wares – formerly unknown upon the central plateau – such as cotton, cocoa, skins, many-coloured feathers, turquoises and finally gold. So luxury could arise in Tenochtitlan, luxury of clothes and ornaments, luxury in eating, luxury in houses and furniture, a luxury founded on the great quantities of every kind of merchandise that continually converged upon the capital from all quarters of the confederation.

On the other hand, an empire formed in this way, with some of its members (Oaxaca, for example) only very recently subjugated, was in the nature of things most uneasy. There was always some city trying to regain its former independence, refusing the tribute and massacring the *calpixqui* and his men.[10] Then a military expedition would have to be sent to restore order and punish the rebels. More and more the Mexican citizen ceased to be

the peasant-soldier of the early days and became a professional fighting-man, continually in the field. The huge
empire, all the vaster in that every journey was a journey
on foot and across naturally difficult country, was like
Penelope's tapestry, always incomplete, always needing more
work; so the Mexican, who in any case was of a warlike
temper, rarely laid aside his arms. The great extent of the
territory meant either that the emperor had to prolong the
campaigns indefinitely, or that he was obliged to keep
standing garrisons in the remoter stations. This was a state
of affairs very far removed from the primitive Mexican
tribe, in which every adult man turned regularly from
military service to the farming of his land, leaving his sword
for his coa.[11] Thus arose a tendency to think that it was the
Aztecs' business to make war, and other peoples' business
to work for them.[12]

Finally, this empire included a great many peoples of
other origins who spoke entirely different languages: it is
true that the central provinces had an essentially Nahua
population, but already the Otomí were living there beside
them, speaking their obscure language and worshipping
their ancient gods of the sun, the wind and the earth, while
to the north it was the Otomí who made up the bulk of the
population of Quahuacan, Xilotepec, Hueypochtla and
Atocpan. In the north-east and the east there were the
Huaxtecs at Oxitipan, Totonacs at Tochpan and Tlapacoyan,
and Mazatecs at Tochtepec. In the south-east there were
Mixtecs at Yoaltepec and Tlachquiauco, and Zapotecs at
Coyolapan. In the borderland of Xoconochco in the south
there were the Mayas; and in the south-west the Tlappanecs
of Quiauhteopan, and the Cuitlatecs and Coixca of
Cihuatlán and Tepequacuilco. Finally, in the west there
were the Mazahua and the Matlaltzinca of Xocotitlán,
Tolocan, Ocuilan and Tlachco.[13] Inevitably the customs
and beliefs of these different nations reacted upon the
ruling tribe. At the time of which we are speaking, the
Mexicans had adopted the feather ornaments of the tropical
races, the amber lip-ornaments[14] of the Mayas of Tzinacantlan,
the particoloured and embroidered clothes of the Totonacs,

the golden jewels of the Mixtecs, as well as the Huextecs' goddess of carnal love and the feast that the Mazatecs held every eighth year in honour of the planet Venus.[15] Their religion was open, their pantheon hospitable: all the little local gods of the agricultural peoples, such as Tepoztecatl, for example, the rustic god of the harvest and strong drink worshipped at Tepoztlán,[16] easily found their way in. Indeed, some rites were accompanied by hymns in the languages of the other countries.[17]

Thus, at the time when the Spaniards came to interrupt its course, there was a historical and social evolution in train which had already transformed the Mexicans from a simple agricultural but wandering tribe, all at one level in a common poverty, into a ruling city-state, supreme over many different countries and nations.

The old tribal society had been profoundly changed by the advent of a class of merchants, who were now beginning to enjoy important privileges, and by the development of the royal power. Official morality extolled the frugality of former ages, just as vainly as it had done in the last days of the Roman republic, and sumptuary laws struggled in vain against the ostentation of luxury.

On the fringe of the rich and brilliant cities, however, the peasant – Nahuatl, Otomí, Zapotec, etc. – continued to lead his patient and laborious life in obscurity. We know almost nothing about him, this *maceualli* whose labour fed the citizens. Sometimes he is to be seen in sculpture,[18] dressed only in a loin-cloth, for embroidered cloaks were out of his reach. He was of no interest to the native or the Spanish chronicler, with his hut, his maize-field, his turkeys, his little monogamous family and his narrow horizon, and they mention him only in passing, between their descriptions and their histories. But it is important to speak of him at this point, if only to make his silent presence felt, in the shadows beyond the brilliance of the urban civilisation: and the more so because after the disaster of 1521 and the total collapse of all authority, all concepts, the whole frame of society and all religion, he alone survived, and he alone still lives.

CHAPTER ONE

THE CITY

Origin and situation. The foundation of Mexico-Tenochtitlan:
the myth of the eagle and the serpent: islets and lakes—Extent
and population. The capital at the beginning of the sixteenth
century: regions and districts: number of inhabitants: the
centre and the suburbs—General appearance; roads and
traffic. Flat roofs and façades: streets and canals: the
causeways across the lake—Public buildings, squares and
market-places. The heart of the capital: the great Teocalli
and the holy city: the imperial palace: the markets: the great
market of Tlatelolco—The problems of a great city.
The supply of drinking water to Mexico: aqueducts: the
danger of flooding: dikes: the town's sanitation. Tenochtitlan
as a young capital. Was the Aztec city an overgrown pueblo
or an American Alexandria?

ORIGIN AND SITUATION

There is some degree of mystery about the city's very name,
for the double term Mexico-Tenochtitlan is not easily
explained. Tenochtitlan offers no great difficulty: it is the
place of the *tenochtli*, the hard-fruited prickly-pear, which,
in the glyph[1] that stands for the name of the city, is
represented by a cactus growing on a rock. But what is the
meaning of Mexico? Some, like Beyer,[2] look for the answer
in the remaining elements of the glyph, that is to say in the
eagle which is perched upon the cactus and which holds a
serpent in its beak: for them this eagle is the symbol of
Mexitl, another name for Uitzilopochtli, the great national
deity. Others[3] disagree with this etymology, and basing
themselves upon the authority of Father Antonio del
Rincón,[4] find in the name of the town the root *metztli*, the
moon, and *xictli*, the navel or centre. Mexico, according to
them, means '(the town) in the middle (of the lake) of
the moon', Metztliapan,[5] the lake of the moon, being the

I

lagoon's former name. And this reading seems to be confirmed by the fact that the Mexicans' neighbours, the Otomí, called the city by the double name *anbondo amedetzânâ*:[6] now *bondo* is the Otomí for prickly-pear, and *amedetzânâ* means 'in the middle of the moon'.

An eagle, poised upon a cactus and devouring a serpent: the arms of the present Republic of Mexico are no more than a faithful copy of the glyph that represented the Aztec city. We find it again, among other places, in the *Codex of 1576*,[7] wound about with reeds and reed-thatched huts. And in the *Codex Mendoza*[8] there is the eagle and the cactus again (but without the serpent) with the caption 'Tenochtitlan'. Each time it is in fact a picture that evokes the origin of the city, a wonderful yet very modest origin: for even at the height of their glory the Mexicans never forgot that their town had been founded in a swamp by a despised and humble tribe.

One of the traditional accounts tells how the old men first discovered, *intollihtic inacaihtic*, 'in the middle of the rushes, in the middle of the reeds', those plants and animals whose presence the god Uitzilopochtli had foretold – a white willow, a white frog and a white fish,[9] etc. 'And when they saw them the old men wept and said, "So it (our town) is to be here, therefore, since we have seen those things that Uitzilopochtli told us of." But the next night the god called the priest Quauhcoatl (Eagle-Serpent) and said to him, "Oh Quauhcoatl, you have seen all that is there, down in the reeds, and you have wondered at it. But listen: there is still another thing that you have not seen. Therefore go at once and seek out the *tenochtli* cactus upon which an eagle stands in his joy . . . It is there that we shall fix ourselves; it is there that we shall rule, that we shall wait, that we shall meet the various nations and that with our arrow and our shield we shall overthrow them. Our city of México-Tenochtitlan shall be there, there where the eagle cries and spreads his wings and eats, there where swims the fish and there where the serpent is devoured: México-Tenochtitlan; and there shall many things be brought about".'

2

Quauhcoatl at once called the Mexicans together and told them the words of the god: and so, following him, they thrust their way into the marshes, among the water-plants and the rushes, and suddenly 'by the side of a cave they saw the eagle, poised on a cactus, eating with delight . . . and the god calling to them said, "Oh Mexicans, it is here." And they wept, crying, "At last we have been worthy (of our god); we have deserved (the reward); with astonishment we have seen the sign: our city shall be here".' This happened in the year *ome acatl*, two – reed, the year 1325 of our era.[10]

The *Codex Azcatitlan*[11] symbolises the beginning of the Mexicans' life at Tenochtitlan by a picture of Indians in boats, fishing with hook and line or with nets, while other Indians with sticks drive the fish towards the open nets: around them are water-birds and tufts of reeds. This must in fact have been the manner of life of the Mexicans of that period. It was in no respect different from that of the little riparian tribes outside the towns, which gave up the greater part of their time to fishing and wildfowling. They were called *atlaca chichimeca*, the lake-dwelling savages.[12] They were armed with nets and with the *atlatl*, the spear-thrower, which is used to this day for the taking of wildfowl. They had their gods – Atlaua, 'he who carries the *atlatl*', Amimitl (from *mitl*, an arrow, and *atl*[?], water), and Opochtli, 'the left-handed man', 'he who throws darts with his left hand' – gods who were still known in Mexico in classical times.[13]

In the eyes of the townsfolk of Colhuacán, of Atzacapotzalco or of Texcoco, the Mexicans cannot have looked any better than the other 'lake-dwelling savages'. They came to the urban tribes on dry land when in the first place they needed beams, planks and stone to build their town, and they paid in fish and water-animals.[14] 'Meanly, wretchedly, they built the house of Uitzilopochtli. The oratory that they raised up to him was very small, for living in a foreign land, among the rushes and the reeds, where could they have found stone or timber? The Mexicans came together and said, "Let us buy stone and timber with whatever lives in the water, the fish, the axolotl, the frog, the crayfish, the *aneneztli*, the water-snake, the water-fly, the worm of the

3

lake, the duck, the *cuachilli*, the swan and all the birds that live on the water. With these we shall buy the stone and the timber".'¹⁵ At the beginning of the sixteenth century the memory of this time was celebrated once a year, during the feast of the month *Etzalqualiztli*. The priests went to bathe ceremonially in the lake, and one of them, the *chalchiuhquacuilli* (literally 'the priest of the precious stone', that is to say, 'of the water') uttered the ritual formula, 'This is the place of the serpent's anger, the humming of the water-mosquito, the flight of the wild-duck, the murmur of the white rushes.' At this everybody leapt into the water, splashing with hands and feet and imitating the cries of waterfowl. 'Some called like ducks (literally 'spoke duck' – *canauhtlatoa*) others like herons, ibis or egrets.' And this same rite was repeated on four consecutive days.¹⁶

There is every reason to believe that the place where Quauhcoatl and his companions saw the eagle and the serpent was the same as that which, in the sixteenth century, was to become the site of the temple of Uitzilopochtli; that is, somewhat to the north-east of the present cathedral and at about three hundred and thirty yards in the same direction from the middle of the large square that is now called the Zócalo. All the traditions agree in stating that the first temple, which was no more than an 'oratory', *ayauhcalli*, was built exactly on this spot: the succeeding rulers spared nothing to give Uitzilopochtli a temple worthy of him, but the buildings, the pyramids and the holy places of the subsequent reigns always arose on the same emplacement, on the same sacred ground pointed out by the god himself. The imperial palaces were built round this religious centre of the nation; and from here, too, radiated the main lines of the city's development. The Mexican city is above all the temple: the glyph that means 'the fall of a town' is a symbolic temple half-overturned and burning. The very being of the city, the people and the state is summed up in this 'house of god', which is the literal meaning of the Aztec *teocalli*.

The original centre of Mexico rested on firm and even rocky ground: the temple was built 'by a cave', *oztotempa*. It was in fact the top of an island in the middle of the swamp

4

in a wide bay of the lake. Around Tenochtitlan the shore made a sweeping curve, a great arc studded with towns and villages – Atzcapotzalco and Tlacopan to the west, Coyoacán to the south, Tepeyacac to the north. The great salt lake of Texcoco stretched eastwards, and on the south stood the fresh-water lakes of Xochimilco and Chalco. Other islands and islets rose above the surface of the bay around Tenochtitlan, particularly the island which was at first called Xaltelolco (sand-hillock) and then Tlatelolco (earth-hillock). This stood immediately to the north of the site of the temple of Uitzilopochtli. The island of Tlatelolco was separated from the island of Tenochtitlan by no more than an arm of the lake, which was afterwards spanned by a bridge.

It must have been a most prodigious labour for these first generations of Mexicans to adapt the network of islets, sand-banks and mud-banks, deep and shallow marshes – to organise it for the purposes of living. The Aztecs were obliged, as an amphibious people in an amphibious environment, to fabricate their own earth by piling up sludge on rafts made of rushes; they had to dig canals, make embankments, build causeways and bridges: and as the population increased what are now called urban problems arose, and they became more and more difficult to resolve.

The fact that a great city could be founded in such conditions, and that it could grow, created by a people with no land, is a proof of truly miraculous ingenuity on their part and of astonishing perseverance. The pride that they later showed was not without its justification; for how great a distance there was between the wretched hamlet of straw huts cowering in the reeds and the shining metropolis of the sixteenth century. It is scarcely surprising that the Aztecs should have been so strongly moved by the splendid destiny that had changed them from a poor and solitary people into the richest and most powerful.

EXTENT AND POPULATION

At the time of the Spanish conquest the City of Mexico covered both Tenochtitlan and Tlatelolco. This 'Greater Mexico' was a recent creation. Tlatelolco had been peopled

5

by an offshoot from the Mexican tribe, who had founded their own city under a dynasty that came from Atzcapotzalco – a city that prospered in war and trade. But the Mexican rulers could not bear the presence of a rival town for long, a rival and a relative not a bowshot from them. The Tlatelolcans themselves provided the pretext for the quarrel: their king Moquiuixtli, who had married a sister of the emperor Axayacatl, treated his wife with contempt; he was also an ambitious, restless man, and he strove to ally himself with other cities in the valley against Mexico. Relations reached such a pitch of bitterness that war broke out: in 1473 the Aztecs invaded Tlatelolco and took the great temple. Moquiuixtli was hurled from the top of the pyramid and dashed to pieces. From that time on Tlatelolco lost its separate identity and was incorporated into the capital under the orders of a governor.[17]

As a consequence the city stretched southwards from the northern limits of Tlatelolco, opposite the shore-village of Tepeyacac, as far as the marshes which gradually merged into the lake: the southern boundary of the urban area was shown by a series of named localities – Toltenco ('at the edge of the rushes'), Acatlan ('the place of the reeds'), Xihuitonco ('the meadow'), Atizapan ('whitish water'), Tepetitlan ('beside the hill') and Amanalco ('the pool'). In the west, the city stopped at about the line of the present Calle Bucareli, at Atlampa ('the water's edge') and at Chichimecapan ('the river of the Chichimecs'). In the east it stretched as far as Atlixco ('at the surface of the water') where the open water of Lake Texcoco began. The whole was in the form of a square with each side measuring about 3,200 yards, and it covered some 2,500 acres: it is worth recalling, for the sake of comparison, that Rome, within the Aurelian Wall, contained 3,423 acres. This entire area had been transformed by two centuries of labour into a geo-metrical network of canals and raised earthworks organised around two principal centres, the great temple and the square of Tenochtitlan and the great temple and the square of Tlatelolco; and about several secondary centres, the different districts or quarters.

6

Few subjects are as obscure as these quarters of Mexico. It can be taken for a fact that the unit called the *calpulli* ('group of houses') or the *chinancalli* ('house surrounded by a hedge') was at the base of Aztec society, and it was therefore shown in the territorial division that is the visible image of that society in terms of land. The Spanish chroniclers usually translated this by *barrio*, a quarter; and modern American authors use the word clan.[18] In my opinion the old Spaniards understood the facts better than the modern archeologists. 'Clan' brings to mind various laws of marriage and lineage, or even a totem, and it seems to me less appropriate to the situation as it is known than 'quarter', which stands for a territorial entity. The *calpulli* was above all a territory, the common property of a certain number of families which shared it among themselves in order to exploit it according to laws that we shall treat later on. It had the elements of an autonomous administration under the command of the *calpullec*, an elected head; and it had its own temple.

It is likely that the *calpulli* remained the essential nucleus of the tribe during its migration and up until the foundation of the city. How many were there then? We know the names of seven early *calpulli*, but it cannot be absolutely asserted that there had not been more of them. Tezozomoc[19] lists fifteen at the time when the Aztecs on their march were about to reach Tula, that is to say, at the end of the twelfth century. There were perhaps twenty at the beginning of the urban period; but that does not prove that their number may not have increased between the fourteenth and sixteenth centuries.[20] In any case one must add the *calpulli* of Tlatelolco after it was annexed: we know seven of these, which were merchants' quarters; but it is reasonable to suppose that there were others. And lastly there were some quarters, as for example that of Amantlan, occupied by specialists in feather-mosaic, which seem to have been incorporated into the city comparatively lately. However it may be, the plan of Mexico drawn up by the learned Alzate[21] in 1789 shows no fewer than sixty-nine named localities in Tenochtitlan and Tlatelolco: it cannot be affirmed that all these localities

7

corresponded with an equal number of *calpulli*, but it is certain that many of them did.

Apart from this, a new kind of division was instituted a little after the foundation of Mexico. The traditional accounts attribute it to Uitzilopochtli himself.[22] The whole city was cut into four sections in relation to the great temple: in the north, Cuepopan ('the place of the blossoming of the flowers'); in the east, Teopan ('the quarter of the god', that is to say, 'of the temple'); in the south, Moyotlan ('the place of the mosquitoes'), a particularly suitable name, for it was there that the canals and the streets ended in marshes which, in colonial times, were called Ciénaga de San Antonio Abad and Ciénaga de la Piedad; and in the west Aztacalco ('beside the house of the herons'). This subdivision into four great sections had become so much a part of daily life that the Spaniards kept it throughout the whole colonial period, merely giving the four regions Christian names: Santa María la Redonda (Cuepopan), San Pablo (Teopan), San Juan (Moyotlan) and San Sebastián (Aztacalco).

It is clear that this division into four parts, ascribed to the chief god of the tribe, had a primarily administrative and governmental character. It was a controlling network superimposed upon the multiplicity of the *calpulli* old and new: each of these great sections had its own temple and a military chief appointed by the central authority. In this the new section was essentially different from the *calpulli*, which elected its head: furthermore, the new section possessed no land.

Thus the whole urban area was organised about its principal and secondary centres: the *calpulli*, each with its temple and its *telpochcalli* ('young men's house', a kind of religious and military college); the four sections, with their temples; and finally the great *teocalli* of Tenochtitlan and Tlatelolco, the imperial palaces and the government buildings.

What was the city's population? No census has come down to us, although the Aztec emperors had the means of knowing at least the number of families living in Mexico. The conquerors estimated the number of households or

8

inhabited houses at figures ranging from 60,000 to 120,000.[23] It remains to be decided how many persons, upon an average, made up a household. Families were large, and the ruling class was polygamous. Torquemada allows that a household contained from 4 to 10 individuals, and if one follows him one has the average of 7 for each house. But this figure is probably an underestimate, for many Mexicans had some of those servants of inferior status whom we inaccurately term slaves. I admit that my figure is arbitrary, and I deeply regret it, but as a better one is lacking, it may be accepted that Tenochtitlan-Tlatelolco counted 80,000 to 100,000 households of 7 persons, or a total population of from 560,000 to 700,000 souls. Let us say that the population was certainly above 500,000 and probably below 1,000,000.

Of course, we are speaking here only of the capital itself: but it is a fact that at the period in question many of the towns and villages on the dry land were no more than suburban satellites of the city. Even when they had kept the outward forms of self-government, as Tlacopan had done, their real standing was that of mere dependencies of the capital. This was the case with Atzcapotzalco, Chapultepec, Coyoacán, Uitzilopochco, Iztapalapan, Colhuacán, Mexicaltzinco, Iztacalco, etc. – that is to say, practically everything that now makes up the Federal District of the Republic of Mexico.

They were rich suburbs, as the Spaniards noted when they arrived.[24] Cortés remarks[25] that the towns on the shore stretched right down into the lake itself, which seems to show that their population was increasing, and that in order to make room the people on the dry land were building out in the manner that was usual in Tenochtitlan. It was, therefore, an enormous conurbation, which, having spread itself on the shore, was now eating its way into the lake – a vast urban area that embraced more than 1,000,000 human beings.

GENERAL APPEARANCE; ROADS AND TRAFFIC

As Bernal Díaz says, the conquistadores 'saw things unseen, nor ever dreamed': all the eye-witnesses concur in the

9

astonishing splendour of the city. Even Cortés, the most coldly calculating of them all, is free in his praise of the beauty of the buildings; and he particularly notices the gardens, sometimes embanked, sometimes at ground level. He speaks of the wide, straight streets, and the traffic of the boats on the canals beside them; of the aqueduct bringing fresh water into the town; and of the size and activity of the markets.

The proud hidalgo, writing to Charles V, goes so far as to say that the Indians 'live almost as we do in Spain, and with quite as much orderliness.' He adds, 'It is wonderful to see how much sense they bring to the doing of everything.'[26]

On the 12th of November, 1519, four days after their entry into Mexico, Cortés and his chief captains went to see the market and the great temple of Tlatelolco with the emperor Motecuhzoma II. They went up the 114 steps of the *teocalli* and stood on the platform at the top of the pyramid, in front of the sanctuary. Motecuhzoma took Cortés by the hand 'and told him to look at the great city and all the other towns near by on the lake and the many villages built on the dry land . . . This great accursed temple was so high that from the top of it everything could be seen perfectly. And from up there we saw the three causeways that lead into Mexico – the causeway of Iztapalapan, by which we had come four days earlier; the causeway of Tlacopan, by which we were later to flee, on the night of our great defeat[27] . . . and that of Tepeyacac. We saw the aqueduct that comes from Chapultepec to supply the town with sweet water, and at intervals along the three causeways the bridges which let the water flow from one part of the lake to another. We saw a multitude of boats upon the great lake, some coming with provisions, some going off loaded with merchandise . . . and in these towns we saw temples and oratories shaped like towers and bastions, all shining white, a wonderful thing to behold. And we saw the terraced houses, and along the causeways other towers and chapels that looked like fortresses. So, having gazed at all this and reflected upon it, we turned our eyes to the great market-place and the host of people down there who were buying and selling: the hum and the murmur of their voices could have been heard for more than a league. And among us were soldiers who had been in many parts of the world, at Constantinople, all over Italy and at Rome; and they said they had never seen a market so well ordered, so large and so crowded with people.'[28]

The witnesses all record the same impression: lofty towers rising everywhere above the white, flat-roofed houses; a methodical, crowded busyness, as of an ant-heap; a perpetual coming and going of boats upon the lake and the canals. Most of the houses single-storeyed, low, rectangular, flat-roofed. Indeed, only great men's houses were allowed to have two floors; and in any case it is obvious that buildings raised upon piles in a yielding soil were in danger of collapsing as soon as they passed a given weight, except in the comparatively rare case of their being built on a solider island or islet.

The majority of the houses, with their windowless façades hiding a private life led in the interior courtyards, must have been like those of an Arab town, except that they were built along straight roads and canals. In the suburbs there were probably still to be found the primitive huts of the early days, with their walls made of reeds and mud, and their roofs of grass or straw: but on the other hand, the nearer one came to the great *teocalli* and the imperial palaces, the grander and the more luxurious the houses became; there were the palaces of the high officials and those that the provincial dignitaries had to keep up in the capital, and then the official buildings such as the House of the Eagles, a sort of military club, the *calmecac*, or higher colleges, the *tlacochcalli*, or arsenals.

There was no monotony in all this. Here and there, from among the close-packed roofs, the pyramid of a local temple would rise up: in some streets the houses served as stalls for jewellers, or for goldsmiths, or for workers in feathers: in others there would be the warehouses of the merchants. And although there was little free space apart from the great squares, Mexico was not a town without verdure: each house had its own inner court, and the

Aztecs have always had a passion for flowers. There were still the mixed flower and vegetable gardens of the country round the suburban huts, sometimes made on the floating *chinampas;* and the flat roofs of the great men's palaces were crowned with green.

'The principal streets,' writes Cortés,[29] 'are very wide and very straight. Some of these, and all the smaller streets, are made as to the one half of earth, while the other is a canal by which the Indians travel in boats. And all these streets, from one end of the town to the other, are opened in such a way that the water can completely cross them. All these openings – and some are very wide – are spanned by bridges made of very solid and well-worked beams, so that across many of them ten horsemen can ride abreast.'

This description is confirmed by another witness[30]: half of each street was surfaced with beaten earth, like brick paving, and the other half was occupied by a canal. He adds, 'There are also great streets where there is water and nothing else; and these are used only for boats and barges, according to the custom of the country; for without these no one could move about the streets nor come out of their houses.' And he speaks of the people 'talking as they go along, some on the land, the others on the water.' This whole network of streets was cut by wooden bridges which could be removed if necessary, as the Spaniards found to their cost when the Aztecs drove them out of the town.

Throughout its whole extent, even to its centre (for one could row into the palace of Motecuhzoma) Mexico was a city of lake-dwellers, and it was joined to the shore by the three raised causeways that Cortés and Díaz speak of. The northern causeway, starting from Tlatelolco, reached the land at Tepeyacac, at the foot of the hills where the sanctuary of Tonantzin, the mother-goddess, 'our revered mother', used to be, and where there is now the basilica of Our Lady of Guadalupe. The western causeway linked Tenochtitlan with the satellite town of Tlacopan. The third, to the south, made a fork, of which the south-west arm finished at Coyoacán, and the eastern at Iztapalapan. At the junction of the arms stood a two-towered redoubt, surrounded by a high wall with two gates in it, and entirely commanding the approaches. It seems that it was only the southern causeway that had been fortified in this way: for it was from this side that the forces of Uexotzinco, an unconquered city on the other side of the volcanoes, might one day launch an attack.

These raised roads were as much dikes as causeways, and the shallowness of the lake had made the building of them comparatively easy: the construction had begun with two parallel lines of piles, and then the space between them had been filled with stones and beaten earth. Here and there the dike was broken to let the water flow under wooden bridges, for the lake had quite violent currents at times, and it would have been dangerous to bottle them up. The roads that were thus formed by the top of the dikes were amply wide enough, as Cortés says,[31] for eight horsemen abreast: the one that ran from Iztapalapan to Mexico was about five miles long, and, according to Bernal Díaz,[32] it 'ran so straight that it bent neither little nor much.'

The causeways showed the main lines along which the city had developed from its original centre: one axis ran from north to south along the line from Tepeyacac to Tlatelolco to the great temple of Tenochtitlan and so to Coyoacán; and another from west to east, from Tlacopan to the middle of Tenochtitlan. Eastwards the town had been stopped by the open lake, and one had to go by water to Texcoco, the starting-place for the inland journey towards the mysterious Hot Lands, which had always fascinated the Indians of the high central plain.

PUBLIC BUILDINGS, SQUARES AND MARKET-PLACES

There were certainly maps of Mexico in the days before Cortés. It is impossible that the Aztec administration, which had scribes continually keeping the land-registers and tax-accounts up to date, should have neglected the capital itself. Besides, we know that the first duty of each *calpullec* was the keeping and if necessary the revision of the 'paintings' which showed his district and its subdivision among the families.

Unfortunately, none of these documents has been preserved. The Mexican national museum of anthropology and history does have one precious fragment, the 'agave-paper map', which is certainly only a little later than the conquest; but the piece that is left shows no more than a small part of the town to the east of Tlatelolco. Such as it is, however, this plan[33] gives a good idea of the structure of the districts, with their equal plots marked off by canals and streets and cut by the main traffic-arteries. I only mention the clumsy plan attributed to Cortés for the sake of completeness: it is almost entirely useless, with its childish embellishments and its little pictures in which the villages around the city are shown crowned by towers in the European manner.

Furthermore, as the buildings of Tenochtitlan were the victims of a systematic vandalism almost without a parallel in history both during the siege and immediately after the surrender of the emperor Cuauhtemotzin, it is exceedingly difficult to say exactly where the open spaces were, or to describe their surrounding edifices. One can only base oneself upon the more or less exact accounts of the chroniclers and upon the results of that amount of archeological digging that has been possible in the heart of the modern city; though one may also argue by analogy and reconstitute the main lines of the public buildings of Mexico by the example of the Aztec architecture outside the capital which the conquerors left alone, especially the pyramid of Tenayuca.[34]

The central square of Tenochtitlan seems to have coincided almost exactly with the present Zócalo of Mexico City. It was therefore a rectangle of some 175 by 200 yards, with its shorter sides on the north and south. The northern side was limited by a part of the precinct of the great temple, which at this point was dominated by the pyramid of a temple of the sun; the south was bordered by a canal running from east to west; the east by the houses of high dignitaries, most probably of two storeys; and the west by the front of the imperial palace of Motecuhzoma II, which stood where the palace of the president of the republic now stands. The palace which had belonged to Axayacatl (1469–1481) and in which the Spaniards stayed when they first arrived in Mexico, stood immediately to the north of the houses of the dignitaries, and its western front looked on to the precinct of the great temple. This huge square was reached by the canal already mentioned, by the causeway from Iztapalapan, which ran along the side of Motecuhzoma's palace to end at the south gate of the temple, or by a variety of smaller streets. The causeway from Tlacopan followed very nearly the line of the present Calle Tacuba, and running along the side of Axayacatl's palace, came out in the western precinct of the temple.[35]

The subsoil of the modern Zócalo as well as the foundations of the buildings that surround it are literally crammed with the remains of Aztec sculpture, statues and pieces of broken monuments and bas-reliefs. It has been possible to dig out some of them, particularly the stone of Tizoc, the famous Aztec calendar, and the *teocalli* of the holy war. Others, whose position is known, are still waiting to be recovered: yet many others are certainly lost for ever. Although it is somewhat spoiled by shops and commercial buildings, this great central square is splendid enough today, with its cathedral and the presidential palace; but what a prodigious effect it must have had upon the beholder in the Tenochtitlan of Motecuhzoma. State and religion combined their highest manifestations in this one place, and they gave a deep impression of their majesty: the white fronts of the palaces, their hanging gardens, the variegated crowds perpetually coming and going in the great gateways, the crenellated wall of the *teocalli*, and standing away one beyond another in the distance like a people of unmoving giants, the pyramids of the gods, crowned by their many-coloured sanctuaries, where the clouds of incense rose between banners of precious feathers. The upward sweep of the temples and the long tranquillity of the palaces joined there, as if to unite both the hopes of men and the divine providence in the maintenance of the established order.

One of the prime duties of the sovereign since the beginning of the city had been 'the defence of the temple of Uitzilopochtli'. It was this task that the magnates had specifically entrusted to the second emperor, Uitziliuitl

(1395-1414), and to Itzcoatl, the true founder of the Aztec power.[36]

It seems that the third ruler, Chimalpopoca, wished to enlarge the temple; and perhaps, if the weakness of his city and his own personal misfortune allowed it,[37] he did begin to build: but the first really important works were undertaken in the reign of Motecuhzoma I Ilhuicamina.[38] This emperor had the idea of asking the neighbouring cities to join in the enterprise, and more or less willingly Colhuacán, Cuitlahuac, Coyoacán, Mizquic and Xochimilco agreed to supply the necessary materials, particularly stone and lime. The people of Chalco, however, refused their help, and this was one of the causes of the long war that ended in their defeat.

The work lasted two years. The temple was built on a pyramid, whose top was reached by three flights of steps: the chief flight was on the south face, the others on the east and west, and the sum of all these steps was 360, which was the number of days in the year with the unfortunate five last days cut off – that is to say, 120 steps in each flight. The building was inaugurated in 1455 after the victory of Motecuhzoma I over the Huaxtecs, and the Huaxtec prisoners were the first of the temple's sacrifices.[39]

That, at any rate, is the tradition: but it may be asked whether this does not assign an earlier date to the temple than the truth allows. For if in fact the edifice had already reached its full size in the time of Motecuhzoma I, it is difficult to see what the labours of the subsequent reigns can have accomplished. There is every reason to think that the *teocalli* of Uitzilopochtli was built up in successive stages, like most of the Mexican pyramids: similarly it is most probable that the temple, as it was rebuilt by Motecuhzoma Ilhuicamina, was not as large as it was to become in later days.

Axayacatl did something towards the equipment of the building that his predecessor had left him: he set up the huge sacrificial stone, the *quauhtemalacatl*, ('the disk of stone of the eagles') which was said to have been brought from Coyoacán by 50,000 men with ropes and rollers. But

it was in the reigns of Tizoc and Auitzotl[40] that the great
teocalli was finished and assumed the appearance in which
it was first to be seen by the Europeans.

In the national museum of Mexico there is a sculptured
stele that commemorates its inauguration. This shows the
two emperors, each with the hieroglyphic of his name,
and it is dated *chicuei acatl*, 'eight – reed', or 1487 by our
reckoning. Tizoc, who had apparently begun the new
work, had only been dead one year.

In the *Codex Telleriano-Remensis*[41] we see two stages in
this undertaking. Under the reign of Tizoc, in *naui acatl*,
'four – reed' or 1483, 'the first stone was laid in the great
temple that the Christians found when they first came into
this country.' In the painting that shows the following year,
macuilli tecpatl, 'five–flint', the glyph that means the year
has a line connecting it with a drawing of a pyramid made
of four elements raised on a four-angled base, with two
blood-stained stairways: a cactus, the symbol of Tenochtitlan,
stands upon the topmost platform. The Spanish gloss reads,
'The village of Tzinacantepec rebelled against its overlords,
the Mexicans. They attacked it and made such a butchery
that scarcely a soul was left alive, for all the prisoners were
taken to Mexico to be sacrificed there in the great temple,
which was at that time still unfinished.'

For 1487 the glyph of the year *chicuei acatl*, 'eight–
reed', is joined to a temple, but this time it is certainly a
finished temple, with two sanctuaries side by side on the
top of the pyramid, one with red on its roof and around its
door, the other with blue. The meaning of these details will
become apparent later. A line joins the temple to a *tlequauitl*,
a fire-stick; and from the fire-stick escape flames and
smoke, which symbolise the ceremonial new fire that was
lit for the inauguration of the shrine. Another line leads
from the fire-stick to the glyph for Tenochtitlan, and this
succession of pictures may thus be read, 'In the year eight –
reed the (double) *teocalli* of Tenochtitlan was inaugurated.'
At the side of these there is a man wrapped in an embroidered
cloak; he is seated upon a kind of chair with a back, the
royal *icpalli*, and above it there is a sign representing a

fabulous water-creature of the lake, the *auitzotl:* this is the emperor of the same name. And finally, below the picture of the temple and around it there are warriors crowned with white feathers and down, the ritual ornaments of the human sacrifices, together with names of the towns from which they came – Xiuhcoac, Cuetlaxtlan and Tzapotlan. Below the warriors is written the sign *xiquipilli* (8,000) twice, and the sign *centzontli* (400) ten times, which is 20,000 altogether. The drawings may be interpreted, 'On this occasion Auitzotl caused 20,000 warriors to be sacrificed: they came from Xiuhcoac, Cuetlaxtlan and Tzapotlan.' The Spanish gloss is somewhat inexact: it reads, 'The great temple of Mexico was finished and made perfect. The old men say that in that year were sacrificed 4,000 men brought from the provinces overcome in war.'

We shall return to the sacrifices later, and for the moment we shall confine ourselves to stating that the great temple, in the form that the Spaniards found it in 1519, had been inaugurated by Auitzotl 32 years before. Unfortunately the descriptions and accounts written after the conquest are often obscure: under the name of 'great temple' they treat sometimes the temple of Uitzilopochtli and the complex of religious buildings in the middle of the city, and sometimes the temple of Tlatelolco. We must endeavour to distinguish between these different buildings.[42]

To begin with the temple of Uitzilopochtli itself: it was in fact a double temple, as the *Codex Telleriano-Remensis* shows it – and this picture is confirmed by several other documents, for example, the illustrations of the text of Sahagún in the Madrid manuscript, and the *Codex of 1576.* The pyramid rested upon a rectangular base whose north-south axis was 110 yards long and its east-west axis 88: the pyramid was made up of four or perhaps five elements, each stage being smaller than the one below it. Only the western face of the pyramid had steps, a very wide double stairway edged by balustrades which finished almost vertically before reaching the platform at the top. The stairs had a balustrade at the edge which began with great serpent's heads: one of these heads was recently exposed in an excavation near the cathedral. The stairway had 114 steps, and it was one of the highest known in Mexico – the temple of Texcoco had one of 117 and that of Cholula 120, according to Bernal Díaz. The height of the pyramid was probably about 100 feet.

The two sanctuaries were raised side by side upon the flat top of this enormous plinth: the one on the north, painted white and blue, was sacred to Tlaloc, the very ancient god of rain and green growth; the one on the south, ornamented with carved skulls painted white on a red background, to Uitzilopochtli. Each opened towards the west by a wide door that had the sacrificial stone in front of it.

The twin roofs, pyramidal in shape, were made of a wooden frame covered with cement and lime, and they were prolonged skywards by a kind of wall or crest very like those that are found upon Mayan buildings and which are designed to increase their apparent height.[43] The roof of the sanctuary of Tlaloc was encircled by a wavy wreath of shells to symbolise water, while that of Uitzilopochtli was decorated with butterflies—fire and sun. Where the balustrades ran up to the platform there were statues of men with their hands arranged to hold the poles of the banners that were hoisted on certain great holidays[44] – banners made of the splendid feathers of tropical birds. These flag-holders were a particular characteristic of Toltec architecture and sculpture, which the Aztecs had adopted.[45]

Serpents' heads, side by side, formed a 'hedge of snakes', *coatepantli*, all round the pyramid: this was also typically Toltec.[46]

Such was the monument that rose in the centre of the city and the empire; colossal yet harmonious in its dimensions, surrounded with veneration and with terror. It was said that uncountable golden jewels and gems had been hidden in the foundations, mixed with the stones and the cement by the order of the emperors: Bernal Díaz avers that this tradition was true and that when the Spaniards destroyed the *teocalli* they found the buried treasure.[47]

At the time of which we are speaking, the double temple of Tlaloc and Uitzilopochtli was not alone. By its size and its height it was the dominant member of a veritable religious city studded with pyramids and enclosed by a serpent-headed wall (*coatepantli*) which must have measured some 440 yards in length from east to west, and 330 in width. This wall ran along the side of the central square and then by the palace of Motecuhzoma, following the present Calle de la Moneda. Eastwards it went by the modern Calle de Carmen and the Correo Mayor, westwards by the streets of the Monte de Piedad and of Santo Domingo. To the north it gave upon a canal parallel to that which bordered the square and the imperial palace, as we have seen. The wall had three or perhaps four gates; they were fortified and 'all the rooms were filled with weapons of different kinds.'[48] They were guarded by a garrison of picked men. The south gate was the starting-point of the causeway to Iztapalapan and Coyoacán, the north of the causeway to Tepeyacac, and from the west gate started the causeway to Tlacopan.

Sahagún[49] lists no fewer than 78 buildings or classes of building forming part of the *templo mayor*, that is to say, the religious quarter enclosed by the *coatepantli*; but one wonders whether there is not some exaggeration here, or rather some mistake – whether the good father has not included buildings under this heading that were in fact outside the wall, elsewhere in the city. One's suspicion is strengthened by the fact that some of the buildings that he mentions have the same name as some of the districts of Tenochtitlan or even of Tlatelolco, and that in the same list he speaks of the houses for fasting and meditation which were attached to the local temples in the *calpulli*. But however that may be, we can nevertheless try to establish the different categories that were to be found among the buildings inside the wall.

To begin with the temples in the full sense of the word: other great gods had their dwellings close to Tlaloc and Uitzilopochtli – there was Tezcatlipoca, 'the smoking mirror', whose temple raised its pyramid by the southern edge of the enclosure, opposite the imperial palace; Tezcatlipoca, the protean god of the night, of war and of youth, who was also called Yoalli Eecatl, 'the night wind', Yaotl, 'the warrior' and Telpochtli, 'the young man'; and there was Quetzalcoatl, 'the precious-feathered serpent', the hero who brought civilisation, the god of the wind. His temple was 100 yards east of the great pyramid, and in a line with its chief stairway. Unlike all the others, it was a round building, having the form of a cylinder raised upon a pyramidal base. The way in was by a door carved and painted to resemble the open jaws of a serpent. 'Some way from the great pyramid,' writes Bernal Díaz, 'there was a smaller tower which was also a house of idols: or rather it was a positive hell, for in the doorway was one of those terrifying mouths that one sees in paintings. They say that hell has such mouths, with huge teeth, to swallow down the damned . . . hell was always the name of that house, for me.'[50]

Once can easily form an idea of the appearance of the temple of Quetzalcoatl by thinking of the round tower of Calixtlahuaca, in the region of Toluca, in the Matlaltzincas' country, which was built under the rule of the Aztecs.[51] Cylindrical constructions are rare in Mexico, which is more the country of the pyramid and the sharp-cut angle, and when they were built it was generally for the wind-god, who was thought to prefer them, because they did not spoil the current of the air. As to the snake's mouth entrance, an impressive example of this is to be seen in the doorway of the Aztec temple at Malinalco.[52]

We can also place the temple of the mother-goddess Ciuacoatl, 'snake-woman', and the *Coacalco*, 'at the temple of the serpent': they stood side by side in the north-west corner of the enclosure. The *Coacalco* was a pantheon: 'It was here that lived the gods of the cities (*altepeteteo*) that the Mexicans had conquered. They made the gods prisoner and brought them back and set them in this temple; and it was here that they were kept, in the *Coacalco*.'[53] Indeed, the Aztecs were most eclectic in matters of religion, and they surrounded their national god with the greatest possible number of other gods, from every part of the empire.

Lastly, we know that the temple of the sun stood at the south-west end of the group, opposite the palace of Axayacatl.

A great many subsidiary buildings were attached to the temples – places for prayer, penance or sacrifice. One of these was the *quauhxicalco*, 'the place where there is the *quauhxicalli*' or bowl for the sacrificed heart of the victims; and here the emperor and the priests fasted and did penance by thrusting agave-thorns into their legs and offering the blood to the gods. Others were the *tzompantli*, where the skulls of the sacrificed men were shown. And there was the *temalacatl*, a huge round of stone laid flatways upon a low pyramid, where courageous prisoners, tied to it by a loose rope, fought their last fight against the Aztec warriors. The *calmecac* were at the same time monasteries and schools. The priests lived in them, austere men, worn out by fasting, severe in their black robes and long hair; and it was here too that the young men of the ruling class learnt the rites, the writing and the history of their country. Each temple had its own *calmecac*, where the priests and their pupils lived together.

There were many springs that came up inside the enclosure, and in addition, as Díaz points out, the aqueduct from Chapultepec ran in by a roofed-over channel to fill a pool. By night the priests of the fire bathed in the Tlilapan, 'the dark water': another spring, Toxpalatl, provided drinking-water not only for the priests but also for the generality. The high-priest of the *Coacalco*, and he alone, bathed in the stream or pool that was called Coaapan.54

But the religious quarter also contained some more secular buildings. To begin with there was the *tlachtli*, the court for the ball-game that was an amusement of the upper classes and at the same time a kind of ritual mime. The long parallel walls of the court stretched in an eastward direction, and it lay to the west of the temple of Quetzalcoatl, between it and the outer wall. A very beautiful statue has been found on this site, Xochipilli, 'the prince of flowers', the god of youth, music and games. The ball-game was esteemed by all the civilised nations of ancient Mexico: the people of

Tenochtitlan had taken it from their neighbours in the valley, who, in turn, had had it from the Toltecs, who were passionately addicted to the game.

There were several buildings called *tlacochcalli* or *tlacochcalco*, 'house of the javelins', which served as arsenals, not only for the possible defence of the temple, but for general military operations. They were guarded by soldiers, and a high military official, the *tlacochcalcatl*, was responsible for them.

Two houses were used as inns 'for the lords of the Anahuac, for those who came from distant cities. And Motecuhzoma honoured them highly, giving them presents, splendid cloaks, precious necklaces or magnificent bracelets.'⁵⁵ And finally there was the *Mecatlan*, a building specially for the school of the *tlapizque*, the musicians who played the flute or other wind-instruments on ceremonial occasions, and for their rehearsals.

This, in all its living complexity, was the shape of the vast collection of houses, high and low, of towers, walls and roofs, embroidered with bas-reliefs, brilliant with whiteness and colour. Here was the birth-place of the city, when it came into being around a reed-woven hut; and it was here that the city was to perish, under the thunder of guns and the roar of the blazing temples.

But as the city and the state had grown, so too their rulers, like their gods, had exchanged poverty for wealth, the reed hut for the palace. It seems that each emperor was determined to build his own house. The palace of Auitzotl, to the north of the great *teocalli*, was still standing when the Spaniards came to Mexico; so was the palace of Axayacatl, where they stayed. This one, as we have seen, was opposite to the western side of the wall of serpents. As for Motecuhzoma II, he lived in the huge palace called 'the new houses' (*Casas nuevas*), whose size and luxury plunged the adventurers into astonished admiration.

This palace, which was to the east of the square, occupied a rectangle each of whose sides measured some 220 yards. This, too, was a town in itself, with many gateways through which one could go into it, either on foot or by boat. 'I went several times to the emperor's residence,' says a witness,[56] 'merely to look at it: each time I walked about until I was quite tired, but even so I never saw the whole of it.' It must be conceived as an arrangement of buildings, some, if not all, of two storeys, grouped round oblong or square interior courts with gardens in them.

The sovereign's apartments were on the upper floor, according to the *Codex Mendoza*, which also shows us the rooms kept on the same floor for the kings of the associated cities, Texcoco and Tlacopan. The ground-floor housed what one might now term the prime movers in public authority and government[57] – the supreme civil and criminal courts and the special tribunal that judged dignitaries accused of crimes or of serious misdemeanours, such as adultery; then the council of war, which was attended by the chief military commanders; the *achcauhcalli*, the place for the officials of the second rank, who carried out the judicial orders; the *petlacalco* or public treasury, where there were large stocks of maize, beans, grain and other victuals, as well as clothes and all kinds of merchandise; and the 'hall of the *calpixque*', the officials responsible for the exchequer. Other parts were used as prisons, either for prisoners of war or for ordinary criminals.

But besides these there were a great many halls and courts which were attuned to that luxurious and sophisticated way of life that the Mexican emperors had grown used to – a way of life that the higher dignitaries imitated, no doubt, as far as their means would allow them. The young men would come from the local schools in the evening to sing and dance, while skilful singers and musicians were ready in another room, in case the emperor might have some desire to be gratified: they were ready with drums and flutes, bells and rattles, everything their master could ask for. Here, also, were the craftsmen whose delicate fingers chiselled the jade or melted gold or built up the feather mosaics piece by piece; farther on there was the *totocalli*, 'the house of birds', which resounded with the song of all the winged jewels of the tropics; elsewhere jaguars and pumas roared from their wooden cages. The rarest flowers from all the regions had

24

been planted in the gardens, and medicinal herbs; and there were great sheets of water with ducks, swans and egrets.

'Motecuhzoma,' says Cortés, 'had a palace in the town of such a kind, and so marvellous, that it seems to me almost impossible to describe its beauty and magnificence. I will say no more than that there is nothing like it in Spain.'[58] These are very strong words from a Spanish hidalgo addressing himself to Charles V. But the descriptions of Bernal Díaz, which have a simplicity that vouches for their truth, are quite as enthusiastic.[59]

Later on we shall speak of the details which allow one to form some idea of the manner of life of the rulers of the Mexican state; for the present it is enough to have shown Authority by the side of Religion in our general picture of the city, and to imagine the extent of the amazement and wonder of a country-man, an Indian from the coast or from the mountains, coming to Mexico and gazing upon the forest of the *teocalli* pyramids or the succession of façades and terraces of the imperial palace. The effect of magnificence that all these must have produced was rendered all the greater because of the innumerable bas-reliefs, statues and sculpture of all kinds, mostly religious but sometimes profane, which adorned the buildings, peopled the sanctuaries and the great halls, and confronted the beholder upon the walls and in the squares. In spite of the wholesale destruction in the sixteenth century, what is left of it in the national museum astonishes one by its abundance, its size and its perfection.

The central square of Tenochtitlan, like those of the other districts, had also to serve as a market-place. 'This town has many squares,' says Cortés, 'on which there are always markets, and in which they buy and sell.' 'But,' he adds, 'there is another, twice the size of the town of Salamanca, completely surrounded by arcades, where every day there are more than sixty thousand souls who buy and sell, and where there are all kinds of merchandise from all the provinces, whether it is provisions, victuals or jewels of gold or silver.'

This obviously means the market place of Tlatelolco. The people of Tlatelolco had always been known for their devotion to trade, and after the town had been annexed it became the chief business centre of Mexico. 'When we reached the great square called Tatelulco,' says Bernal Díaz, 'as we had never seen anything like it, we stood amazed by the infinity of people and goods, and by the method and regularity of everything.' The author of the *Relation abrégée* states that 20,000 to 25,000 buyers and sellers came there every day, and that every fifth day there was a great market attended by 40,000 or 50,000.

All accounts speak of the extraordinary variety of the enormous market in the same way, and all agree as to its orderliness. Each kind of merchandise had its own customary and defined place, in street-like rows, 'in just the same way as it happens in my own country, at Medina del Campo,' writes Bernal Díaz, 'when they have the fair.' In one place there would be jewels of gold and silver for sale, and precious stones and the many-coloured feathers brought from the Hot Lands; in the next row there would be slaves, resigned and waiting for their purchasers, some untied, some wearing heavy wooden collars; farther on, men and women bargaining over cloaks, loin-cloths and skirts, made of cotton or the cloth obtained from the fibre of aloes.

Shoes, ropes, the skins of jaguars, pumas, foxes and deer, raw or tanned, were piled up in the places kept for them: and there was a quarter reserved for the feathers of eagles, sparrow-hawks and falcons. Maize, beans, oil-bearing seeds, cocoa, peppers, onions, a thousand kinds of green-stuff; turkeys, rabbits, hares, venison, ducks and the little mute hairless dogs that the Aztecs so loved to eat; fruit, sweet potatoes, honey, syrup from maize-stalks or the juice of the agave; salt; colours for dyeing and writing, cochineal, indigo; earthenware of every shape and size, calabashes, vases and dishes of painted wood; flint and obsidian knives, copper axes; builder's wood, planks, beams, firewood, charcoal, resinous torches; paper made of bark or aloes; cylindrical bamboo pipes, charged and ready for smoking, all the produce of the lakes, from fish, frogs and crustaceans to a kind of caviare of insect-eggs, gathered from the surface of the water; matting, chairs, stoves . . .

'What more can I say?' cries Bernal Díaz. 'There were even several boats for sale, which, saving your reverence, were filled with human excrement; they were moored in the marshes not far from the market, and they were used for tanning skins. I say this, although I know very well that it will make a certain kind of person laugh.' On every hand there was this great accumulation of provisions, an unheard-of plenty of all manner of goods; and up and down between the stalls the dense crowd, unhurrying, grave; not a noisy crowd, but one that hummed or mumured, as Indian crowds do to this day. In this market-place, says Cortés, 'there are places like apothecaries' shops, where they sell medicines ready to be taken, ointments and poultices. There are barbers' shops, where one can be washed and trimmed; there are houses where, upon payment, one may eat and drink.' And there were women who cooked on their stoves in the open air, and offered the customers their stews or spiced maize-porridge, or sweetmeats made of honey with those excellent maize-cakes called *tlaxcalli*, the Mexican tortilla; or savoury tamales, whose steamed maize crust was stuffed with beans, meat and pimentoes.

One could wander all day long in this festival of trade, taking one's meals there and meeting one's friends and relations; and many did, strolling up and down the alleys lined with tottering mounds of fruit or many-coloured clothes all spread out. One could talk at length to an Indian woman squatting behind her vegetables or amuse oneself with the savage aspect of an Otomí come down from the hills to sell a few hides; or one could gaze enviously upon a *pochtecatl*, a merchant, just back from the fabled regions of the south-east, with his parrot-feathers, his jewels of translucent jade and his air of wealth.

The impassive guardians of the market, the *tianquizpan tlayacaque*, paced up and down the vast square, silently overseeing the crowd and the tradesmen. If any dispute arose, a buyer protesting that he was cheated, for example, or someone seeing his stolen goods exposed for sale, then

27

instantly everybody concerned was taken off to the court that sat without interruption at one end of the market, where three judges continually took turns and gave their verdict on the spot. If a wrongdoer were fined he would send for his family, and they might be seen coming, gasping under the load of *quachtli*, the lengths of cloth that were used for money. And the crowd, satisfied, would return to its round, moving like a nation of ants between the covered galleries that lined the square, at the foot of the tall pyramid of the temple of Tlatelolco.[60]

THE PROBLEMS OF A GREAT CITY

So huge a town and so numerous a population must have set its rulers problems undreamed of by its founders, two centuries earlier. The question of feeding it presented no difficulty, judging by the plenty in the market-places; and in fact innumerable boats perpetually converged upon it, loaded with provisions. It may be observed, in passing, that water-transport was by far the most effective kind, in a country that did not possess a single pack-horse, cart-horse, cart or any other land-vehicle, nor any creature that could take the horse's place.

But the grave problem of water was exceedingly difficult to resolve. Nature has so made the valley of Mexico that it suffers from two opposing disadvantages: it suffered then, as it does today, from either too much water or not enough – flood or drought. In the rainy season, unbelievably violent storms fill the bottom of this huge basin in a few minutes with a mass of water that can only escape very slowly. In the dry season there is great difficulty in supplying the city with drinking water and water for the gardens. Evaporation was gradually lowering the water-level, and already the part of the lake round Mexico was quite shallow: though indeed at that time the climate of the valley must have been better than it is today, upon the whole, and less subject to violent extremes. The drying-up of the city's own immediate lagoon as part of the struggle against the danger of flooding, has done nothing to improve the climate, either.[61]

In the beginning, the Mexicans can have had no difficulty

at all with drinking-water: the springs on the central island were amply sufficient. As we have seen, they still answered part of the city's needs in the sixteenth century. The water of the lake itself, however, was useless, being too brackish; and when the unfortunate defenders of the city were reduced to trying it, it only made their sufferings worse.[62]

As the population increased, the springs were no longer enough. The only solution was to bring in water from the springs that flowed on the mainland. The Aztecs were well acquainted with the spring of Chapultepec, to the west of Tenochtitlan: it was a place of unfortunate memory for them, for it was there, at the beginning of the fourteenth century, when they were still a nomadic tribe, that they met with the most appalling defeat in their history, and had their chief Uitziliuitl the elder taken together with his two daughters, to die in slavery at Colhuacán.[63] But under Motecuhzoma I, Chapultepec ('the hill of the grasshopper') had become a dependency of the capital, together with its wood of famous trees and its rocks, with a copious spring rising at their feet.

Perhaps for some time the Mexicans were satisfied with carrying over pots of this water by boat, but very soon this must have appeared quite inadequate and the idea of the aqueduct must have arisen. The aqueduct was built under Motecuhzoma I, and it ran from the spring to the very middle of the city, in the enclosure of the great *teocalli*, a distance of rather more than three miles. It was made of stone and mortar, and, as all the accounts agree, it had two channels, each the width of a man's body. Only one was used at a time, so that when, after a given period, it had to be cleaned, the water could be turned into the other.

It is clear that the aqueduct had to pass over several canals, because of the way in which the city was laid out. Cortés, describing this, seems to have been particularly struck by the ingenious construction of the hollow bridges, 'as big as an ox', which spanned the water-ways. Practised water-drawers balanced themselves upon these water-bearing bridges, and for a fee, they poured drinking-water into the jars that the boatmen below held up to them. The boatmen then rowed off to sell the water throughout the city. There were also public fountains; or at least there was one principal fountain in the middle of the city: women went there, to fill their pitchers.[64]

As the number of people still increased, so, in its turn, the aqueduct of Chapultepec became inadequate. The construction of the second, which was begun and finished under Auitzotl, shows both the amount of the town's expansion and the intelligent activity of its rulers. This aqueduct, which brought the water from Coyoacán, ran alongside the Iztapalapan causeway.

The carrying-out of this work had been preceded by a most unfortunate venture which shows the delicacy of the natural balance between the lake and the islands. The events made so strong an impression upon people's minds at the time, that the account, as we now have it, is heavily charged with magic. In fact, Auitzotl proposed taking the water of a spring named Acuecuexatl, which welled up in the territory of Coyoacán, between that city and Uitzilopochco.

According to Tezozomoc, Auitzotl sent messengers to seek the lord of Coyoacán; he was a well-known wizard, and before their horrified eyes he changed himself into an eagle, a tiger, a snake and a whirlwind of fire. The messengers, however, managed to slip a rope about his neck, and so throttled him. The work was begun at once, and presently the aqueduct was ready to carry the water right into the middle of the town.

A great feast celebrated the finishing of the work: one of the high-priests drank the water of the spring on his knees, while his acolytes sounded their instruments and the 'singers of Tlaloc' sang hymns to the beat of a wooden gong, in honour of the water-gods. 'Let thy water be welcomed in Mexico-Tenochtitlan, lying among the reeds of the lake,' they sang; and farther off, human sacrifices were offered up. Finally, the emperor himself, crowned with gold, welcomed the coming of the water to Tenochtitlan, offering it birds, flowers and incense. 'Oh Chalchiuhtlicue ("wearer of a green stone skirt" – water-goddess)' he cried, 'welcome to the home of Uitzilopochtli!'

But the Acuecuexatl began to seethe, and the water rushed out with a continually increasing violence. The aqueduct overflowed, and by the end of forty days the situation was grave; the lake was continually rising. The fishermen gave the alarm, and then the flood began, destroying houses and even menacing the emperor, who was obliged to take refuge in the great temple. On the shore and the islands, the fields of maize were ravaged, and there was the prospect of famine: many people were drowned, and others began to leave the city.

Both Tezozomoc, a Mexican chronicler with a strong tendency to exalt his own people and their former rulers, and Ixtlilxochitl, whose history is obviously biased in favour of Texcoco, record that Auitzotl, brought to this pass and fearing that the discontented Mexicans would rebel, went to ask the help of his ally, Nezaualpilli, king of Texcoco. Nezaualpilli said, 'You would never have had this misfortune, if you had followed the advice of the lord of Coyoacán in the first place, instead of having him killed.'

He then took command of the technical and magical operations: several high officials were sacrificed and their hearts thrown into the spring, together with gems, gold and embroideries; then fifteen divers went down and succeeded in blocking the holes by which the water came out with such violence. Following this a kind of cement casing was built over the dangerous pool, to shut it in for ever.

The flood cost the emperor and the city a great deal: there were uncountable houses to be rebuilt, and among them Auitzotl's palace itself; 10 loads of *quachtli*, a small fortune, to each of the divers; 200,000 loads of maize distributed to the hungry populace; 32,000 boats provided for the people so that they could carry away whatever could be saved from the water, until it should go down again; and lastly the distribution of a great many clothes to the distressed. Ixtlilxochitl even claims that it was the cause of the emperor's death, for 'being in a room on the ground floor, which opened on to the gardens, and the water rushing in with such force, he was obliged to flee; and he

31

hit his head so hard on the jamb of the door that he wounded himself badly, and in the end he died of it.'[65]

This was certainly the best-known of the floods in the days before the coming of the Spaniards; but it was certainly not the only one. The city ran the risk of another every rainy season; for whenever the rivers that flowed into the lake of Texcoco were in flood, particularly the Acolman, the water surged into the lagoons that surrounded Mexico. It was against this danger that Motecuhzoma I built a dyke ten miles long in 1449, according to the plan and the advice of Nezaualcoyotl, king of Texcoco; it ran north and south from Atzacoalco to Iztapalapan, and it protected Tenochtitlan from the overflowing of the great lake. Considerable remains of it can still be seen.

It may therefore be said that the Mexicans solved the first of their two great problems, that of drinking water; but that the solution of the second, the danger of flooding, was precarious and incomplete: indeed, even now it is still not entirely done away with, in spite of modern machinery.

There is another question that should be looked at for a moment – the question of urban sanitation. Tenochtitlan no more had main-drainage than the Rome of the Caesars or the Paris of Louis XIV, so the foul waters flowed into the canals and the lake; fortunately the lake had enough in the way of currents to ensure a certain degree of outflow. In certain places, 'on every road' says Bernal Díaz, there were public latrines with reed walls against the public gaze: no doubt the boats mentioned by the same conquistador in his account of the market came from here. In passing, it may be observed that the Aztecs understood the manuring of the ground with night-soil.

Garbage was dumped at the edge of the town, in the marshy waste-lands, or buried in the inner courtyards. The upkeep of the streets was the responsibility of the local authorities in each quarter, under the general supervision of the *Uey Calpixqui*, an imperial official who issued directions, in the manner of a prefect. Every day a thousand men were employed in the cleaning of the public thorough-fares, which they swept and washed with such care that according to one witness you could walk about without fearing for your feet any more than you would for your hands.[66] It is quite certain that at the beginning of the sixteenth century the city appears to have been healthy, because of the abundance of water, the cleanly habits of the people, and the mountain air. There is no mention of a single epidemic in the *Codex Telleriano-Remensis*, which nevertheless carefully sets down all remarkable happenings and calamities, very heavy rains, earthquakes, comets and eclipses of the sun: the same applies to the *Codex of 1576* and the *Codex Azcatitlan*. The first great epidemic ever known in Mexico was when a Negro from Cuba, who came with the Spaniards, brought the smallpox: it devastated the country, and carried off the emperor Cuitlahuac.

TENOCHTITLAN AS A YOUNG CAPITAL

Modern observers differ widely in their interpretation of the scene that has just been described. What in fact was Tenochtitlan? A very big Indian village, a swollen *pueblo*? Or an Alexandria of the western world? 'Although socially and governmentally Tenochtitlan was distinctly an American Indian tribal town, outwardly it appeared the capital city of an empire,' says Vaillant.[67] Oswald Spengler, on the other hand, classes Tenochtitlan among the 'world cities', the symbols and the materialisation of a culture whose greatness and whose decadence is summed up in them.[68]

I must admit that I do not know what is meant by 'an American Indian tribal town'. If it means that Mexico was not really the capital of an empire, and that behind the brilliant setting there was nothing more than what might be found in any Arizona village, then it appears to me that it is refuted by the most unquestionable facts. There is as much difference between Mexico and Taos or Zuñi as there is between the Rome of Julius Caesar and the Rome of the Tarquins: the adult must not be confused with the embryo.

But neither can it be claimed that Tenochtitlan was one of those rich, sophisticated and ossified cities which are the elegant tombs in which their own civilisation stiffens as it dies. It was the young capital of a society in full development,

33

of a civilisation in full progression, and of an empire that was still in the making. The Aztecs had not reached their zenith; their rising star had scarcely passed the first degrees of its course. It must never be forgotten that the town was destroyed by the Spaniards before it had reached its two hundredth year, and that its true rise only began with Itzcoatl, less than a century before the invasion.

It is true that in so short a time the evolution of men and institutions had been extraordinarily rapid; and this evolution had certainly been hastened by the vitality of a young nation with a rich cultural inheritance in its hands. But their vitality, far from diminishing, continued to increase and to give continual signs of its presence; the time of weariness and decline had not yet come. Nothing had even begun to weaken their upward impetus before the irruption of the Europeans stopped it dead.

It is for this reason that the Mexico of 1519 has nothing of the look of a city that is finished, a dead soul in a dead stone shell. It is a living organism that has been animated these two hundred years by a raging lust for power. The empire is still growing towards the south-east; the social structure is in a flux of change; the form of government, less and less that of a tribe, is becoming more and more that of a state. There is no hint of old age in this picture. The Aztec world is only just reaching its maturity; and the capital, neither primitive nor decadent, is the true image of a people which, although it still keeps its tribal cohesion, is looking from the height of its domination forwards to new horizons.

Let us look at this town again, and listen to it. There is nothing feverish in its unceasing, orderly activity; the crowd, with its brown faces and white clothes, flows continually along the silent façades of the houses, and from time to time one catches the scent of a garden through an open doorway; there is not much talking, and that little is in murmurs which scarcely rise above the quiet brushing sound of bare feet and sandals. If one looks up, there are the sharp lines of the pyramids against the brilliant sky, and farther on the two great volcanoes rear up their dark forests and their eternal snow. Men pass by, trotting with their foreheads bowed against the band that supports their burden: there are women with baskets of poultry or vegetables. Beside them the canoes glide past without a sound upon the canal. Suddenly the cry of 'The emperor' runs from mouth to mouth, and the imperial retinue comes into view; the crowd opens, and with lowered eyes the people throw flowers and their cloaks under the feet of the emperor as he comes, attended by dignitaries, in a glory of green feathers and golden jewels.

Even at noon it is cool in the shadows of the walls, and at night it is positively cold. The streets are not lit at night: and the night, as everyone knows, is the time for the fierce, uncanny beings that loom at the crossroads, for Tezcatlipoca, who challenges the fighting-men, and for the baleful *Ciuateteo*, the she-monsters that haunt the shadows. But unlike our European towns of the same period the city does not suspend all life until the morning, for in Mexico the night is the most important time for visiting, and the red light of torches is to be seen in the doorways and reddening the darkness over the inner courtyards. It is at night that there are parties to celebrate the return of caravans, and at night the priests get up at regular intervals to celebrate their services. The darkness, already torn by the flames from the huge tripods loaded with resinous wood on the steps of the *teocalli*, reverberates with the sounds of flutes and voices from noble or commercial banquets, and the beating of the temple gongs.

It is a vivid, complex life, the reflection of a many-faceted, much-stratified society with powerful currents running through it; and to understand it we must turn from the physical surroundings in which it was lived to the society itself.

CHAPTER TWO

SOCIETY AND THE STATE AT THE BEGINNING OF THE SIXTEENTH CENTURY

The ruling class. Dignitaries, warriors, officials, priests: the Mexican 'nobility'—The rising class of traders. The monopoly of foreign trade: origin of the honours allowed to the merchant guilds: the traders' place in the social system—The craftsmen— The common people. Rights and duties of the ordinary citizen: the possibilities open to him: the case of the landless peasant— The slaves: the misleading nature of the word: how a man became a slave: manumission—Wealth and poverty. Standards of living. Ownership and usufruct of land: personal estate: taxes and tribute: wealth and expenditure of the rulers: public service and private fortune: luxury, comfort and frugality— The sovereign, the great dignitaries, the council. Beginnings of the Mexican dynasty: election of the emperor: the prerogatives and functions of the Ciuacoatl: other great dignitaries and high officials: the Tlatocan, or supreme council.

During its migration and after its arrival in the central valley the Mexican tribe retained a fairly simple and essentially equalitarian social structure. The *Mexica*, a people of soldier-peasants, sometimes stayed for several years in fertile places;[1] sometimes they fought to gain possession of arable land; and then, carrying their few belongings on their backs, they would begin their march again.

Such a life did not call for any marked differentiation in social function, nor for the appearance of an organised authority. The head of each family was both a warrior and a farmer, and he joined with all the others in the palavers which made the important decisions; and as for the Aztecs' standard of living, it was the same for all. They were all equally poor.

The only germ of a ruling class that existed at this period was to be found in the priests of Uitzilopochtli, the god-bearers, who joined some degree of military command and general authority to their priestly functions. But this rudimentary organisation was sufficient; and when the Mexicans, in an attempt to imitate their more developed neighbours and to raise themselves to the rank of the cities, provided their nation with a king, the result was catastrophic.[2] At the time of the foundation of their city they had the same social and political organisation as that which they had known throughout their wanderings.

How great a change there was between this and the beginning of the sixteenth century! The Mexican community had become differentiated, complex and stratified: the different sections had widely differing functions, and the authority of the ruling dignitaries was very great. The priesthood, high in honour and importance, no longer had its military and civil aspect. Trade now dealt with a great volume of valuable merchandise, and the influence of the traders was increasing. Wealth and luxury had made their appearance, and misery with them.

The old simple lines of tribal organisation had been overlaid by those of a state, with its ability to administer and to conceive and execute a foreign policy; and at the head of this stood a single man, the *tlatoani*, the emperor, with his counsellors and his officials about him, a man so high and splendid that the common people might not look upon him.

The change was very great, and it had come about in a very short time: tribal democracy had been replaced by an aristocratic and imperialistic monarchy.

THE RULING CLASS

The ruling class, the top level of the social stratification, was itself divided into several categories according to function, importance and standing. Thus a high-priest was the equal of a general, but both would look down upon a poor 'parish priest' or a village tax-gatherer. Yet all of them stood apart from what Spaniards called the plebeians, the *maceualtin* (*maceualli* in the singular), who had neither authority nor office.

The word *tecuhtli* – 'dignitary', or 'lord' – was applied to the upper level of the ruling class when the army, administration or judiciary was concerned: it was used for the chief generals, officials of the highest rank in Mexico (the head of the exchequer, for example) and in the provinces, the chiefs of the districts of the capital, and the judges who dealt with the most important cases in the large towns. If the former ruler of a city that had been absorbed by the empire remained in his place under the authority of Tenochtitlan, he was a *tecuhtli*. The emperor himself was a *tecuhtli;* and the glorious title was often borne by the gods – Mictlantecuhtli, 'the lord of the world that is under the ground', for example, or Xiuhtecuhtli, 'the turquoise lord', the god of fire.

The priests, for their part, were only rarely distinguished in this way. As we shall see, they had their own hierarchy, which was no less splendid and respected than that of the other divisions.

In the early days, the *tecuhtli* was elected, or rather nominated, seeing that the choice of the electors nearly always fell on a member of the same family for any given appointment. The succession to the headship of a district, for example, came about 'not by inheritance, but, at his death, by the election of the most honourable, wise, capable and aged man . . . If the dead man has left a son who is fit for the position, he is chosen: it is always a relation who is elected, providing that there is one and that he is suited for the post.'[3]

By the time of Motecuhzoma II, however, the only offices that were really filled by election were the very highest – those of the emperor and of the four 'senators' who attended him. In all other cases it was either a straightforward appointment of his own servant by the emperor or a nomination on the part of the districts or the cities – a nomination which held good only if it were confirmed by the central authority.

In practice it was generally a son or a nephew or even a brother of the local *tecuhtli* who succeeded him in his

village, town or district; but although the outward show of
tradition was respected, in fact this was no longer an election
but a presentation, and in the last resort it was the emperor
who appointed the man of his choice. Power no longer came
from below, but from above: the new machine of the state
had absorbed the last traces of the democratic beginnings.

A *tecuhtli* was always a man of importance, whether he
governed a village, a town or a city. It was the *tecuhtli* whom
the Spaniards (bringing with them a Jamaican word) termed
the 'cacique'. He had distinguishing clothes and jewels: his
name carried the respectful termination -*tzin:* he lived in a
teccalli, a palace modest or luxurious as the case might be,
maintained by the people of the village or the town who
owed him 'wood and water', as the expression went, and
domestic service. Land was set aside for him and worked
on his account; the income from it, which he received,
might be called his salary. Apart from this, the emperor
allowed him 'victuals and pay', stuff, clothes and provisions,
in return for which he was obliged to present himself before
the emperor whenever he was called for.

What were his functions? In the first place, he represented
his people before the higher authorities: he was to 'speak
for the people under his care'[4] and to defend them, if it
was necessary, against excessive taxation or any encroach-
ment upon their land. Secondly, he judged law-suits,
appeal lying to Mexico or Texcoco. Then, as a military
commander, he led the contingents that he was required to
furnish in war. Finally, he was there to maintain order, to
oversee the cultivation of the fields, particularly those which
were set aside to produce the tribute, and to see that this
tribute was paid to the *calpixque* of the imperial administration.

To accomplish all this, especially if his district were
important, he in his turn had the right of appointing local
officials, so long as he paid them himself out of the produce
of his lands and his allowances. The *tecuhtli*, his family and
his children, paid no taxes.

There used to be a great difference, in the France of
earlier days, between the manner of life of the country

39

squires in Brittany or Gascony and that of the great lords around the king, and a great difference in their real importance: in the same way the *tecuhtli* of a distant Mexican village was of no great account compared with one of those in Motecuhzoma's train. But whereas the French noble was sure of leaving his title to his descendants, the *tecuhtli* was not. He held it only for himself and for his lifetime, and at his death the double process of local nomination and central confirmation might give his office to a distant relative, or even to someone entirely outside his family. And in fact, many cities, particularly in the neighbourhood of Mexico, had had a *tecuhtli* directly appointed by the emperor.

Each district or *calpulli* in the capital had its own chief, the *calpullec*, who was elected for life, preferably from the same family, by the inhabitants, and confirmed by the emperor. He had a council of elders, the *ueuetque*, who were probably the oldest and best-known heads of families, and 'he never did anything without taking the opinion of the elders.'[5] His duties were in every way like those of the *tecuhtli* of a village or a city: he was particularly required 'to be able to protect and defend' his fellow-citizens. But his chief task was the keeping of the register of the communal land belonging to the *calpulli*, which was shared out in parcels among the various families. As we shall see, each family had the usufruct of its piece and could farm it and take the harvest under certain conditions: the duty of the *calpullec* and his council was to see that these conditions were respected, and to record all the alterations of the sharing of the land in their books, by means of emblematic pictures and hieroglyphs.

By reason of his office, the *calpullec* had to meet quite heavy expenses. The frequent district councils met in his house, and he was expected to offer the elders food and drink: even today, in a Mexican village, if an Indian who has an official position does not do the thing handsomely he loses face; it was the same then. In compensation, the head of the district did not pay taxes, and the people of his *calpulli*, taking it in turn, did the work of his land and of his house.

There is no doubt that here we are in contact with a very old institution in the Mexican tribe: the *calpulli* is the true nucleus, and its chief and elders represent the earliest form of the Aztec territorial organisation. It is equally sure that at the time of which we are speaking the *calpullec*, although he was still a highly honoured figure, found his authority growing less and less real as it was nibbled away on all sides.

He was elected to his office by his fellow-citizens, but he only retained it by the sovereign's favour. In theory he was at the head of all local activities, but he had to yield the temple to the *quacuilli*, the district priest, who belonged to the ecclesiastical chain of command, and the 'house of the young men' to the military instructors appointed from above. Torquemada[6] says that he was obliged to go to the palace every day to take his orders: 'he waited for the *Uey calpixqui*, who was the *mayordomo mayor*, to speak to him and tell him what the great lord (the emperor) ordered and commanded.' There were officials under him whose duty it was to oversee groups of twenty, forty or a hundred families for the payment of taxes and the organisation of collective labour, such as cleaning or public works. At least theoretically they were under him; but one has a distinct impression that they really belonged to what one may call a bureaucratic administrative system which was outside his control. 'The number of civil servants (*oficiales*) that this nation had for every little thing was so great and all the registers were so well kept that there was nothing wanting in either the accounts or the rolls (*padrones*); for there were clerks and minor officials (*mandoncillos*) for everything, even the sweepers. The whole city and its districts were divided up, for the man who was in charge of a hundred houses chose and appointed five or six other agents under him and shared the hundred houses between them so that each, looking after twenty or fifteen, could direct and command (the inhabitants) in order to provide the taxes and the men necessary for the public works: and so the officials of the city (*oficiales de la república*) were so many in number that it was impossible to count them.'[7]

This picture of Mexican officialdom, which is strangely

reminiscent of the administrative system of the Inca empire of Peru, leaves one little illusion as to the amount of independence that the *calpullec* could enjoy, with the *Uey calpixqui* above him and the bureaucracy below. He was a traditional chief, a survivor from a former day, and he now found himself incongruously attached to a centralised administration which belonged not to the local communities but to the state.

Finally, although it may be conceded that at the beginning he had some military powers, they had almost all been taken away. In practice the contingents from the various quarters were grouped in four corps, agreeing with the four great regions of the city, Teopan, Moyotlan, Aztacalco and Cuepopan; and these corps were under commanders far more imposing than the local chiefs. In a country that was perpetually at war the army offered brave and ambitious men a career particularly rich in honours and power.

It goes without saying that in Tenochtitlan every man, whatever his origin, either was a warrior or wished to be one. The officials had been, or were going to become, warriors: the priests, at least when they were young, went off to war in order to take a prisoner; and some of them, the *tlamacaztequiuaque*, were both priests and fighting-men:[8] as for the traders, as we shall see, their calling had none of the tameness that it has with us, but was more like an armed reconnaissance or a colonial expedition.

A boy-child was dedicated to war at his birth. His umbilical cord was buried together with a shield and some little arrows, and in a set speech he was told that he had come into this world to fight.[9] The god of the young men was Tezcatlipoca, who was also called Yaotl, 'the warrior', and Telpochtli, 'the youth'; and it was Tezcatlipoca who ruled over the *telpochcalli*, 'the houses of the young men', where the boys went when they were six or seven. There was one in each district, and the education that they gave was essentially an education for the war in which the Mexican boy longed to shine. When they were ten, the boys had their hair cut with a lock left on the napes of their necks; the lock was called a *piochtli*, and they were not allowed to cut it off until they had managed to make a prisoner in battle, even if it meant two or three joining their efforts to do so.

The warrior who had accomplished this first exploit carried the title of *iyac* from then onwards. 'I am an *iyac*,' said Tezcatlipoca;[10] so the young warrior already rivalled his god. He cut off his lock and let his hair grow so that it fell over his right ear. But he had still only risen a single rank, and if he did not do better in the two or three succeeding campaigns he would be obliged to retire and give up soldiering. He would have to devote himself to his piece of land and his family, a dismal fate; he would never be allowed to wear dyed and embroidered clothes, nor jewellery. He would only be a *maceualli*.

But if on the other hand he were favoured by the gods, if (as a Mexican would have said) he had been born under a fortunate sign, he would go on as a fighting-man. When he had taken or killed four of the enemy he would have the title of *tequiua*, 'one who has (a share of the) tribute'; that is to say, he would reach that upper category of men who participated in the allotment of the revenues. He would become a commander and he would join the councils of war: he would have the right to wear certain feather head-dresses, and bracelets made of leather. The higher ranks would be open to him and he might become a *quachic*,[11] a *quauhchichimecatl*, 'chichimec-eagle', or an *otomitl*, so called from the old, rough, warlike tribe that lived in the mountains north of Mexico. Lastly, he might become a member of one of the two higher military orders, that of the 'jaguar-knights', Tezcatlipoca's soldiers,[12] who wore the skin of a jaguar in battle, and that of the 'eagle-knights', whose helmet was an eagle's head, and who were the soldiers of the sun.[13]

In the eleventh month of the year, *Ochpaniztli*, the emperor himself distributed the honours and rewards. 'They all stood in even ranks before Motecuhzoma, who was seated upon his eagle-matting (*quauhpetlapan*): indeed he sat upon eagle's feathers and the back of his seat was jaguar's skin . . . Everyone stood before him and saluted him: at his feet he had all kinds of weapons and badges of distinction,

43

shields, swords, cloaks, loin-cloths. They stood before him and saluted him: and each in turn received his gifts. Then they went aside to adorn themselves and put on their decorations. It was to the great chiefs that he (the emperor) gave these splendid ornaments . . . When they had all been equipped in this way they formed their ranks again in front of Motecuhzoma . . . And the decorations that they had received were their rewards, and they served to bind them (to the service) . . . And the women who watched, the old women, the beloved women, shed burning tears, and their hearts were filled with sorrow. They said, "Here are our beloved children: and if in five or six days the word *Water and burning* is said (that is to say, war) will they ever return? Will they ever find their way back? Indeed, they will be gone for ever." ' [14]

But these lamentations, which were traditionally allowed, do not seem to have diverted the warriors from their no less traditionally honoured and glorified career. For them death in battle, or better still, death on the stone of sacrifice, was the promise of a happy eternity; for a warrior who was killed in the field or on the altar was sure of becoming one of the 'companions of the eagle', *quauhteca*, one of those who accompanied the sun from its rising to the zenith in a procession that blazed with light and was splendid with joy, and then of being reincarnated as a humming-bird, to live for ever among the flowers.

At the summit the military hierarchy merged with that of the state. One of the emperor's titles was *tlacatecuhtli* 'lord of the men', that is to say 'of the warriors', and his primary function was that of commanding not only the Mexican armies but those of the allied cities. The most important of the great dignitaries who were about him had offices that were essentially military, at least to begin with: in time of war, four of them commanded the contingents that were supplied by the four regions of the capital.

Of these 'four great ones' two stand out by reason of the honours that they received; the *tlacateccatl*, 'he who commands the warriors', and the *tlacochcalcatl*, 'the man of the javelin-house'. The titles seem to imply that the first had a military command and that the second was responsible for the arsenals (*tlacochcalli*) in which the weapons were kept. Generally they were near relations of the sovereign, and it was often from them that the emperor was chosen: Itzcoatl, Axayacatl, Tizoc and Motecuhzoma II were *tlacochcalcatl* at the time of their election, and Auitzotl was *tlacateccatl*. They had a splendid and magnificent dress – embroidered cloaks, jewels, plumes. Their houses and their way of life were based on the emperor's. They were among the first to receive when presents were given and the spoil of subjected provinces shared out. They had both great standing and great wealth.

This was also the case according to their rank with all the soldiers who distinguished themselves. As they rose in the hierarchy their fame grew, and as they earned the right to wear more and more splendid ornaments and clothes so at the same time they received gifts in kind and the rents of various estates. They were not only free from the duty of farming their own shares of land as ordinary men had to do, but they were given other shares, mostly in conquered country, which were worked for them.

They were wealthy men, with their fine houses, many servants, brilliant clothes and jewels, well-filled store-houses and coffers. But it must be remembered that this was a wealth that came only after honourable achievements and as a consequence of them. A man was wealthy because he was honoured, not honoured because he was wealthy. Besides, honourable achievement was the only means to wealth, for a man of the ruling class.

The Spaniards believed these military chiefs to be a nobility that attended upon the emperor – the equivalent of the European nobles at the court of the king of Spain or of France. But they were clearly mistaken; for the court of the Aztec emperor was made up not of hereditary magnates with great estates or inherited wealth, but of military or civil officials who enjoyed privileges that were attached to their office.

This ruling class continually renewed itself, taking recruits from the general body of the people; and this was

45

its great strength. Any warrior who managed to capture his four prisoners became a *tequiua* and thus a member of the upper classes, whatever his origin. Furthermore, the emperor filled the higher ranks by promotion according to merit, and often at the end of a battle or a war he would make a whole batch of superior officers: Motecuhzoma II made two hundred and sixty at once after his victory over the men of Tutotepec.[15]

Tezozomoc states that all the plebeians who had distinguished themselves in the war against Coyoacán were promoted to the highest ranks after the submission of the city, and that at the same time each was given the income of one estate or more.[16] Moreover even those very important offices of *tlacochcalcatl* and *tlacateccatl*, which have already been mentioned, were so filled that one at least was held by a soldier who had risen from the ranks – *criado en las guerras*, as Sahagún has it.[17]

In a society that was so hungry for renown, a society in which renown based upon services rendered counted for so much to everybody (the remarkable exception of the business-men will be dealt with later), the fighting-men had an enviable and an envied position. When a father treated his son to one of those improving lectures that were so usual among the Aztecs he always proposed them as the model for imitation. Their superiority was continually made evident, not only by their clothes and marks of rank, but by their privileges on ritual and ceremonial occasions. In the eighth month of the year, which was called *Uey tecuilhuitl*, 'the high feast of the dignitaries', for example, only 'the captains and other brave men accustomed to the usages of war' were allowed to join in the great sacred dance that took place at night, at the foot of the pyramids in the holy city, by the light of huge braziers and torches held up by the young men. They danced by pairs, and each pair of warriors was joined by a woman (one of the *auianime*, the companions of the unmarried soldiers) with her hair loose on her shoulders, dressed in a fringed, embroidered skirt. The dancers wore jewels according to their rank: a *quachic* had the right to a lip-ornament in the shape of a bird, an *otomitl* to one shaped like the leaf of a water-plant. They all wore turquoise disks in their ears. The dance went on for several hours; and sometimes the emperor came to take part in it.[18]

In the following month, *Tlaxochimaco*, there was an equally solemn dance in honour of Uitzilopochtli, in front of his *teocalli*; but this dance was at noon, for Uitzilopochtli was the god of the sun at its height. Here the warriors were arranged according to their rank, first the *quaquachictin* and the *otomi*, then the *tequiuaque*,[19] then the young men who had made one prisoner, then the 'elder brothers', the distinguished solders who acted as instructors, and lastly the youths from the district schools. 'And they held hands, one woman between two men and one man between two women, as in the dances of the common people in Old Castille; and as their dance wound about they sang. The most seasoned in war, who were in the first row, held their women by the waist, as if they were embracing them; but the others, the less distinguished (in military rank) were not allowed to go so far.'[20]

There were many other occasions upon which the warriors were the centre of admiring public attention and honour: it was the case, for example, when, every four years, there was the celebration of the feast of the god of fire, and the emperor and his chief ministers, covered with ornaments of gems and feathers, danced the 'dance of the dignitaries'; or on the days that had the sign *ce xochitl*, 'one – flower', when the sovereign gave them rich presents, amid songs and dances; or, of course, every time the victorious army came home from an expedition, making its entry into the city by one of the raised causeways, with welcoming elders and the din of *teponaztli* and trumpets attending them from as far out as the shore of the lake.

If it is true that these dignitaries did not form a nobility in the European sense of the word, it is equally true that at the time of which we are speaking there was an inclination to make distinctions hereditary – distinctions that were originally attached only to an office. The son of a *tecuhtli* did not fall to the level of a *maceualli*, of a plebeian; by the

47

right of his birth alone he had the title of *pilli*, whose primary meaning is 'child' or 'son', but which had acquired the sense of 'son (of a *tecuhtli*)', or, as the Spaniards would say, of *hidalgo*, 'son of somebody (of importance)'.

In theory the *pilli* had no privileges, and in order to rise in the army, the administration or in religion he was to work as hard as any *maceualli*. In fact he had many advantages from the beginning, derived from the standing of his father and a higher education in the *calmecac* instead of the local school. It was among the *pilli* that the emperor most readily found his officials, judges and ambassadors; and the *pilli* as a group may be placed half-way between the people and the ruling class, forming a reservoir that could be drawn upon to meet the constantly increasing needs of a constantly growing administration.

A nobility was therefore coming into being. But still it must not be forgotten that the *pilli* who did nothing outstanding during his lifetime left his children no distinction. The prestige of the *tecuhtli* scarcely lasted beyond one generation unless it were revived by fresh exertions.[21]

As the empire grew and the undertakings of the state became more and more varied so necessarily the duties of its servants became more specialised. It is very difficult to form an exact opinion of the functions of those officials whose titles have come down to us: it is likely that most of these titles no longer had any relation to their literal meaning, resembling in this the titles used in the Roman or Byzantine empire, or in France in the days of the kings. The *tlillancalqui* was probably no more 'the keeper of the dark house' than the Constable of France was the person in charge of the stables. But for all that, we can discern three classes of officials in the time of Motecuhzoma II.

In the first place there were the governors of certain cities or strongholds. Although they had the military title of *tlacochtecuhtli*, 'the lord of the spears', of *tlacateccatl* and even *tlacatecuhtli*, or more rarely *tezcacoacatl*, 'he of the mirror-serpent', or *tlillancalqui*,[22] their duties must to a large extent have been civil and administrative. Several towns had two governors at the same time – Oztoman, for example, and Zozolan and Uaxyacac (Oaxaca) – so it is likely that one of the governors looked after the administration and the other the command of the garrison.

The generic name for the officials occupied with administration and more particularly with the taxes was *calpixque*, 'house-attendants', translated by the conquering Spaniards and the chroniclers as 'major-domos'.[23] They were chosen from among the *pilli*, and their principal duty was to organise the cultivation of the lands set aside for the payment of the tax, and to receive the grain, merchandise and provisions that each province was to furnish at fixed intervals and see to its transport as far as Mexico.

They were obliged to send the emperor reports upon the state of agriculture and commerce: if a famine should break out, it was for them to tell the emperor and under his orders to exempt the province from the payment of tax or even to open the public stores of corn and distribute it to the people. They were also responsible for the erection of public buildings, for the maintenance of the roads and for the supply of servants for the imperial palaces.

In each province the *calpixqui* lived in the chief town, together with his staff, which included a large number of scribes, able to keep the tribute-registers up to date and to draft reports: and no doubt he had deputies in the towns and principal villages of his province.

Bernal Díaz' account gives some idea of the powers of these officials, and of their formidable authority. The first time the Spaniards met any *calpixque* was at Quiauiztlan, in the country of the Totonacs, a nation subject to the empire.[24] 'Some Indians from the same village came running to tell all the caciques who were talking with Cortés that five Mexicans had been seen, the tax-gatherers of Motecuhzoma. On hearing this they went pale, and began to tremble with fear. They left Cortés to himself and went out to welcome them. In all haste they adorned a room with foliage, prepared some food and made a great deal of cocoa, which is the best drink that is to be found among them. When these five Indians came into the village they passed by the place where we were with so much confidence and

49

pride that they walked straight on, without speaking either to Cortés or any of the others of us. They wore rich embroidered cloaks, loin-cloths of the same nature, and their shining hair was raised in a knot on their heads: each had a bunch of flowers in his hand, and he smelt to it; and other Indians, like servants, fanned them with fly-whisks.' And these arrogant representatives of the central authority had no hesitation in calling the Totonac chiefs before them and violently reprimanding them for having presumed to negotiate with Cortés.

Lastly, the third category of appointed officials, the judges, were nominated by the sovereign either from the experienced and elderly dignitaries or from among the common people. At Texcoco half the higher judges were of noble family and the other half of plebeian origin.[25] All the chroniclers agree in praising the care with which the emperor and his fellow-kings chose the judges, 'taking particular care that they were not drunkards, nor apt to be bribed, nor influenced by personal considerations, nor impassioned in their judgments.'[26]

Their office had an extraordinary respect and authority: at their disposition there was a kind of police-force which, upon their orders, could arrest even the highest officials, in any place whatsoever. Their messengers 'travelled with greatest speed, whether it was day or night, through rain, snow or hail.'[27] Their scribes recorded every case, with the claims of either side, the testimonies and the sentences. They were very much honoured: but woe to the judge who let himself be bought – from reproof it was but a short pace to dismissal, and sometimes to death. A king of Texcoco had a judge executed for favouring a grandee against a working-man.[28]

All these people, military or civil officials, soldiers, administrators, judges, serving dignitaries or the sons of great men waiting for a post, together with the host of messengers, attendants, clerks and constables who surrounded them, depended upon the secular power. They depended upon the emperor, the head of the state; and they were so many cogs in the huge mechanism of the empire. Beside them, intimately linked by family ties, by education and by the common depth of religious faith, but depending upon another power, was the clergy – beside the servants of the state there were the servants of the gods. The ruling class was divided into these two parallel hierarchies: the one side conquered, administered and judged; the other, by its faithful service in the temples, caused the kindness of the gods to rain down upon the earth.

Every young *pilli* was well acquainted with the priestly order from his childhood, since he was brought up in a *calmecac*, a monastery-school, where he had shared the life and the austerities of the priests. The sons of tradesmen could also go to the *calmecac*, but on something of a supernumerary or marginal footing.[29] It would seem, then, that the priesthood was only open to members of the ruling class, or at a push to traders' sons: yet Sahagún[30] insists upon the fact that sometimes the most venerated priests came from very humble families. It must therefore be granted that it was possible for a *maceualli* to enter the novitiate if he wished: perhaps if he showed an unusual vocation for the priesthood while he was still at the local school his masters could transfer him to the *calmecac*.

The novice, literally the 'little priest', was dedicated to Quetzalcoatl, who above all others was the god of the priests. When he was between twenty and twenty-two years old, if he decided not to marry and to enter fully into the clerical career, he became a *tlamacazqui*, a priest, and from then onwards he could assume this venerated title, which was in fact the attribute of Quetzacoatl,[31] god, king and high-priest of the legendary Tula. It was also the title given to Tlaloc, the ancient god of rain and fecundity, to the lesser divinities who attended him, and to the splendid, beneficent young god of music and dancing.[32] To be entitled *tlamacazqui* was, to some degree, to be already the equal of a god.

Most of the priests probably never went further than this stage. As they became old they would undertake some permanent but subsidiary duties, such as beating upon a drum or helping in the sacrifices; or else they would take

51

charge of a 'parish', and peaceably end their days conducting the services of the local temple. Their rank in the hierarchy was termed *quacuilli*.

Others, on the other hand, reached a higher level, and acquired the title of *tlenamacac*. They could be members of the electoral body that chose the emperor, and it was from among them that the highest dignitaries of the Mexican church were taken.

Two high-priests, equal in power, reigned jointly over this church. The one, *quetzalcoatl totec tlamacazqui*, 'the plumed serpent, priest of our lord', was in charge of the worship of Uitzilopochtli; the other, *quetzalcoatl Tlaloc tlamacazqui*, 'the plumed serpent, priest of Tlaloc', of that of Tlaloc. The two gods dominated the great *teocalli* together, as we have seen; and in the same manner their two high-priests dominated the religious hierarchy.

The title of 'plumed serpent' which they had in common sealed them with that sanctity which the myth recognised in the Toltec god-king Quetzalcoatl; and, in short, they were his representatives and successors. 'Among these priests,' says Sahagún,[33] 'the best were chosen to become the supreme pontiffs, who were called *quequetzalcoa*, which means successors of Quetzalcoatl . . . No heed was paid to birth in this choice, but only to morals and observance of religion, knowledge of doctrine and purity of life. Those were chosen who were humble, righteous and peaceable, earnest and reasonable, not given to levity, but sober, severe and scrupulous in morals, full of love and charity, compassion and friendship for all, god-fearing and devout.' This, it must be admitted, is uncommonly warm praise, coming from the pen of a Catholic monk.

These two high-priests were, according to the same authority, 'equal in status and in honour'; and they were surrounded by the deepest respect – the emperor himself went in person to visit them. Their double presence at the head of the religious world consecrated the union of the two basic ideologies of Mexico, which the Aztecs had brought together when they became the ruling nation. On the one side there was Uitzilopochtli, the solar god of war and near relation of the hunting gods, the pattern of the soldier and the prototype of the sacrificed victim who is to be reborn for a carefree immortality as a bird: and on the other Tlaloc, the old rain-god and god of the farmer's plenty, who without fighting makes the maize spring up and all the plants that men eat, the benign wizard who keeps famine and drought away. On the one hand the religion of the warlike nomad and on the other that of the settled peasants, each with its own vision and its own paradise.

Under the two high-priests there were many 'prelates' who were responsible either for some given branch of religious activity or for the worship of some particular god.[34] The most important of them, the secretary-general of the church, as it were, had the title of *Mexicatl teohuatzin*, 'the venerable (*-tzin*) Mexican in charge of the gods'; he was chosen by the two *quequetzalcoa*, and 'he controlled other less important priests, somewhat like bishops, and he saw to it that everything to do with divine worship in all places and provinces was carried out diligently and perfectly, according to the laws and customs of the former pontiffs . . . he controlled all matters concerning the worship of the gods in the provinces subjected to Mexico.' His competence also included the discipline of the priestly body and the supervision of the education given in the *calmecac*. His assistants were the *uitznauac teohuatzin*, who was principally concerned with ritual, on the one hand, and on the other the *tepan teohuatzin*, who attended to questions that concerned education.

A treasurer, the *tlaquimiloltecuhtli*,[35] had care of the holy vessels and other religious objects, and of the temples' estates. The wealth of the gods was enormous: there were not only the buildings and their land, the statues, the countless implements of worship, which were of great value, and the offerings of provisions and clothes, continually brought by the faithful, but also the agricultural land which the ecclesiastical corporations let out or had worked for them, and their share of the tribute from the subjected provinces.

The piety of the emperors rained gifts upon the temples.

53

At Texcoco[36] fifteen important villages and their dependencies were set aside solely for their maintenance and repair and for supplying them with wood for their never-extinguished fires. At Mexico there was the same arrangement:[37] some villages furnished the temples with maize, wood, meat and incense, and paid no other kind of tax. The temples, therefore, had special granaries beside them; and these contained important reserves not only of the provisions for the priests but also of those which they gave to the poor and sick – they had hospitals at Mexico, Texcoco, Cholula and other places. The management of all these properties must have called for a very considerable staff of scribes in the treasurer's department.

There appear to have been an exceedingly large number of priests assigned to the various gods: no deity would have been satisfied with less than his own 'household', a chief priest, ministrants and novices. The four hundred gods of drink and drunkenness were served by an equal number of priests, under the guidance of the *Ometochtzin*, the 'venerable two-rabbit', whose name was the same as that of one of these gods. This was a very general practice; each priest bore the name of the god he served and whom, serving, he incarnated. The rites had proliferated to an enormous extent, and a host of priests busied themselves over the accomplishment of this or that particular task; for the division of labour had reached a very high pitch: for example, the *ixcozauhqui tzonmolco teohua* was responsible only for the supplying of wood to the temple of the fire-god, and the *pochtlan teohua yiacatecuhtli* for the organisation of the feast of the god of the merchants.

Clearly it was essential that the calendar of feasts should be kept up to date, and the sequence of ceremonies exactly followed: this very important duty was entrusted to the *epcoaquacuiltzin*, 'the venerable minister of the temple of the rain', who, in spite of his limiting title, had authority, under the *uitznuac teohuatzin*, over the entirety of the religious scene, at least in its material aspect.

Women were by no means excluded from the priesthood. Some twenty or forty days after her birth, a girl might be brought to the temple by her mother; the woman would give the priest a censer and some *copal* (incense), and this would establish a reciprocal agreement. But it was only when she was a grown girl (*ichpochtli*) that the novice would go into religion, with the title of priestess – or literally 'woman-priest', *ciuatlamacazqui*. As long as she kept this title she was bound to celibacy: but it was quite possible for her to marry 'if she were asked in marriage, if the words were properly said, if the fathers, the mothers and the notables agreed.'[38] An unusually solemn marriage service took place, and then she left the temple for her home. But it appears that many preferred to give themselves up entirely to religion.

One finds a great many priestesses ministering on various occasions in the traditional accounts. The feast of the great goddess Toci (our grandmother) was directed by a woman, a *ciuaquacuilli*: another priestess, called the *iztacciuatl*, 'the white woman', was in charge of the physical preparation of certain ceremonies, particularly the sweeping of the holy places[39] and the lighting of the fires.

During *Quecholli*, the fourteenth month, a great many women went to the temple of Mixcoatl, the hunter and warrior, to take their children to the old priestesses there: they took the children and danced with them in their arms. Then the mothers, having made the priestesses a present of sweetmeats or delicacies,[40] took their children away again. This ceremony lasted all the morning.

During the month of *Ochpaniztli* it was the young priestesses of the goddess of maize who played the most important part in the religious celebrations. Each of them represented the goddess, and each carried seven ears of maize wrapped in rich cloth[41] on her back: their faces were painted, their arms and legs adorned with feathers. Singing, they went in procession with the priests of the same goddess; and at sunset they threw handfuls of coloured maize and calabash seeds to the crowd, who struggled and scrambled for them, because they were a token of wealth and plenty for the coming year.

Torquemada[42] states that some of these young priestesses

took vows for one year or more to win some favour from heaven, such as the healing of an invalid or a happy marriage: but it seems that they never took vows for ever. They were guarded, supervised and taught by old women, and they looked after the temple, offering incense before the images of the gods at nightfall, at midnight and at dawn; they also wove cloaks for the priests and the idols.

From priesthood to divination, to medicine and at last to magic, so good shades into evil, respect into fear and hatred: on its shadowy frontiers the world of religion merged with that of the malignant warlock and the sorcerer.

Divination in the true sense of the word was not only permitted but practised, by a particular class of priests called *tonalpouhque*. They were educated in the monastery schools, for it was there that a knowledge of the characters used in the divinatory calendar was taught; and indeed this knowledge formed an integral part of the higher education. In this context it is worth remembering the importance of augury in the palmy days of Rome. But it seems that these soothsayers did not become members of a temple when they were qualified; they set up on their own account. Neither business nor income can have lacked, for every family necessarily went to a soothsayer whenever a child was born: furthermore, there was no important occasion in life, marriage, leaving for a journey or a military expedition, etc., whose date was not fixed by the soothsayers, either at the request of private persons or of officials. Each of these consultations was paid for by a meal, by presents, 'several cloaks, some turkeys and a load of victuals.'[43]

The doctors, men and women, were officially recognised, although their sphere was not always far from that of the black magicians; and they openly took part in many ceremonies. The midwives should also be mentioned: these women helped at the birth of the child, but more than that, they harangued it with the necessary moral and religious speeches, and (the soothsayers having been duly consulted) endowed it with its 'baptismal' name. They had a highly respected position in society; and no doubt they were quite well-to-do.

56

Finally, at the opposite pole of the religious world from the priests, there were the magicians, the sorcerers,[44] the formidable experts in spells, who were believed to have such wide and multifarious powers. They could change themselves into animals; they knew magic words 'that bewitch women and turn affections wherever they choose'; and their spells could kill from a great way off. There were men magicians and women magicians; and they kept their dark practices hidden. But for all that they were known well enough for people to come by night to buy their aid. It was said that their power came from their having been born under a malignant sign – 'one – rain', or 'one – wind' – and that for their purposes they always waited for a day that came under a sign favourable to them. The figure nine, which was the figure of the night-gods and of hell and of death, was particularly auspicious for them.

One of the most frequently-mentioned crimes of sorcery consisted of theft – fifteen or twenty magicians would combine to rob a family. They would come to the door by night, and by means of certain charms they would strike the people of the house motionless. 'It was as if they were all dead, and yet they heard and saw everything that happened . . . The thieves lit torches and looked through the house to find what there was to eat. They all ate quite calmly, and none of the people could hinder them, for they were all as who should say turned to stone and out of their senses. Then when the sorcerers had eaten and thoroughly satisfied themselves they went into the store-room and granaries and took everything they found there, clothes, gold, silver, precious stones and feathers . . . and it is even said that they did a great many foul things to the women of the house.'

The sorcerers, then, were severely condemned by public opinion and severely punished by the law. If they were caught they were either hanged or sacrificed before an altar, their hearts being torn out.[45] In the reign of Chimalpopoca a man of Cuauhtitlán and his wife were sentenced to death because they had stupefied a peasant from Tenayuca by charms, and had stolen his maize during his sleep.[46]

Apart from this minority of dangerous outcasts all the classes that have just been mentioned, warriors, officials and priests, had the common character of directors in society and state. Together they made up a ruling order: it was an order of recent origin, vigorous, and continually strengthened by the new blood brought in by the plebeians, who could accede to the highest offices, whether they were military, adminstrative or religious. Birth played its part, but it was still personal merit that raised a man, and lack of it that lowered him. The Mexican always bore in mind that honours were no more stable than running water, and that a man born noble might die a slave.[47]

It appears that an aristocratic reaction took place at the beginning of the sixteenth century, under the reign of Motecuhzoma II, and that the reactionaries tried to expel the sons of plebeians from the higher places: according to the documents, however, this affected only the embassies that went abroad, for 'it was not decent that the *maceuales* should go into kings' palaces'.[48] It is possible that this reaction might have gone on to the point of bringing a purely hereditary nobility into existence: but there was a strong influence that worked in the other direction every day – the continual pressure of war and conquest, which brought brave and ambitious men up to the top.

When one reflects upon this ruling class's way of life one is much struck by the fact that one of its essential sections, the priests, lived in austere poverty, and that the others, the soldiers and the civil servants, only came by wealth, in the form of estates, houses, slaves, clothes, victuals, jewels, etc., as a consequence of their rank or office. Wealth was not pursued for itself; it came as a function of increasing power and official expenses. It was an income and not a capital. The only thing that really counted in the *tecuhtli's* eyes was reputation.

Another class existed, however, in which these values were reversed, a class preoccupied with wealth, not only indifferent to prestige but averse to it. It was a class below the level of the ruling class, but it was in the act of rising towards it – a class so different, with its own customs, its laws and organisation, that it almost belonged to another world.

A RISING CLASS: THE TRADERS

A very great many Mexicans engaged in trade, some from time to time, and some continuously. There were the peasants who sold their maize, vegetables and poultry in the market; the women who sold all sorts of cooked meals in the streets; the merchants who sold cloth, shoes, drink, skins, pots, rope, pipes, and various useful objects; and the fishermen who daily brought in their fish from the lake, and frogs and shellfish. These small and medium traders did not form a distinct class of the population. The name of *pochteca*, traders, was kept for the members of the powerful corporations which were in charge of foreign trade and which had the monopoly of it.

They organised and guided the caravans of porters which went from the central valley to the remote, almost legendary provinces on the Pacific coast or on the Gulf. There they sold the produce of Mexico – cloth, rabbit's-hair blankets, embroidered clothes, golden jewels, obsidian and copper earrings, obsidian knives, cochineal dye, medicinal herbs and herbs for making scent, and they brought back such luxurious things as the translucid green jade, *chalchiuitl*, emeralds, *quetzalitztli*, sea-shells, tortoiseshell to make the stirring-spoons for cocoa, jaguar and puma skins, amber, parrot, *quetzal* and *xiuhtototl* plumes. Their trade, therefore, consisted in the export of manufactured goods and the import of luxurious foreign commodities.

It may be observed, in passing, that these exchanges are not in themselves enough to explain the economic relations between the Cold Lands of the centre and the Hot Lands of the south-east. Jewels of gold were exported, but gold was not imported: cotton cloth was sent out, but cotton yarn was not brought in. It was the tribute or the taxes that the provinces were obliged to pay that provided Mexico with its raw materials: for example, the Mixtec province of Yoaltepec had annually to send in 40 gold discs, each a finger thick and about 2 inches across; the province of Tlachquiauco 20 calabashes of gold-dust and those of

59

Quauhtochco and Ahuilizapan 1,600 bales of cotton.[49] These raw materials were worked up in Mexico, and having become cloth or jewels they continued their journey towards the south on the shoulders of the porters led by the *pochteca*.

There were merchant guilds[50] in some ten towns or large villages of the central plateau – Texcoco, Atzcapotzalco, Uitzilopochco, Uexotla, Cuauhtitlán, Coatlinchan, Chalco, Otumba, and of course at Tenochtitlan and Tlatelolco. It was in Tlatelolco before the Mexicans annexed it and while it was still independent that the *pochteca* seem to have had the greatest influence. They lived in seven districts, and one of these was called Pochtlan, which gave them their name: each of the districts had a commercial court or 'seat' – literally a mat, *petlatl*. If Chimalpahin is to be believed, it was only in the year 12 *tecpatl*, 1504, that '*inpeuh pochtecayotl Mexico*' – that trading began in Mexico:[51] he means, no doubt, that at this late date the guild was officially organised, after the manner of the *pochteca* of Tlatelolco and at their instigation, they having been Mexican citizens for thirty-one years.

The Tlatelolcan merchants, for their part, had begun in the early days of the fifteenth century, when the *tlatoani* Tlacateotl, who came to the throne in 1407, reigned over their city; and we are told that it was they who first brought fine cotton cloth to the then still countrified people of the lake-city.[52] Under the second ruler of Tlatelolco, Quauhtlatoa (1428–1467) they imported lip-ornaments, feathers, and the skins of wild animals; under Moquiuixtli, their last independent sovereign, the list of the goods that they brought back from their distant long voyages was much longer, and cocoa figures prominently in it, having by then become the usual drink of the better sort of people. The guild had at its head two chiefs, the *pochtecatlatohque*, 'merchant lords', whose name carried the honorific suffix –*tzin*.

After the annexation of Tlatelolco, the traders of that city and those of Tenochtitlan were closely associated, although the two bodies retained their individuality. Their chiefs, who numbered three or five, were old men; and for this reason they no longer went out on the tiring and perilous voyages, but entrusted their goods to the younger *pochteca* to be sold on their account. They supervised the departure of the caravans and presided over the ceremonies at their going and their coming back; they represented the guilds before the emperor, and they judged all law-suits within the trading class, not merely cases to do with commerce but cases of every kind. Their courts could pronounce all sentences, including that of death.

This privilege was all the more striking because in matters of justice there were no other exceptions whatever in Mexican society, and the emperor's courts judged everybody, from the *tecuhtli* to the *maceualli*. The *pochtecatl* alone stood outside this rule. In many respects the traders formed a nation within a nation: unlike the soldiers and even the priests they did not draw recruits from the common people – they were traders from father to son. They all lived together in the same districts, and they married among themselves. They had their own gods, their own feasts, and they worshipped in their own manner, for during their long journeys they had no priests but themselves.

We have seen the very marked graduation that existed in the ruling class: the same applied to the merchants, and there were many ranks interposed between the chiefs and the young trader setting out on his first voyage. There were the *tecuhnenenque*, 'travelling lords', respected for their long and dangerous expeditions; the *naualoztomeca*, 'disguised traders', who wore the clothes and spoke the language of the hostile tribes in order to reach the mysterious Tzinacantlan[53] to buy amber and *quetzal* plumes; the *tealtianime*, who had offered slaves in sacrifice; the *teyaualouanime*, 'those who surround the enemy', and the *tequanime*, the 'wild beasts'. The last two sound strange, applied to traders; but the truth is that their commerce was a continual adventure. The farther they were from Mexico the more dangerous their life became. They were thought to be spies as well as merchants – as indeed they were – and they had to contend with the hostility of the tribes who were as yet unconquered. Their goods aroused the cupidity of the highlanders: brigands attacked their caravans; and the *pochtecatl* had to transform himself into a warrior in order to survive.

This in fact was the original cause for the rise of the merchant class in the social system of the ancient city. In the reign of Auitzotl a column of Mexican traders was surrounded in a village of the Anahuac Ayotlan, on the Pacific side of the isthmus of Tehuantepec. They were besieged by contingents from different tribes, but fighting continuously they held out for four years, and when the future emperor Motecuhzoma, who was then *tlacochcalcatl*, came at the head of a Mexican army to extricate them he met the victorious *pochteca* on the road, laden with the spoils of their attackers.

With their hair down to their waists and their air of exhaustion and of triumph, these merchant-warriors made an extraordinary impression in Mexico, where they were received by the emperor with great magnificence. When they were welcomed at the palace, they laid at Auitzotl's feet the standards and the insignia made of precious feathers that they had captured in battle. He called them 'my uncles' and at once gave them the right to wear jewels of gold and feather ornaments – a right that was limited to their particular holidays, however, whereas the ruling class had the privilege without any restrictions.

According to Sahagún the spokesman who answered Auitzotl in the name of the merchants said, 'We, your uncles, the *pochteca* who are here, we have risked our heads and our lives, and we have laboured day and night; for although we are called traders and although we seem to be traders, we are captains and soldiers who, in a disguised fashion, go out to conquer.'54 This is a remarkable speech, for it must be seen as the expression of a kind of legal fiction designed to allow the merchants certain social advantages and to justify to the soldiers what would formerly have appeared intolerable effrontery. In fact, it was untrue to say that the *pochteca* were camouflaged soldiers: they were primarily and above all merchants. But the very conditions of their trading sometimes brought them into military action; and in this respect the siege that they were able to withstand in the isthmus of Tehuantepec was of decisive importance in their history. This side of their life was really quite secondary, in spite of everything, but nevertheless it was this side that was most emphazised from that time onwards. Auitzotl and after him Motecuhzoma II saw how useful these tireless traders could be to the empire; for it may be said that in these two reigns conquest followed the caravan, and the flag took the place of the merchant's cloth. As a recompense the trader was officially supposed to have taken up his calling only to dissemble his true character, which was that of a warrior – a pious falsehood that nevertheless allowed the mercantile class to rise in a society of whose fundamental principle it remained fundamentally ignorant.

And indeed what a total opposition there was between the way of life of a *pochtecatl* and that of the ruling class. The one was wholly taken up with service and reputation, the other with the pursuit of personal gain. The high official wore the embroidered cloak and the plume of his rank with pride; the trader went meekly along in a patched and homely garment. If one met him with his porters and their costly burdens he would softly deny that he could be the owner – he was only an intermediary. On his return from a voyage he would bring his goods to the warehouse by night, secretly over the water of the lake, and store them under the name of a relation or a friend.

Suppose that a *pochtecatl* should find himself growing rich, and decide to give a banquet. He would invite his equals and his betters in the commercial world; but he would have to put up with a great deal of offensiveness on their part – they would pull his goods about, flatly accusing him of having stolen them, and all this would have to be accepted with humble tears. It was only after he had undergone this treatment that he was allowed (or indeed obliged) to show his generosity in the feast that he offered – a feast of such proportions that the guests, and even the inhabitants of the whole quarter, could eat and drink for two days, and then carry the leavings home.

But apart from these exceptional occasions the traders

63

'did not parade their wealth, but on the contrary, they were lowly and humble. They did not wish to be thought rich, nor to have the reputation of wealth; they desired neither honours nor fame, and they walked humbly, without raising their eyes. They went in worn-out cloaks, and they feared honour and renown above all.'[55]

This humility that they put on, this desire to remain unnoticed, was the currency in which they paid for their social rise – the coin with which they bought pardon for their real and ever-growing importance; for the ruling class would bear their rivalry only if they avoided all open conflict. If the *pochteca* grew haughty in their richness, the emperor 'sought some transparent excuse to bring them down and put them to death, not that they were guilty, but out of hatred for their arrogance and pride; and he shared out their goods in presents to the old warriors.'[56] In other words, death and deprivation hovered over the head of the trader who forgot his rôle and made the mistake of showing off his wealth.

Nevertheless, their rise was sure. Their children could already go to the *calmecac* with the children of the dignitaries. During the month that was sacred to Uitzilopochtli the merchants were allowed to sacrifice slaves that they had bought to the great national deity, after the warriors had sacrificed the prisoners that they had taken in battle. Thus the *pochtecatl* imitated the *tecuhtli*, although it was on a somewhat lower level. If a trader died when he was on his voyage, his body was burnt, and he was presumed to have joined the sun in heaven, as if he had been a warrior killed on the battlefield. The god of the *pochteca* was worshipped together with the other great deities, and he had a special hymn.[57] And finally, if it is true that the traders had to pay a tax levied on their goods, they were nevertheless exempt from manual labour and personal service.

In a society basically concerned with war and religion, therefore, a recently-formed mercantile class was steadily climbing towards the top. It still had a very long way to go, and it was obliged to be very careful to avoid a violent hostile reaction. But this class supplied the increasing luxury of the others, and it had become indispensable: its wealth became an instrument of greater and greater power as the ruling class progressively abandoned the frugality of the earlier generations, never to return.

Although it is necessarily guess-work, one can speculate upon what would have happened if the foreign invasion had not cut short all development by destroying the whole of Mexican society and the state itself. Perhaps these 'merchant lords', who already had such important privileges, their own courts and the badges of honour that Auitzotl had granted them, would have become the chiefs of a bourgeoisie that would either have become part of the ruling class or would have displaced it and taken its power.

But perhaps on the other hand the aristocracy would have reinforced its position by crushing any further attempt at rising. All that can be said is that there was nothing rigid about the structure of the Mexican community in 1519; it was in a state of flux, and perhaps the most mobile element in it was the class of *pochteca*. The class represented the principle of personal capital as opposed to that of income attached to office, of wealth as opposed to renown, of luxury as opposed to austerity. It was repressed, and it took to deceit and hypocrisy; but already the grandees condescended to go to the merchants' feasts and accept their presents,[58] much as the French nobles of the *Ancien Régime* mixed with the wealthy tax-farmers. Even very important dignitaries married their daughters, at least as secondary wives: this was the case with Nezaualpilli, king of Texcoco, whose favourite was 'the woman they called the lady of Tula, not that she was of noble lineage, for she was only a merchant's daughter.'[59]

THE CRAFTSMEN

The farther down the social level, the more scanty the information. Neither the native historians nor the Spanish chroniclers have troubled to describe the life of the lower orders.

The craftsmen formed a numerous class with its own quarters and organisations, below that of the *pochteca* but in some respects allied to it. Not very much is known about the useful but unexciting guilds such as those of the quarry-men or salters, which are sometimes mentioned, but in passing and without detail. The only groups that were much noticed were those outstanding ones devoted to the so-called minor arts of the goldsmith, the jeweller and the maker of feather-mosaics. These craftsmen were known by the name of *tolteca*, 'the Toltecs', for the origin of their crafts was assigned by tradition to the ancient Toltec civilisation, the civilisation of the god-king Quetzalcoatl and the marvellous city of Tula.

Quetzalcoatl 'discovered great treasures of emeralds, of fine turquoises, gold, silver, coral, shells and (the plumes of) *quetzal, tlauhquechol, zaquan, tzinizcan* and *ayocan* . . . (in his palace) he had mats of feathers and precious gems and silver' wrote the Aztec editor of the annals of Cuauhtit-lán.[60] And Sahagún goes farther – 'They were called Toltecs, which means exquisitely skilled workmen . . . they were all craftsmen of the first order, painters, lapidaries, feather-workers . . . They found mines of those gems which in Mexico they call *xiuitl*, that is to say, turquoise . . . also gold and silver mines . . . and amber, crystal, and the stones called amethysts, pearls, and all kinds of stones that they made into jewels.'[61] 'They knew a great deal; nothing was difficult for them. They cut the green stone (*chalchiuitl*), they melted the gold (*teocuitlapitzaia*) . . . and all these crafts and sciences came from Quetzalcoatl.'[62]

As we have just seen, the generic term for their techniques was *toltecayotl*, 'the matter of the Toltecs' or 'the Toltec thing', and from this these artisans drew their honourable name.

Besides, their claim to an illustrious origin was by no means entirely without foundation. The nomadic Aztec tribe that in 1325 had only just settled in the marshes certainly had no such craftsmen among its members, and those who subsequently became members of the tribe can only have been drawn from the survivors from earlier times. Ixtlilxochitl[63] states that the people of the little towns of the lake such as Colhuacán or Xochimilco preserved the ancient arts of Tula after that city's fall, as well as its language and customs. The lapidaries, for example, were held to descend directly from the men of Xochimilco.[64]

A strange air of foreignness hung about these craftsmen. For the other Mexicans, who were members of a particularly homogeneous tribe, they were men of a remote, different and even mysterious origin. It was said that the feather-workers, who made the exquisite feather-mosaics for the great men, their head-ornaments, plumes and insignia, were the original people of the country. They and their god Coyotlinaual, 'he who is disguised as a wolf', had founded Amantlan, their village, about the temple where his image stood, beautiful with gold and plumes and dressed in the skin of a wolf.

In the historical period this village of Amantlan was never anything but a district in the capital, but there are traces that seem to show that it was absorbed by Mexico as the result of a war. The hymn in honour of the great Mexican god, *Uitzilopochtli icuic*, has these lines, 'Our enemies the men of Amantlan (*Amanteca toyaohuan*), gather them together for me: they shall be in their houses, the enemies.' And the Aztec commentator states explicitly 'Their houses shall be burnt down' – that is, 'They shall be conquered'.[65] This old sacred poem, therefore, retains a vestige of the period at which the *Amanteca* were not part of the city, but were still enemies upon whose heads the wrath of Uitzilopochtli was to be called down.

The goldsmiths too, the *teocuitlahuaque*, had their aura of mystery; and although they were also called Toltecs their customs, strangely enough, seem to link them with another nation, far more remote and exotic in the eyes of the Aztecs. Their great god was Xipe Totec, 'who was the god of the people of the coast, properly speaking the god of Tzapotlan',[66] who carried a golden shield in his hand 'like those of the men of the coast'.[67] He was worshipped in a temple called Yopico, 'the Yopi ground': and Yopi was the name of a people whose country lay on the west side of the mountains, stretching from them to the Pacific between the Mexicans and the Mixtecs – a people who were able to remain largely independent of the Aztec empire. These Yopi, who were also called *Tlappaneca*, 'painted men', because they dyed their bodies, were classed as barbarians – that is, they did not speak the Mexican language. 'They lived in a poor and sterile country, famine-struck, harsh and rugged; but they knew the precious stones and their virtues,' says Sahagún.[68] Consequently they were considered rich, in spite of the poverty of their soil. The working of gold was brought to central Mexico at a late period, and some of the finest examples of the art have been found in the Mixtec country; so bearing this in mind, one is led to suppose that the goldsmiths, with their god from the coast in his golden cloak,[69] brought with them a southern influence that was essentially foreign to the original Aztec culture.

At the date of which we are speaking they were quite certainly embedded in the Mexican community, but still as a distinct body, with their own customs. The feather-workers of Amantlan associated with almost nobody except the traders of Pochtlan, their neighbours; with them, however, they feasted at a common table. The feather-workers, like the *pochteca*, were allowed to sacrifice a slave after the prisoners of war in the month *Panquetzaliztli:* the whole guild clubbed together to buy the victim. In the month *Tlaxochimaco* they held their own feast, in honour of their local god and of the four other gods and two goddesses of their guild, and they vowed to devote their children to the same trade that they followed.

These workmen, with their simple tools, their exquisite taste and their infinite patience, could produce masterpieces: Albrecht Dürer saw some of the presents given by Mote-cuhzoma to Cortés and by him sent to Charles V, and he wrote, 'These objects are so valuable that they have been set at a hundred thousand florins. In all my life I have never seen anything that rejoiced my heart so much; I have found an admirable art in them, and I have been astonished by the subtle spirit of the men of these strange countries.'

Some of these craftsmen worked directly for the emperor in the palace, as Bernal Díaz describes them;[70] others worked at home, receiving the stones, feathers or metal from the great men or the traders and working them up into jewels or ornaments. Each workshop consisted only of one family: the feather-workers' wives, for example, spun and embroidered, made rabbits'-hair blankets or devoted themselves to the dyeing of the feathers. The children stayed with their parents to learn their trade.

The social standing of the *tolteca* was modest; they made no claims to power or wealth. But it was not without a certain esteem. Young dignitaries did not think it beneath them 'for their exercise and recreation, to learn some arts or accomplishments, such as painting, engraving on stone, wood or gold, or the working of gems.'[71] It seems that the artist was very well paid. It is true that the case is exceptional, but on one occasion each of the fourteen sculptors who made the statue of Motecuhzoma II received clothes for himself and his wife, 10 loads of calabashes, 10 loads of beans, 2 loads each of peppers, cocoa and cotton, and a boatload of maize, before he began; and when the work was finished, 2 slaves, 2 loads of cocoa, some crockery and salt, and a load of cloth.[72] It is likely that at the various stages the craftsmen received very considerable remuneration. But on the other hand they were subject to tax, although, like the traders, they were not obliged to provide personal service or agricultural labour. Furthermore, their guilds enjoyed what may be termed the right of corporate personality, and their chiefs represented them before the central authority and the law.

Here again, then, we are dealing with a class whose privileges raise them above the plebeian mass. But the distinction between them and the traders is that in this case we find no trace of that more or less repressed tendency to rise in the social scale, nor of any of the tension that existed between the ruling class and the traders, nor the habits of concealment of the *pochteca*. The craftsman had nothing to hide: he did not have to ask pardon for his importance, for he neither had nor claimed it. He had his own place in this complex society, and he seems to have meant to stay there; for whereas the trading class was dynamic, that of the artisans was static, happy to remain in the position where its immunities and the general respect for its abilities had placed it, one step higher than those with no privileges, just above the common people.

THE COMMON PEOPLE

The Aztec word *maceualli* (*maceualtin* in the plural) stood, in the sixteenth century, for any person who did not belong to any of the social categories that have just been mentioned and yet who was not a slave – the 'common people' or the 'plebeians', as the Spaniards often translated it. It appears that in the beginning this word simply meant 'worker'. It comes from the word *maceualo*, 'to work to acquire merit', from which is derived *maceualiztli*, which does not mean 'work', but 'an act meant to acquire merit' – it is the word used to describe those dances which were performed before the images of the gods in order to acquire merit in their eyes.[73] It is obvious that it had no pejorative sense. Literature is full of examples in which the meaning of *maceualtin* is just 'the people', without any implication of inferiority. Yet it is certain that in time the word did take on a slightly contemptuous ring: the *maceualli* was thought to be common: *maceuallatoa* meant 'to speak boorishly', and *maceualtic* meant 'vulgar'.[74]

In a great city, although there might be some thousands of officials, merchants and craftsmen, there were a very great many more *maceualtin* – the vast majority of the population. They were full citizens, members of the tribe and the district, but they were liable to certain inescapable duties: their position can best be shown by a list of their rights and corresponding obligations.

As a Mexican and a member of a *calpulli* of Tenochtitlan or Tlatelolco, the *maceualli* had a right to a life-interest in the plot upon which he built his house and in the piece of land that he cultivated. His children could go to the local school. He and his family took their ritual and traditional part in the ceremonies of the district and the city; and when the authorities handed out food and clothes he had his share. If he were courageous and intelligent he could rise out of his class and become honoured and wealthy. He had a vote in the election of the local chiefs, although in the last resort their appointment depended upon the emperor.

But in so far as he remained a plebeian, and if he did nothing to distinguish himself in the first years of his life in the world, he was subject to grave obligations. To begin with there was military service; although no Mexican thought of this as a burden, but rather as something that was both an honour and a religious rite. And then the *maceualli* was inscribed on the rolls of the urban officials and at any time he could be called upon for communal work – cleaning, maintenance, the building of roads, bridges and temples. If the palace needed water, or wood for its fires, a fatigue-party of *maceualtin* was ordered at once. Furthermore, our *maceualli* was required to pay taxes, which were assessed within each district by the chief and the elders of the council, together with officials who supervised the payment.

Yet it must be admitted that compared with the *maceualtin* of the subject-towns or even more of the countryside, the *maceualli* who belonged to any of the three confederate cities at the head of the empire, Mexico, Texcoco and Tlatelolco, was in a privileged category. He paid taxes: but on the other hand he must have been largely compensated for this by his share in the distribution, very like the Roman dole, of clothes and provisions that were provided by the tribute of the provinces. His tribe was the ruling nation, and in his degree he benefited from the system: it was the provincial who paid. It was the peasant, with his unpolished speech and manners, who was the real plebeian: it was always his labour that was requisitioned, always his harvest that was laid under contribution. He bore the whole weight of the social edifice. Nevertheless this population of free men, in the town and in the country, had a status which was not without a certain dignity, however humble it may have been; a status, moreover, which prevented no man from rising above the common level if his personal courage or good fortune enabled him to do so. No one could take the land he worked away from a *maceualli*, nor expel him from his *calpulli*, except as a punishment for serious crimes or offences. Apart from natural disasters or war, he did not run the risk of starving, nor of dying far from his accustomed surroundings, his neighbours and his gods.

As for the chances of success and improvement, it has already been shown that they were quite considerable: the army and the less accessible priesthood could lead to the highest offices; and the protection of a great man opened the way to a great number of employments, less brilliant, it is true, but still respectable and no doubt lucrative – ushers, guards, messengers, minor officials of all kinds. Or the emperor's favour or the kindness of a noblewoman might completely change a plebeian's life. This happened to a man named Xochitlacotzin, a gardener in the suburbs of Mexico, in the reign of Motecuhzoma II: although he was a plebeian he would not give way to the emperor, who was delighted by his integrity and made him a lord, observing that he looked upon him as a kinsman.[75]

Chimalpahin tells how a daughter of Itzcoatl fell in love with a *maceualtzintli*, a 'little plebeian', of Atotonilco; she married him, and because of this royal marriage he became lord of his village.[76]

This is to say that no impenetrable walls separated the classes, and that the humblest life was not without its hope.

Beneath the plebeian freemen and above the lowest class of all, the slaves, there was still another category, that of the landless peasants. Their name, *tlalmaitl*, literally 'hand of the earth' whence 'rural manual labour', is translated 'farm-labourer' or 'day-labourer'.[77] It is hard to see how this class can have come into being, since every member of the tribe had a right to a piece of arable land. Perhaps these landless peasants were what we now call 'displaced persons', victims of the wars and coups d'état which had been so frequent in the cities of central Mexico in the preceding two or three hundred years. Having fled from their tribe they may have offered themselves to some Mexican dignitary who provided them with land: or perhaps they were families who stayed when the farm-land of conquered cities was given to Aztec lords. However that may have been, the *tlalmaitl* lived on the land that was allowed him with his family, and if the tenure of the estate passed on to inheritors he remained, being bound to the soil. In return for this land that he worked for himself he provided 'water and wood', domestic service, and paid a rent, either by giving up part of his harvest or by working a separate field for the great man whose dependent he was. What we have here, therefore, is share-cropping or tenant farming.

Unlike the *maceualli* the *tlalmaitl* was not a citizen. He did not have the citizen's rights: but he did not have the citizen's expenses, either. He paid no taxes and he could not be called on for labour; that is, he owed nothing to the city and nothing to the *calpulli*. In short, he looked only to the man who had granted him his land.

There were two points, however, in which his status resembled that of the plebeian: he was liable for military service (a most important exception); and he was under the civil and criminal jurisdiction of the Aztec ruler. He was not, therefore, entirely given up to the authority of a private person.[78] He was still a free man.

THE SLAVES

Below everyone, lower than anybody else, at the bottom of society, we have what for want of a better word must be called the slave, *tlacotli – tlatlacotin* in the plural. He was not a citizen; he was not a subject: he belonged like a chattel to his master. In this particular his condition resembled slavery as it was understood in western antiquity or, until not long ago, the modern world; but in many others Mexican servitude was quite unlike the accepted notion of slavery. 'The manner in which slaves are made by these natives of New Spain is very different from the practices of the European nations,' writes Father Motolinía, ' . . . It even seems to me that those who are called slaves (in Mexico) do not fulfil many of the conditions of a slave properly so called.'[79] When the Spaniards introduced the kind of slavery current in Europe into Mexico after the conquest the wretched Indians, who were branded on the face with red-hot irons, put down the mines and used worse than animals, must have envied the lot of the former slaves: they had certainly not gained by the change.

What were the distinguishing characteristics of the slave status in Mexico at the beginning of the sixteenth century? The first was that the slave worked for another man, as a farm-labourer or as a servant, or perhaps as a porter in the merchants' caravans. The women slaves spun, wove, sewed or mended clothes in their master's house, and they were often among his concubines. The *tlacotli* had no pay for his work. But he was housed, fed and clothed like an ordinary citizen. 'They treat their slaves almost like their children.'[80] And there are examples quoted of slaves promoted major-domo and given the charge of great estates and command over free men. Better still – and here we leave the classical idea of slavery altogether – the *tlatlacotin* could possess goods, save money, buy land and houses and even slaves for their own service. There was nothing to forbid marriage between slaves and citizens. A slave could marry a free woman; and not infrequently a widow would marry one of her slaves, who would thus become head of the family. All children were born free, including those both of whose parents were slaves. No inherited shame was attached to this state; and the emperor Itzcoatl, one of the greatest in Mexican history, was the son of a slave-woman, by Acamapichtli.

Furthermore, the state of slavery was not necessarily perpetual. Many were freed at their master's death, by his will; others were emancipated by the emperor or one of his fellow-kings – Motecuhzoma II and Nezauapilli, for example, decreed very considerable manumissions.[81] Any slave who was about to be sold could try to regain his liberty: if he escaped from the market, nobody except his master and his master's son might stop him without being enslaved himself; and if once he succeeded in getting into the palace the royal presence instantly released him from all bonds, and he was a free man.

Others again could buy themselves out of slavery, either paying their master back the price he had given for them (which justifies the statement that slaves could become free and prosperous[82]) or in having themselves replaced by another member of their family – several brothers could, in turn, undertake the service of the same master. So slavery here had nothing of the hopeless character that it had in other times and other places: it was a state that might be only temporary.

But how did a man become a slave? In replying to this question one realises that there were many kinds of slave and that the status of the different kinds differed widely. Prisoners of war or at least those who were not sacrificed as soon as the campaign was over, were sold as slaves either at Tlatelolco or at Atzcapotzalco. It is said that the richest traders were those who raided the unsubjected tribes for slaves. Some cities were obliged to supply a given number of slaves as a tax; and they certainly obtained them outside the empire by armed expeditions. Cihuatlán on the Pacific sent Tarascan and Cuitlatec prisoners to Mexico; Zompanco sent Tlappanecs and Teotitlán Mixtecs. All these slaves, foreigners classed as barbarians and prisoners of war primarily intended for death before the altar, might be considered as so many victims under suspended sentence; and most of them ended their lives stoically upon the bloody stone at the top of a pyramid.

Slavery could also originate as a punishment for certain crimes and felonies.[83] Mexican justice knew nothing of the long sentences of imprisonment so familiar to our courts: but the man who stole from a temple or in the palace, or who burgled a private house, became the slave of the temple, the lord or the private person, unless he ransomed himself by paying back the amount of his theft, if necessary with his family's help. Slavery, too, was the punishment of those who kidnapped children to sell them as slaves; of those who prevented a slave from escaping to the palace to free himself; those who sold goods that did not belong to them; those who plotted against the emperor. And in the more remarkable case of a man who took another's slave as his mistress, if she died in childbed, he was enslaved to replace the woman whose death he had brought about.

But contemporary documents seem to show that the most

75

numerous class was that of the voluntary slaves. A free man, or a woman, had the disposition of his person, and by a solemn deed he could sell himself to another. Those who decided upon this course were sometimes drunken and idle creatures, tired of working their land, which in any case was taken from them by the *calpulli* when it had been left uncultivated for three years, or sometimes players of the ball-game or *patolli*, ruined by their addiction to it, or sometimes women who having played the whore 'for nothing most of the time'[84] ended by selling themselves to be sure of food and a roof, and to be able to dress well.

The act of giving up one's liberty was accompanied by a ceremony which was at the same time a protection. It took place in the presence of at least four aged and respectable witnesses; and there were always many people there to watch the final settlement. The future slave received his price, which at this period was usually one load of *quachtli*, that is, twenty pieces of cloth. He remained at liberty so long as he had not spent it all, and this was generally a year or a little over, which is one of the few exact figures that we have for the cost of living in Tenochtitlan. When everything was gone he gave himself up to his master and began his servitude.

Another form of slavery arose from the indebtedness that one or more families might contract with a private person or a dignitary. A poor family might sell one of its sons as a slave and replace him by another child when he reached a marriageable age. Or again in a time of famine the wretched starving people might engage themselves to perform certain services in perpetuity for a master and his heirs – sowing, harvesting, sweeping the house, or carrying the wood. Four or five families would join to provide a slave for these duties; he would undertake them for some years and then be replaced by some other member of the same families. The master paid an additional three or four *quachtli* at each replacement, and gave some maize. This was a very old custom, and it was called *ueuetlacolli*, 'the old servitude': its disadvantage was that in exchange for a single sum, paid once and for all, and a few small supplementary payments, it brought into being a compulsory and permanent liability. For this reason it was done away with in 1505, at the time of the great famine, by Nezaualpilli; and the abolition appears to have become general over the whole of the empire. At the time of the Spanish conquest a family would still provide one of its members as a slave in payment of a debt: if the slave happened to die, the debt was cancelled. These slaves, therefore, were unusually well treated.

The sale of the slave was also strictly regulated. Generally speaking a master did not sell his slaves: if he became poor, he would send them off to trade on his account between Mexico and some more or less distant village; in order to do this, the slaves moved about quite freely. It was only the idle and vicious slave who could be sold; and even then it was necessary to have admonished solemnly him three times before witnesses in order to record his dishonesty or his refusal to work. If he did not improve his master had the right to put a heavy wooden collar on his neck and lead him to the market to be sold.

When three successive masters had been obliged to get rid of him the slave faced the most shocking fate possible to his condition: from that moment he could be bought to be sacrificed. The *pochteca* and the artisans, who could not capture prisoners of war, provided themselves with victims in this way. Sahagún[85] describes these sad processions of slaves plodding dully along the road to their death, ritually bathed, luxuriously dressed and adorned, stupefied by the 'divine' *teooctli* that they had drunk, to end their lives on the stone in front of the statue of Uitzilopochtli. Yet they did not rebel: this manner of death seemed not only normal and inevitable to the ancient Mexicans, since those who were born under certain signs were foredoomed to such a fate, but even honourable. The slaves, plumed and ornamented, on the point of death, were the physical reflection of the gods: they *were* gods. Their wretched outcast lives finished in apotheosis.

But in fact there was little chance of a slave dying thus. The great majority of slaves, it seems, either managed to free themselves, even if it were only at their master's death, or else lived a life that was at least without danger and beyond the reach of misery. They were above all people who had escaped from their responsibilities, who had given up the rights and the duties of freedom.

No military service, no taxes, no *corvées*: no duties towards the state or the district. I say it again, they were well treated: furthermore, they were held to be under the protection of Tezcatlipoca – his 'well-beloved children'. The sign *ce miquiztli* was sacred to the great god, and on this date the slaves were given presents, and no one presumed to reproach them for fear of being brought to slavery by the wrath of Tezcatlipoca. 'The masters of the slaves gave strict orders to the whole household not to vex a slave in any way. It was said that if anyone reproached a slave on one of those days he would bring poverty on himself, and sickness and misfortune, and deserved to fall into slavery for having misused a well-beloved son of Tezcatlipoca . . . and if it happened that a slave freed himself and grew rich, and that the slave-owner became in his turn a slave, it was said that this was the will of Tezcatlipoca, who had heard the slave's prayer and had had pity on him, and had punished the master for his hardness to his servants.'[86] In this way beliefs, laws and customs all joined to protect the slave, to make his condition easier and to increase his chances of emancipation.

At the beginning of the sixteenth century the number of *tlatlacotin* seems to have been increasing, a phenomenon which is explained by the greater tribute, the growth of trade to distant parts and the difference between standards of living. In a complex society whose ancient organisation had almost completely crumbled away, the rise of some to power and wealth had as its counterpart the depression of others – the very poor and the misfits sank, as it were, to the lowest level, beneath which there was nothing. Yet it is only justice to repeat once more that even this bottom-most state was not without its hope.

WEALTH AND POVERTY: THE STANDARDS OF LIVING
In the *Codex Telleriano-Remensis*[87] wealth is symbolised by

a wicker-work chest, *petlacalli*, filled with green stones: and indeed the idea of material possessions tended more and more to take the manageable form of pieces of jade, gold, or cloth: personal estate, as we should say now, was taking the place of real estate. It is none the less true, however, that in the eyes of the ruling class in the sixteenth century land, arable land, still remained the basis of all wealth. As a dignitary rose rank by rank so he acquired rights over a larger and larger area of real estate.

In theory no one was the owner of a piece of ground. The land belonged collectively either to the *calpulli*, or to public institutions such as temples, or to the city itself. There was no private ownership of land, but a collective ownership with individual rights of user. 'These lands,' says Zurita,[88] referring to those of each district, 'are not the private possession of each member of the district, but the common possession of the *calpulli*, and the individual cannot dispose of them; but he enjoys them for his lifetime and he can leave them to his sons and heirs.' It is clear that what we are concerned with is a heritable usufruct.

The register of the land and its distribution was kept up to date by the chief of the *calpulli*: he and the elders saw to it that each family was allowed the plot that it needed. If a man did not cultivate his piece for two years running he was severely admonished; if he took no notice of this, the next year he was deprived of his right and the land that had been his returned to the common stock. The same happened when a family left the district or died out. The *calpulli's* proprietorship covered all the land within its boundaries, even that which was not cultivated: there was no indeterminate ground, nothing without an owner. The chief and his council could let land to men who were not members of the district, but the rent was paid into the communal purse and not to a private person.

But although the ownership was collective, the usufruct was individual. Every adult married man had the right, and the indefeasible right, to be given a plot and to work it. He was inscribed on the rolls at the moment of his marriage, and if he had not already inherited the right of working his father's land, the *calpulli* was obliged to provide him with a piece. And at his death he left his children not the piece of land, but the right of farming it.

Such was the primeval law of the Mexican city, the law of the democratic tribe: every free man was provided with a piece of land and was required to work it. In time, and as the differentiation of social function increased, many exceptions to the ancient rule came into being: the dignitaries, the officials and the priests did not cultivate the fields to which they had a right; the traders and the artisans were excused manual labour. Moreover, arable land was exceedingly rare in Mexico, on the islets of the lake, and it was only on the shores that the *maceualtin* could have their patches allotted to them. Many Mexicans led an entirely urban existence.

It must be conceded, however, that the cases in which a family had its land taken from it were quite rare. The same maize-field, the same market-garden stayed from generation to generation in the hands of the same family. No doubt the *calpulli* retained the ownership, but in practice, the citizen who followed his father and his grandfather in the same holding really felt himself at home. At the time immediately before the Spanish invasion it appears that the sale of land was provided for by law.[89] Arising from the traditional collective ownership, private property was in the act of coming into existence.

This development is all the clearer if one takes the possessions of the other communities and cities, rather than those of the *calpulli*. The growth of the sovereign's power and the conquests of the *Mexica* and their allies are the two related bases for the evolution; for they brought into being a wide variety of land-holdings with differing regulations – *altepetlalli* belonging to a town, *tecpantlalli* or land set aside for the palace, *tlatocamilli* or fields 'of the military command', *yaoyotlalli*, the fields 'of war'.

In all these cases we are concerned with estates that were cultivated either by slaves or by the plebeians of a subjected city, and whose produce was devoted 'to the needs of the republic'.[90] The Indians of the valley of Toluca, for example, cultivated a field 1,600 yards long and 800 wide on behalf of the Mexican emperor. Thus an important stock of land was at the disposal of the emperor and his allied kings, and they could allocate the income either to a temple or as pay to an official, a judge or an officer. In a society that did not have money, pay consisted essentially of the income from a piece of land. There are a great many examples of estates being given to warriors as a reward for their achievements.[91]

At the time of which we are speaking an important development was beginning to make itself apparent; for although in theory property was still communal, in fact the land that had been attributed by way of life-interest to a *tecuhtli* was transmitted by him to his heirs. These estates then became *pillalli*, 'land belonging to *pilli*'; that is to say that the sons of dignitaries who already by their birth had a kind of right to be preferred in the higher appointments were also allowed the advantage of inherited revenues. A private domain was building itself up at the expense of the public domain. It would be an exaggeration to say that the emperor and the dignitaries were great landed proprietors, for in fact an over-riding law of communal possession was felt to exist: but it would be equally mistaken to assert that this law alone was recognised in practice.

At this time Aztec society was in a state of flux, of transition, and the taking of land into private hands was continually coming, as it were, to the surface: the customs and practices of real life grew more and more unlike those of tradition; for whereas the old way established one general standard for all by the sharing of communal land, inequality in landed wealth had in fact become the rule. While the *maceualli* made the best of his plot, the high officials enjoyed important possessions in several provinces, following the example of the emperor, who owned country houses and pleasure gardens in many places.

This inequality was no less striking in what may be termed liquid wealth. Although there was no money, certain commodities, goods or objects ordinarily served as measures of value and as means of exchange – the *quachtli*, or length of cloth, with its multiple the load (twenty lengths); the cocoa-nib, the small change of the Aztecs, with its multiple the *xiquipilli*, a bag holding or supposed to hold eight thousand of them; little T-shaped copper hatchets[92] and quills filled with gold-dust. Apart from these exchange-goods, the treasure of the emperor or a private person consisted of an immense variety of agricultural products, such as maize, beans, oil seeds, many-coloured feathers, precious and semi-precious stones, jewels, clothes, ornaments, etc. This wealth was derived from two sources, tribute or tax, and commerce. And it is at this point that the traders come upon the scene.

The whole population of the city and the empire paid taxes, except dignitaries, priests, *pilli*, children, orphans, paupers[93] and, naturally, the slaves. The Mexican *maceualtin* paid principally in work; the traders and the artisans in commodities or the goods of their trade; and they paid every twenty or every eighty days. The tribute that each city or village was obliged to pay varied widely according to the circumstances in which it had been incorporated into the empire, and according to local resources.

According to the Indian conception of it, the original institution of tribute was based upon a true contract, a contract of redemption. The conqueror had unlimited rights over the conquered: but the victorious city agreed to give up some of them in exchange for a solemn undertaking. After the fighting, very hard bargaining would begin:[94] the defeated would try to come off as lightly as possible, while the Mexicans would threaten the renewal of hostilities. In the end they would come to an agreement, and the victors would never fail to record the adversaries' enforced submission in due form. 'Do not come to us later on and complain that we require too much of you, since now you agree with it,' was the sense of the observations that one finds in the native histories.

Each province, and within each province each city or town, had to supply a certain quantity of objects or produce once or twice a year, and the lists given in the *Codex Mendoza* show how varied these contributions were. One province of the 'Cold Country', Xilotepec, had a yearly tax of 800 loads of women's clothes (that is, 16,000 articles), 816 loads of men's loincloths, 800 loads of embroidered skirts, 3,216 loads of *quachtli*, 2 suits for warriors with their headgear and their shields, 4 large baskets of maize and other grain, and lastly from 1 to 4 live eagles.

The province of Tochpan, on the shores of the Gulf, had to furnish 6,948 loads of cloaks of different kinds, 800 loads of loincloths and 800 of skirts, 800 loads of peppers, 20 sacks of feathers, 2 jade necklaces, 1 turquoise necklace, 2 turquoise-mosaic disks, 2 sumptuous costumes for the military chiefs. Tochtepec, which was the traders' head-quarters on the frontiers of the southern and the eastern countries, paid, besides a great many clothes, 16,000 balls of rubber, 24,000 bunches of parrot's feathers, 80 packets of *quetzal* plumes, 1 shield, 1 diadem, 1 gold headband and 2 gold necklaces, amber and crystal jewels, and cocoa.

The tribute-lists mention cotton and agave-fibre cloth, clothes of all kinds, maize, grain, cocoa, honey, salt, peppers, tobacco, building materials, furniture, crockery, gold from the Mixtec provinces, turquoises and jade from the eastern coast, cochineal, incense, rubber, paper from Quauhnahuac and Huaxtepec, shells from Cihuatlán, live birds from Xilotepec and from Oxitipan. In *quachtli* alone the tribute brought in more than 100,000 loads every year: now, as it has been shown, a load of *quachtli* was reckoned to be the equivalent of a year's living for one person. It was therefore 100,000 'yearly livings' that came into Mexico in this one form, without speaking of all the other products mentioned above. For example, the tribute brought 32,000 large sheets of paper into the capital, 152,320 loincloths, 30,884 bundles of precious feathers, etc.

No doubt a certain proportion of this wealth was shared out among the districts of the capital, which, however, did not (at least in theory) take more than two fifths of the levy, two fifths being reserved for Texcoco and one fifth for Tlacopan. But it is quite sure that the emperor and his chief dignitaries took the lion's share: after the fall of Cuetlaxtlan, Motecuhzoma I, his deputy Tlacaeleltzin and

83

the leader of the expedition allotted themselves three quarters of the tribute raised from this province; only a quarter continued its journey towards the districts, and no once can tell what trifling share actually reached the common people.[95]

Considering the size of these figures, it is natural to suppose that the taxation was very heavy; and this was certainly the impression that the Spaniards received on their arrival, when they heard the complaints and the protests of the Totonacs.[96] But this tribe had been quite recently subjected, and it hated the Mexicans: perhaps its evidence is not to be taken as literally true. One must also remember that some provinces were very densely populated. Alonso de Zurita, an excellent Spanish official and a most accurate observer, particularly states 'In all this there was a great deal of regularity and of attentiveness to see that no one person was more heavily burdened than the rest. Each man paid little; and as there were many men it was possible to bring together great quantities (of goods) with little work and no vexation.'[97]

The towns and the villages of the valley of Mexico were assessed in a manner peculiar to themselves: they were required, each in turn, to see to the upkeep of the palaces of the three allied sovereigns, and to supply them with domestic servants and provisions. Nezaualcoyotl, the king of Texcoco, had divided the country surrounding his capital into eight districts, each of which was obliged to perform these duties for a given period each year, under the supervision of a *calpixqui*.

If Ixtlilxochitl[98] is to be believed the amount that these districts had to provide was very great indeed: a royal household would consume no fewer than a hundred turkeys daily.

It is certain that the rulers and those close to them were able to amass huge quantities of goods from the great inflow of wealth into Mexico and the allied cities which resulted from the tribute: it is equally sure that their expenses were enormous. Both Nezaualpilli at Texcoco, with his immense harem and his forty favourite wives, of whom one alone, the daughter of the Mexican emperor Axayacatl, had more than two thousand people in her service, and Motecuhzoma II at Mexico, who was perpetually surrounded by three thousand attendants in the palace, without counting the eagles, snakes and jaguars which he kept in special quarters and which ate five hundred turkeys a day, lived like potentates in the midst of an abundance from which an ever-increasing train of followers grew rich. But on the other hand, as there was no distinction between the public treasury and the sovereign's private fortune, it was he who gave out food and drink to the whole population during the month *Uey tecuilhuitl*, the time of the gap between harvests when the family stocks were exhausted,[99] and he who emptied his granaries in time of famine and disaster,[100] and he who took upon himself the cost of war, the equipment and the victualling of the troops. And the expenses of each dignitary, in his degree, had to cover not only his own living, but that of his followers as well as the reception of travellers and the feeding of poor people.[101] The wealth of the powerful blossomed out in luxury, but to a large extent the obligations of their office brought about its redistribution.

This was not the case with the traders. As we have seen, the *pochteca* made no display of their wealth, except on the rare occasions when custom and propriety required them to be generous hosts. They had no position to keep up, and they did not redistribute their fortune. This wealth was derived neither from land nor from the taxes but from trade, of which they had the monopoly: it piled up, carefully concealed, in their warehouses, in the form of bundles of precious feathers, chests of green stones and amber, calabashes filled with gold-dust.

Whereas the ruling class spent lavishly, the *pochteca*, leading their comfortable but unspectacular lives, did not have to provide for any needs but their own; they were not called upon to help the common people or the poor, and they were able to accumulate what one now terms capital. The dignitaries, after all, were only high officials who received important grants or salaries but who were obliged to spend by far the greater part merely because of their position: but the traders, on the other hand, formed the primary nucleus of a wealthy class whose fortune was essentially personal.

In the Aztec society of the beginning of the sixteenth century many widely differing standards of living were to be found – the brilliant luxury of the sovereign, and that of the dignitaries in their various degrees, the middle-class comfort of the traders and the frugality of the common people. The poor are too often mentioned in literature for it to be possible to ignore their importance: the happy mediocrity which had been the lot of all Mexicans two centuries earlier was vanishing little by little, as the tribal village grew into the capital of an empire and became the centre towards which all the wealth of a vast country converged. Urban life, the increasing complexity of functions, the increase of the dominions and the accompanying task of administration, and the emergence of commerce all ineluctably and irremediably changed the ancient ways. No doubt the *calpulli* with its democratic organisation must have acted as a powerful stabiliser; but it is equally probable that the little plot of ground that had seemed quite enough to the plain citizen of the fourteenth century appeared wretchedly meagre to the man of the sixteenth. For here too an evolution was beginning, whose development we can only imagine, seeing that it was savagely broken by the European invasion.

THE SOVEREIGN, THE GREAT DIGNITARIES, THE COUNCIL

At the summit, at once the leader in war and the giver of rewards, the representative of the privileged classes and the protector of the common people, the sovereign upheld the rule of the governing class, alternately conciliating and repressing that of the merchants. He was attended by all the outward show of monarchical power, and this show corresponded exactly to the reality: nothing is more futile than the attempts of certain modern authors[102] to deny the evidence of this.

Although the conquistadores may have been uncultivated men, they were excellent observers, and their descriptions are clear; besides, they agree with the native sources, which carefully trace back the genealogy, the coronation and the death of each ruler. One is compelled to recognise the fact that the Mexican city of 1519 was a monarchy: but it remains to be decided what kind of a monarchy it was. Who was the monarch, and how was he appointed?

The Mexican whom we call the emperor was there entitled the *tlatoani*, 'he who speaks', from the verb *tlatoa*, 'to speak': the same root is found in words relating to speech, for example *tlatolli*, 'language', and to power or authority, such as *tlatocayotl*, 'state'; and the two senses come together in the word *tlatocan*, which means the supreme council, the speaking-place and the place from which power emanates. The name *tlatoani* was not given to the ruler by mere chance, for the basis of his power was the art of speaking, of speaking well in the discussions in council and of making with ease and dignity those high-flown, figurative speeches that the Aztecs liked so much. His other title was that of *tlacatecuhtli*, 'chief of the warriors', which referred to a very important aspect of his office – he was the commander-in-chief of the armies of the three confederated cities.

The origins of the Mexican dynasty are obscure, and this obscurity was rendered the darker by the attempts of the Aztec chroniclers at supplying their ruling house with a noble pedigree. They felt obliged to make it appear that the dynasty descended from the great and legendary Toltec kings, although it was in reality a house that had come but lately on the scene. This end was reached by taking a turn through Colhuacán, the lake city of the south where the customs and the language of Tula had persisted: it was quite essential that the first Aztec emperor, Acamapichtli, should be a native of this town, and thus a Toltec; and in order to prove it there were a great many complicated accounts of his rise to power. One of these versions, a particularly interesting one in that it was drawn up after the Spanish conquest by order of the conquistador Juan Cano, who had married doña Isabel, the daughter of Motecuhzoma II, no doubt gives us the official story.

This *Relación*[103] expressly states that the lords of Colhuacán descended from Quetzalcoatl, the 'plumed serpent', king of Tula, and that Acamapichtli was the adopted son of the last legitimate lord of this family. According to another source,[104] Acamapichtli was born at Colhuacán, although his mother was a Mexican. But another woman plays a very important, though somewhat obscure, rôle in the founding of the dynasty: sometimes she appears as the young king's mother by adoption, sometimes as his wife; but always as a señora of great Colhuacán family. There is more than one pointer to show that in former times both nobility and power were inherited through women. But however that may be, the link by which they tried to join the Mexican royal family to a glorious and mythical past was an exceedingly frail one.

After Acamapichtli the turquoise diadem stayed in the family without a break until the end: the second emperor, Uitziliuitl, was his son, and the third, Chimalpopoca, his grandson. After that the power was often inherited by the brother of the late sovereign, or his nephew. The different sources do not always agree as to the exact relationship between the successive emperors,[105] but one point remains upon which there is no possible doubt – the descent is always in one family: it is one single dynasty.

Custom could vary from one town to another: at Texcoco, for example, there was a regular father-to-son descent. But it was still necessary to decide which son should have the throne, and this was not easy in the case of polygamous rulers. It was conceded that one of the king's wives was the 'legitimate' wife, and in theory it was her eldest son who succeeded his father.[106] Yet there was still a considerable amount of room for uncertainty, for, as Zurita says, 'if none of his sons or grandsons was fit to rule, no successor was proclaimed, but the chief lords set about electing one.'[107] For this reason Nezaualcoyotl, before his death, took the precaution of appointing his seven-year-old son Nezaualpilli as his successor,[108] and having him acknowledged king, in the same way that the Roman and Byzantine emperors made their sons associates in the empire to assure them of the crown.

At Mexico, election was customary. Acamapichtli did not

name his successor at the time of his death, 'but left the
republic the task of electing whoever appeared most fit . . .
This custom has always been preserved among the Mexicans.
The sons of the kings have not ruled by right of inheritance,
but by election.'[109] In the beginning it was the whole
nation, or at least the heads of families, who appointed the
sovereign: the city was still small, and the inhabitants few;
they could all be brought together in the central square to
ratify the suggestions of the leaders by acclamation.

As the city and the empire grew larger, so the body that
elected the sovereign grew smaller: it was not the people but
'the senate' who named Auitzotl.[110] At the beginning of the
sixteenth century the electoral college was composed of about a
hundred persons, divided into five categories: the *tecuhtlatoque*
or supreme dignitaries, who numbered thirteen; the *achcac-*
auhtin, officials of the second rank who represented, or who
were supposed to represent, the various districts; two
military categories, the one serving and the other retired;
and then the most important priests, the *tlenamacazque*.[111]
As it will be seen, this college represented only the higher
level of the ruling class of officials, priests and warriors: not
only were the slaves excluded, of course, and not only the
people, but the traders, the craftsmen and even the 'nobles'
– the *pilli*. The election of the emperor was, therefore, in
the hands of a narrow oligarchy.

Sahagún states that there was no poll. It is the same
even now, in the Nahuatl villages of Mexico, when a
municipal official or the head of a confraternity is to be
chosen: the electors discuss it among themselves, suggestions
are put up, and they agree upon a name. There is no
voting, no ballot, as we understand it. When he was proclaimed, the new sovereign had to go through the long and
trying ceremonies of the coronation: in the course of them
he was obliged to do penance before the gods, listen to
many harangues and reply to them by eloquent speeches.[112]
Finally he addressed the people, exhorting them above all
to venerate the gods and flee drunkenness. He then appeared
in all the splendour of the imperial robes, with a triangular
diadem of gold and turquoises on his forehead, wearing a

blue-green cloak and jewels of green stones, and carrying a sceptre in the form of a serpent in his hand.[113]

The speeches exchanged between the newly-elected emperor and the chiefs, and his address to the people give an idea of the Mexican conception of the sovereign dignity. He had undoubtedly been chosen by the magnates, but the official theory was that he had really been appointed by the gods, especially by Tezcatlipoca, he who sees all in his magic mirror; and therefore his first duties were towards them. He thanked them for having selected him, though at the same time he complained, sighing at the weight of such a burden as the government of the empire: he would defend the temple of Uitzilopochtli, and ensure the gods the worship that was their due.

His remaining duties were towards the people: he was traditionally known as 'the father and mother' of the Mexicans. He owed them justice, and he was to struggle for them against famine, so that they might have 'an abundance of the fruits of the earth'.[114] The fundamental ideas of the Aztec monarchy, as they show through the stereotyped official formulæ, are not without dignity; there is a sense of the public good, and the feeling of a real unity between the rulers and the ruled. Furthermore, everything goes to show that the emperors took their duties seriously. Reign after reign, they are to be found in the traditional histories zealous not only in increasing the empire and building temples but also in coming to the help of the unfortunate – there is Motecuhzoma I, for example, distributing food and clothing to the entire population, or Auitzotl sharing out 200,000 loads of maize among the victims of the flood.

The great dignitaries, who were often the closest relatives of the emperor, collaborated with him in the government; and the first among them, who had the curious title of *Ciuacoatl*, 'woman-serpent', was a real vice-emperor. His title was the name of a great goddess, and it is likely that in the beginning the *Ciuacoatl* was no more than her chief priest. It is only in the reign of Motecuhzoma I that the title of *Ciuacoatl* (which is found earlier in Mexico and other cities[115]) suddenly became that of the first dignitary of the state after the sovereign. 'You will help me to rule this Mexican republic,' said Motecuhzoma I to his brother Tlacaeleltzin,[116] whom he had named *Ciuacoatl.*

This great dignitary had the widest powers: he was the supreme judge in martial and criminal law,[117] and he 'had the duty of providing for the requirements of governmental business and the royal finances. He heard cases which were submitted to him on appeal,' says Torquemada, who describes him as the 'high presiding judge'.[118] It was he who named the warriors who were to be rewarded;[119] it was he who organised the military expeditions and appointed their commanders.[120] He convened the electoral college at the sovereign's death and during the interregnum he acted as head of state.[121]

When the emperor left Tenochtitlan to command the troops of the confederacy in person, the *Ciuacoatl* moved into the palace and replaced him in his absence.[122] The honours that were paid him were second only to the emperor's; and he alone might appear before the sovereign without taking off his shoes.[123] He received a very considerable share of the tribute from the conquered cities. He was the *tlatoani's* understudy in everything, and as a symbol of power his black and white cloak[124] came immediately after the blue-green.

It seems that the action of Motecuhzoma I in setting his brother Tlacaeleltzin beside him was a stroke of genius; he had a vigorous personality, and the chroniclers always admire him – Chimalpahin, for example, describes him as *uey oquichtli,* which is exactly rendered by *vir illustris.*[125]

All testimonies agree in extolling his military worth, his statesmanship and his loyalty to the emperor. The office acquired such lustre under him that all those who followed him in it were chosen from his direct descendants, his sons and his grandsons, to the very last of them, Tlacotzin, who lived long enough to lay the submission of Mexico at the feet of Cortés on 13th August, 1521, and to be baptised under the name of don Juan Velásquez.

Beneath the *Ciuacoatl* there were four great military

dignitaries who, with him, were the emperor's chief counsellors: two of them, the *tlacochcalcatl* and the *tlacateccatl*, were often directly related to the sovereign, and it was between them that his successor was chosen. Motecuhzoma II, for example, had the office of *tlacochcalcatl* in the reign of his father, Auitzotl. Some of these dignitaries also had judicial powers: the *tlacateccatl*[126] had cognisance of civil and criminal cases, and appeal lay from him to the *Ciuacoatl*.

And then the Indian and Spanish histories speak of a fairly large number of titles which cannot, in the present state of knowledge, be defined in terms of their function. For example, we know that in his youth the emperor Tizoc had the office of *tlailotlac*,[127] a word which means a foreign tribe and which may have been used for a title, as Germanicus or Parthicus was used among the Romans. The *Mexicatl achcauhtli*, the chief of the officials of the city of Mexico, was one of those who had the terrible responsibility of the final surrender. The *tecuhtlamacazqui*, who is often mentioned among the immediate advisers of the emperor, appears to have been the representative of the priestly order before the central authority. The *petlacalcatl*, 'he (who is in charge) of the chest', took care of the granaries and stores in which the tribute of the provinces was kept; and the *uey calpixqui* had the functions both of prefect of the capital and of chief director of the empire's taxgatherers. In this connection, it seems that plurality of offices was not uncommon: thus the *tlacochcalcatl* Itzquauhtzin, who was serving when the Spaniards arrived, was at the same time governor of Tlatelolco.[128]

Apart from the *petlacalcatl* and the *uey calpixqui*, perhaps because of the purely civilian nature of their duties, the great dignitaries were members of the *tlatocan*, or supreme council of the city. The emperor presided over it, or if he were not there, the *Ciuacoatl;* and this council was consulted before all important decisions – embassies, declarations of war, etc. It also formed the principal nucleus of the college that chose the sovereign. This being the case, it would be absurd to see in it the equivalent of one of our deliberative assemblies, or even of a council of sachems in a North-American Indian tribe.

In the beginning, no doubt, it was made up of delegates elected by the different *calpulli;* but at this period at least part of it was composed of the emperor's nominees, and the rest were co-opted. Here again we have an instance of the change from tribal democracy to an oligarchic régime, whose guardian and whose chief was the emperor. But it must not be forgotten that plebeians could reach the highest honours: although this aristocracy was jealous of its prerogatives it was not ossified; it could still renew and strengthen itself by recruiting new men of value. But it is to be observed that although the plebeian might hope to become a *tecuhtli,* a trader might not: a man born to trade remained all his life a merchant. In modern terms it could be said that the aristocracy had its origin in the people and not in the bourgeoisie.[129]

The Mexican city-state of the sixteenth century, a complex social and political organism, was profoundly different from the wandering tribe which, in 1325, had pitched upon a few islets in the reeds as a refuge: and the difference was not merely quantitative, concerned with the increase of population, territory and resources, but qualitative. The city was not merely the tribe enlarged: it had become something else, a state launched upon a career of aggrandizement, a society in which differentiation was continually growing and in which enmity between the classes was beginning to appear, in which the nature of ownership was changing and in which the ideas of public service and of personal wealth were coming into hidden conflict. But religion, the wonderfully powerful cement binding the various elements of this society, obscured its complexity, and with its living, dominating and unquestioned power imposed a single vision of the world upon the whole community, and by its rites regulated the life of each of its members.

It was by religion that the city and the tribe were one, and by religion that variety was unified. It was religion that gave this town (so strangely modern in many ways) its mediæval face: for the life of the Mexican, within his

93

social and material compass, makes sense only if one perceives the degree to which an all-powerful religion told him his duty, ruled his days, coloured his view of the universe and of his personal destiny.

CHAPTER THREE

THE WORLD, MAN AND TIME[1]

A shifting, threatened world. The myth of the four suns: the supreme Duality: the birth of the sun: the meaning of the human sacrifices: the sacred war: the Mexicans' intensely anxious view of the world—Heaven and earth. The Mexicans as 'people of the sun': Uitzilopochtli: Tlaloc: the earth and the goddesses of the earth: Tlazolteotl, the goddess of love: the moon and the gods of drunkenness: Xipe Totec—Death and rebirth. A constant theme of native thought: vegetation, Quetzalcoatl, the sun: the abodes of the dead—Destinies and signs. The solar year and the divinatory calendar: the Tonalpoualli and the prime axes of the universe: predestination: omens and apparitions: the strong pessimism of the Aztecs—An imperial religion. The Mexican a receptive religion: a welcoming pantheon: syncretism and theological doctrines: belief in a supreme god.

A SHIFTING, THREATENED WORLD

The Mexicans, like some other Central-American peoples,[2] believed that several successive worlds had existed before ours and that each of them had fallen in ruins amid cataclysms in which mankind had been wiped out. These were the 'four suns';[3] and the age in which we live is the fifth. Each of these 'suns' is shown on monuments such as the Aztec calendar or the stone of the suns[4] by a date, a date which is that of its end and which evokes the nature of the catastrophe which ended it: in this way the fourth epoch, for example, the 'sun of the water', which was drowned in a kind of Flood, has the date *naui atl*, 'four – water'.

Our world will have the same fate: its destiny is fixed by the date which has, as one might say, branded it at birth – the date *naui ollin*, at which our sun first began to move. The glyph *ollin*, shaped like a Saint Andrew's cross, which shares the centre of the Aztec calendar with the sun-god's visage, has the double sense of 'movement' and of 'earthquake'. It symbolises both the first motion of the heavenly body when our age began and the cataclysms that will destroy our earth. At that moment the appearance of reality will be ripped open like a veil and the *Tzitzimime*, the monsters of the twilight who await the fatal hour beneath the western sky, will swarm out and hurl themselves upon the last survivors.

The ancient Mexicans believed in two primordial beings who were at the origin of all others, even of the gods: they were Ometecuhtli, 'the Lord of the Duality', and Omeciuatl, 'the Lady of the Duality'; and they lived at the summit of the world, in the thirteenth heaven, 'there where the air was very cold, delicate and iced.'[5] Their unending fruitfulness produced all the gods, and from it all mankind is born. At the time with which this book is concerned these two great divinities had come in some degree to resemble those kings who reign but do not govern: they had been pushed into the background by the vigorous crowd of younger and more active gods. But it was still they who were held to have the privilege of fixing the birth-date of each living being, and thus its fate.

The gods, the descendants of the supreme Duality, in their turn were the creators of the earth: the most important act in this creation was clearly the birth of the sun; and this sun was born from sacrifice and blood. It is said[6] that the gods gathered in the twilight at Teotihuacán, and one of them, a little leprous god, covered with boils, threw himself into a huge brazier as a sacrifice. He rose from the blazing coals changed into a sun: but this new sun was motionless; it needed blood to move. So the gods immolated themselves, and the sun, drawing life from their death, began its course across the sky.

This was the beginning of the cosmic drama in which humanity took on the rôle of the gods. To keep the sun moving in its course, so that the darkness should not overwhelm the world for ever, it was necessary to feed it every day with its food, 'the precious water' (*chalchiuatl*) – that is, with human blood. Sacrifice was a sacred duty towards the sun and a necessity for the welfare of men: without it the very life of the world would stop. Every time that a priest on the top of a pyramid held up the bleeding heart of a man and then placed it in the *quauhxicalli*[7] the disaster that perpetually threatened to fall upon the world was postponed once more. Human sacrifice was an alchemy by which life was made out of death; and the gods themselves had given the example on the first day of creation.

As for man, his very first duty was to provide nourishment *intonan intota tlaltecuhtli tonatiuh*, 'for our mother and our father, the earth and the sun'; and to shirk this was to betray the gods and at the same time all mankind, for what was true of the sun was also true of the earth, the rain, growth and all the forces of nature. Nothing was born, nothing would endure, except by the blood of sacrifice.

The great god-king of the Toltecs, Quetzalcoatl, 'never would (offer up human victims) because he so loved his subjects, the Toltecs, and he presented only snakes in sacrifice, and birds and butterflies.'[8] But Quetzalcoatl was expelled from Tula by the black magic of Tezcatlipoca; and so Mexico was delivered over to the blood-thirsty gods. In the most usual form of the rite the victim was stretched out on his back on a slightly convex stone with his arms and legs held by four priests, while a fifth ripped him open with a flint knife and tore out his heart. The sacrifice also often took place in the manner which the Spaniards described as *gladiatorio*: the captive was tied to a huge disk of stone, the *temalacatl*, by a rope that left him free to move; he was armed with wooden weapons, and he had to fight several normally-armed Aztec warriors in turn. If, by any extraordinary chance, he did not succumb to their attacks, he was spared; but nearly always the 'gladiator' fell, gravely wounded, and a few moments later he died on the stone, with his body opened by the black-robed, long-haired priests. The warriors who were set apart for this kind of death wore ornaments and clothes of a special nature, and they were crowned with white down, as a symbol of the first light of the dawn, of the still uncertain hour when the

97

soul of the resuscitated warrior takes its flight in the greyness towards our father the sun.[9]

But these were not the only forms of sacrifice. Women were dedicated to the goddesses of the earth, and while they danced, pretending to be unaware of their fate, their heads were struck off; children were drowned as an offering to the rain-god Tlaloc; the fire-god's victims, anæsthetised by *yauhtli* (hashish), were thrown into the blaze; and those who personified the god Xipe Totec were fastened to a kind of frame, shot with arrows and then flayed – the priests dressed themselves in the skin.[10] In most cases, the victim was dressed, painted and ornamented so as to represent the god who was being worshipped; and thus it was the god himself who died before his own image and in his own temple, just as all the gods had accepted death in the first days for the salvation of the world. And when ritual cannibalism was practiced on certain occasions, it was the god's own flesh that the faithful ate in their bloody communion.

There is no aspect of the Mexican civilisation that shocks our feelings as much as this. From the first contact between the Indians and the Europeans the horror and disgust that the newcomers felt for the human sacrifices helped them to convince themselves that the native religion came from hell and that its gods were no more than devils:[11] from then onwards they were certain that Uitzilopochtli, Tlaloc, Tezcatlipoca and all the other gods of Mexico were in fact demons, and that everything that concerned them either directly or remotely should be rooted out for ever. The Aztec practice of human sacrifice was a great factor in making the two religions which confronted one another totally irreconcilable, and when the war broke out between the Spaniards and the Mexicans, in giving it a bitter and remorseless character from the moment the helpless conquistadores saw from afar the death of their comrades, whose grinning skulls they later found exposed on the *tzompantli*.

Clearly, it is difficult for us to come to a true understanding of what human sacrifice meant to the sixteenth century Aztec: but it may be observed that every culture possesses its own idea of what is and what is not cruel. At the height of their career the Romans shed more blood in their circuses and for their amusement than ever the Aztecs did before their idols. The Spaniards, so sincerely moved by the cruelty of the native priests, nevertheless massacred, burnt, mutilated and tortured[12] with a perfectly clear conscience. We, who shudder at the tale of the bloody rites of ancient Mexico, have seen with our own eyes and in our own days civilised nations proceed systematically to the extermination of millions of human beings and to the perfection of weapons capable of annihilating in one second a hundred times more victims than the Aztecs ever sacrificed.

Human sacrifice among the Mexicans was inspired neither by cruelty nor by hatred. It was their response, and the only response that they could conceive, to the instability of a continually threatened world. Blood was necessary to save this world and the men in it: the victim was no longer an enemy who was to be killed but a messenger, arrayed in a dignity that was almost divine, who was sent to the gods. All the relevant descriptions, such as those that Sahagún took down from his Aztec informants, for example, convey the impression not of a dislike between the sacrificer and the victim nor of anything resembling a lust for blood, but of a strange fellow-feeling or rather – and this is vouched for by the texts – of a kind of mystical kinship.

'When a man took a prisoner he said, "Here is my well-beloved son." And the captive said, "Here is my revered father." ' The warrior who had made a prisoner and who watched him die before the altar knew that sooner or later he would follow him into the hereafter by the same kind of death. 'You are welcome: you know what the fortune of war is – today for you, tomorrow for me,' said the emperor to a captured chief.[13] As for the prisoner himself, he was perfectly aware of his fate and he had been prepared from his childhood to accept it: he agreed, stoically. More than that, he would refuse a clemency that crossed his destiny or the divine will, even if it were offered him.

Tlacahuepan, the Mexican leader, who was a prisoner of

99

the *Chalca* in the reign of Motecuhzoma I, had distinguished
himself so much by his bravery that when he was captured
his enemies offered him a part of their térritory for himself
and the other Aztecs they had taken. He would not only
have his life, but he would be lord of that section: they
even asked him to command the troops of Chalco.
Tlacahuepan's only reply was to kill himself, shouting to his
fellow-prisoners, 'Mexicans, I am going, and I shall wait
for you.'[14]

The story of Tlahuicole, a lord of Tlaxcala, who was
taken by the Mexicans, was no less famous. They admired
him so much that instead of sacrificing him they entrusted
him with the command of a body of soldiers in the war
against Michoacán: but on his return, covered with honours,
from this expedition, the Tlaxcaltec refused to withhold
himself any longer from his fate. He insisted upon his
death, and died upon the sacrificial stone.[15]

To a less extent this was also the attitude of all the other
victims. It was the attitude of the young man who, having
lived for a year in princely luxury, was to die at the end of
it in front of the image of Tezcatlipoca; and it was that of
the women who calmly danced and sang while the dark-
robed priests behind them waited for the moment to make
their heads fall like ears of maize when they are plucked
from the stem. The sensitivity of the Indians, moulded by
a powerful and very ancient tradition, was not the same as
that of the Europeans of their epoch: the Aztecs were un-
moved by the scenes in their blood-soaked temples, but
they were horror-struck by the tortures that the Spaniards
brought with them from the land of the Inquisition.[16]

It is only these foregoing considerations that allow one
to understand the meaning of war for the ancient Mexicans,
the meaning of the continual war towards which all the
energies of the city were directed. Certainly it is not in-
correct to interpret the history of Tenochtitlan between
1325 and 1519 as that of an imperialist state which steadily
pursues its aim of expansion by conquest. But that is not all.
As the Mexican dominion spread, so their very victories
created a pacified zone all round them, a zone which grew

wider and wider until it reached the edges of their known world. Where then were the victims to come from? For they were essential to provide the gods with their nourishment, *tlaxcaltiliztli*. Where could one find the precious blood without which the sun and the whole frame of the universe was condemned to annihilation? It was essential to remain in a state of war, and from this need arose the strange institution of the war of flowers, *xochiyaoyotl*, which seems to have come into being after the terrible famines which ravaged central Mexico in 1450.

The sovereigns of Mexico, Texcoco and Tlacopan and the lords of Tlaxcala, Uexotzinco and Cholula mutually agreed that, there being no war, they would arrange combats, so that the captives might be sacrificed to the gods: for it was thought, indeed, that the calamities of 1450 were caused by too few victims having been offered, so that the gods had grown angry.[17] Fighting was primarily a means of taking prisoners; on the battlefield the warriors did their utmost to kill as few men as possible. War was not merely a political instrument: it was above all a religious rite, a war of holiness.[18]

At bottom the ancient Mexicans had no real confidence in the future: their fragile world was perpetually at the mercy of some disaster – there were not only the natural cataclysms and the famines, but more than that, on certain nights the monstrous divinities of the west appeared at the cross-roads; and there were the wizards, those dark envoys from a mysterious world; and every fifty-two years there was the great fear that fell upon all the nations of the empire when the sun set on the last day of the 'century' and no man could tell whether it would ever rise again.

In all the cities and throughout the countryside the fires were put out: the close-packed crowds, filled with intense anxiety, gathered on the slopes of Uixachtecatl, while on the mountain-top the priests watched the Pleiades. The constellation mounted towards the zenith: but would it go on? Or would it stop, and would the hideous monsters of the end of the world come swarming out? The astronomer priest made a sign: a prisoner was stretched out on the stone. With a dull sound the flint knife opened his chest and in the gaping wound they spun the fire-stick, the *tlequauitl*. The miracle took place and the flame sprang up, born from this shattered breast; and amid shouts of joy messengers lit their torches at it and ran to carry the sacred fire to the four corners of the central valley. And so the world had escaped its end once more. But how heavy and blood-drenched a task it was for the priests and the warriors and the emperors, century after century to repel the unceasing onslaughts of the void.

HEAVEN AND EARTH

The Aztecs were above all 'the people of the sun'.[19] Their supreme god Uitzilopochtli personified the sun at its height, the blazing sun of noon. His mother Coatlicue, 'she of the serpent skirt', a terrestrial goddess, had borne innumerable stellar gods before him, gods called 'the four hundred of the south', as well as the lunar goddess Coyolxauhqui, the incarnation of the shades of night. According to tradition[20] Coatlicue was miraculously got with child by a ball of feathers that fell from the sky – the soul of a human sacrifice – and her son, born already armed with his fire-snake (*xiuhcoatl*) made his brothers and his sisters flee as the sun chases away the night and wipes out the stars.

The early days of Uitzilopochtli were hard, for then he was no more than the obscure god of a small wandering tribe, travelling on men's backs across the dusty plains of the north. At that time he was 'only a plebeian, no more than a man', * çan maceualli, çan tlacatl catca*, but he was also *naoalli, tetzauitl*, 'a wizard, an apparition (a marvel).'[21] His fortunes improved with those of the tribe that he led, and by the sixteenth century he reigned over the Aztec empire as the sun reigns over the world. 'Thanks to me the sun has risen,' he cried, through the mouth of his priests.[22]

As the god of a tribe of hunters and warriors from the north, Uitzilopochtli belonged to a group of stellar and celestial gods who had been brought down by the northern nations that had invaded Mexico – gods such as Tezcatlipoca, the god of the Great Bear, of the night sky, the protean wizard who sees all in his obsidian mirror, the 'young man', Telpochtli, who protects the young warriors; and Mixcoatl, the god of the Milky Way, the protector of hunters and, under the name of Camaxtli, the national god of Tlaxcala.

It may be that the nomads of the steppes knew only a small number of deities and that their religion was essentially, if not entirely, astral. The settled people of the central plateau, on the other hand, from the remotest antiquity had worshipped the agrarian gods of growth and the rain. The greatest of these was Tlaloc, with his mask of snakes, he who piles the clouds upon the mountain-tops where the *Tlaloque* live, the little rain-gods, and who sends out either the beneficent rain or the devastating hurricane at his pleasure and who can release the horror of drought upon the land. 'Oh my lord, magician-prince, truly it is to you that the maize belongs,' they said to him.[23] He was the supreme god of the peasants as Uitzilopochtli was that of the warriors. And as we have seen his place was on the top of the great *teocalli* of the capital beside Uitzilopochtli's and equal with his: his high-priest ranked with the high-priest of the sun-god. The sun and the rain, the two great forces that rule the world, shared the high place of a city that had been founded by a people of nomadic warriors turned farmers.

Tlaloc's companion Chalchiuhtlicue, 'she who has a skirt of gems', was usually placed beside him, together with Uixtociuatl: Chalchiuhtlicue was the goddess of sweet water and Uixtociuatl of salt water and of the sea – she was the goddess of the guild of salters.

The earth was symbolised by a monster with wide-open jaws which swallows the sun in its setting, the remains of the dead and the blood of the sacrificed. The monster was always put on a level with the 'old god', the father-god associated with the mother-goddess, that is to say Xiuhtecuhtli, the god of fire, 'the lord of the turquoise', sometimes called Otontecuhtli, 'Otomí lord' – the ancient tribe of the central plateau having in effect worshipped a divine pair. But besides these there were a great number of terrestrial deities, 'the mother of the gods', 'our revered mother', 'our ancestress', 'the she-snake', 'the obsidian butterfly', all wonderful and formidable goddesses, sources of life and death: Aztec sculpture represents them with an extraordinary balance of realism in the details and of the most esoteric symbolism in the conception, with features that are half human and half animal, and with macabre ornaments.[24]

They are compared in hymns to the white and yellow flowers that open when the rains come, or described as standing in 'the sacred maize-field', *centlateomilco*, waving the magic bell that makes the grain-bearing plant come up.[25] They are the Great Mothers who gave birth to the young god of maize, Centeotl, and the young gods of music, dancing and flowers, Xochipilli and Macuilxochitl. The two faces of the world and of life, benign and terrifying, are brought together in them.

Not far from them and often represented with the same kind of attributes although she was of a different origin (her cult seems to have been brought in from the Huaxtec country in the north-east) was Tlazolteotl, the goddess of carnal love and of sin and of confession. It was to her that one could, through a priest, confess one's sins; but, unlike the Christian practice, this happened only once in a man's lifetime. The goddess was called *tlaelquani*, 'the eater of filth', that is to say, 'she who eats sins'.

For the ancient Mexicans, as for many other agricultural peoples, there was a close link between the moon and vegetation. Metztli, the moon, had been closely followed in its phases and eclipses by the native astronomers since Mayan times. The terrestrial goddesses were at the same time goddesses of the moon.

There were also uncountable numbers of little local gods who were held to protect the harvests and make them plentiful. Usually each one had the name of the town or village where he was worshipped – Tepoztecatl, for example, 'he of Tepoztlán' – and as a body they were called the Four Hundred Rabbits. The rabbit was held to represent the moon, for it was a rabbit that the Mexicans saw in the dark patches on its face. These rustic gods had their festival at the end of the harvest, and at these feasts the *octli* flowed in abundance: they were therefore also the gods of drunkenness.[26]

While Tlazolteotl came from the north-east, it was probably from the south, from the Pacific coast, that they imported the terrible cult of Xipe Totec, 'our lord the flayed one', the god of the goldsmiths and also the deity of the spring rain, the renewal of nature and the fresh growth. His victims were dedicated to him during the month *Tlacaxipeualiztli* and transfixed with arrows so that their blood should drop on the earth like rain: then they were flayed.

The priests put on their skin, dyed yellow to look like gold leaf, and this magical act, which symbolised the way the earth 'makes a new skin' at the beginning of the rainy season, induced the vegetation to come again. Xipe Totec was called 'the drinker by night' because it was at night that the fertilising rain came down. They called upon him most pitifully, crying, 'Oh my god, why do you make us beg so hard? Put on your golden clothes.' And they thanked him in a heart-felt way – 'My god, your gem-like rain has fallen.'[27]

That was one of the aspects of the eternally-repeated drama of the year, the rebirth of the forces of nature and of growth after they had apparently died in the dry season. The whole of ancient Mexican thought, and their whole vision of the world, turned about this central idea, whether it concerned man or nature.

DEATH AND REBIRTH

Maize and the garden plants are born in the occident, in the western garden of Tamoanchan where the earth-goddesses live, the sources of life. Then they undertake a long journey under the ground (that of germination) praying the gods of rain to guide them on their road: at last they come up in the east, the country of the rising sun and of youth and plenty, the 'red land' of the dawn where the bird *quetzalcoxcoxtli* sings.[23]

Venus, the morning star, is born in the east; then she disappears, and she is seen again as the evening star in the west. She has therefore traversed the world as a shuttle traverses the cloth: she is the symbol of death and rebirth.

In divinity the planet was called Quetzalcoatl, 'quetzal-snake', or 'plumed serpent', a name which can also be interpreted as meaning 'precious twin', since the two appearances of the planet are like two twin stars. Quetzalcoatl sacrificed himself upon a pyre, and a brilliant star was seen to rise from the flames. Under the name of Xolotl, the dog-headed god, he went under the earth, down to the hell of Mictlan, to seek for the worn bones of those long dead, in order to make living men out of them.

Was not Uitzilopochtli, the conquering sun, the rein-carnation of a dead warrior? He was born miraculously, as we have seen, and it was the soul of a man killed in battle or in sacrifice that impregnated his mother the earth. His name 'the humming-bird (*uitzilin*) from the left' means 'the reborn warrior from the south', for the south is the left-hand side of the world, and warriors are reborn in the minute, brilliant body of a humming-bird.

Thus neither nature nor man are to be sent to an ever-lasting death. Resurrecting forces are at work: the sun comes up again each morning after passing the night 'under the holy plain' *teotlalli iitic*, that is to say, in Hades; Venus dies and is reborn; the maize dies and is reborn; the whole world of plants, struck dead in the dry season, arises more beautiful and younger each season of the rains, just as the moon dwindles in the sky and returns according to the rhythm of its phases.

Death and life are no more than two sides of the same reality: from the earliest times the potters of Tlatilco made a double face,[29] one half alive and the other skull-like; and the dualism is also to be found in innumerable documents. Perhaps no people in history have been so much haunted by the grim presence of death as the Mexicans; but for them life came out of death, as the young plant comes from the mouldering seed in the earth.

As for man himself, and what became of him after his death, our knowledge is still somewhat incomplete. It is sure, however, that some kinds of immortality were pro-vided; but without any moral connotation, either of reward or of punishment. The warrior who died in battle or upon the stone of sacrifice became a 'companion of the eagle', *quauhtecatl*, that is to say, a companion of the sun. Every day he would take his place with his fellows in the brilliant and happy company that surrounded the luminary from the time that it rose in the east until the time that it reached the zenith. These immortal soldiers filled their sunlit hours with war-songs and mock battles; and after four years they were reincarnated as humming-birds, flying from flower to flower in the warm air.

As soon as the sun had passed the zenith it came into the western side of the world, the 'female side', *ciuatlampa*, because that was where the goddess-mothers lived and also the women who died in childbirth and who thus became goddesses too, the *Ciuateteo*. It was they, in their turn, who accompanied the sun from the zenith to its setting.

Other dead people had been selected by fate for a very different kind of eternity: those upon whom Tlaloc had set his mark and who had been drowned or struck by lightning or who had died of a disease thought to be brought about by water – dropsy, for example. The peasant god had reserved his own paradise for them – Tlalocan, an idealised vision of the eastern tropics, a green country of flowers and warm rain; it was a garden of repose and plenty, where the blessed lived for ever in a peaceful happiness.

In this way the two ideologies of the two elements that had formed the Mexican people came together; the first element hunters and warriors, worshippers of a sun-god, and the second settled peasants whose deity was the god of the rain. For the first there was the brilliant road from the orient to the zenith, and for the others the mild happiness of abundance without trouble or labour in the moist green tropical paradise.

But what happened to the others, to those who were not singled out either by Uitzilopochtli or Tlaloc? It was but a dreary outlook for these undistinguished corpses, for they had nowhere to go except Mictlan, the underworld which lay beneath the great steppes of the north, in the cold, twilit country. Mictlantecuhtli and his wife Mictecaciuatl reigned there: the Mexican Pluto's face was covered with a bony mask, and he sat among owls and spiders.

Even so, it was not easy for the dead man to reach his last resting-place. He had to wander four years in the underworld, together with a 'soul-companion', a dog that was cremated with him; four years in which he had to undergo the furious attacks of an icy blast, 'the wind of obsidian', escape from voracious monsters, and at last cross the Nine Rivers, on the other side of which began Hades. And there, dissolving as it were into the void, he vanished totally and for ever.

It is likely that our sources have not told us all that there was to tell. Were the emperors and the dignitaries, for example, to go to Mictlan, even if they did die in their beds? What about the priests, who do not appear to come under any of the known headings? It is difficult to conceive that no after-life was envisaged for them. As Uitzilopochtli is shown as the guarantor of the warriors' resurrection and Tlaloc of his peoples', then perhaps Quetzalcoatl, the prototype of the priest, had a future life in store for the ecclesiastics. However that may be, the prime decision of the creating pair, the Lord and the Lady of the Duality, established the ineluctable fate not only of each man's earthly life but also of his eternity. Everything depended upon the sign under which he was born. And it was this belief in signs, the expressions of fate, that had the greatest influence upon the life of every Mexican.

DESTINIES AND SIGNS

From the Mayas, who seem to have been positively hypnotised by time and its majestic passage, onwards, all the civilised nations of Mexico and Central America worked out complex chronological systems, and this for two purposes: the first was to find fixed points in order to understand and foresee the succession of natural phenomena, the seasons and the movements of the stars, and so to regulate the rites that were necessary to their proper sequence; the second was to determine the fate of each man and the fortunes of each undertaking by means of a body of portents which made up a coherent whole quite as 'scientific' for those people as our rational explanations of the world are for us.

The solar year, *xiuitl*, of 365 days, was divided into 18 months of 20 days, to which were added 5 'hollow' days, thought of as exceedingly unfortunate. Each of these months had a name which had reference either to a natural phenomenon or, more often, to the rites which were to be celebrated during it.

The year itself was named after the first day in it: the name was taken from the divinatory calendar, and it already contained concealed within it the potential good or evil of the year.

Given that the number of days in the year, less the hollow days, is 360 and therefore divisible by 20, it is clear that if the year began let us say with the sign *acatl*, the first of the intercalary days had the same sign. But as there were four other intercalary days, the first day of the following year was therefore separated by five intervals from that of the preceding year. As 20 divided by 5 is 4, there were only four signs that could be used for the beginning of the year. In the days of the Aztecs these were the four signs *acatl*, *tecpatl*, *calli* and *tochtli*.

The thirteen fundamental numerals of the divinatory calendar combined with the four signs to allow $13 \times 4 = 52$ beginnings of the year. It was only at the end of this series that the same numeral and the same sign would recur; and then they set about 'binding the years' by lighting the new fire. This period of 52 years, which is sometimes called the Mexican century, was represented by a bundle of stalks tied together.

The Aztecs had learnt, probably from their Pueblan or Mixtec neighbours, to observe the apparent revolution of the planet Venus. Five years of Venus are the same as eight years of the sun. These years were counted by means of the signs of the divinatory calendar. The two accounts, that of the years of Venus and that of the years of the sun, coincided only after 65 of the first, which are the equivalent of 104 of the second – that is to say, at the end of two earthly 'centuries'. This was the longest period in Mexican chronology, and it was called *ce ueuetiliztli*, 'one old age'.[30]

As for the *tonalpoualli*[31] or divinatory calendar itself, the

Aztecs, like the other Mexican nations, based it upon the combination of 13 numbers, 1–13, and 20 names:

cipactli: crocodile or aquatic monster
eecatl: wind
calli: house
cuetzpalin: lizard
coatl: snake
miquiztli: death
mazatl: deer
tochtli: rabbit
atl: water
itzcuintli: dog
ozomatli: monkey
malinalli: dead grass
acatl: reed
ocelotl: ocelot
quauhtli: eagle
cozcaquauhtli: vulture
ollin: motion, or earthquake
tecpatl: flint
quiauitl: rain
xochitl: flower.

Each name of a day was represented by a sign. The combination of the 13 numbers and the 20 signs gave a series of 260 days, the duration of the divinatory year, which, beginning at 1 *cipactli* ended on the day 13 *xochitl*, running without interruption and without the same sign ever bearing the same figure. The continuous sequence of dates in the divinatory calendar and that of the dates in the solar year had no influence upon one another at all. Every day could be named by reference to the two systems: for example, 8 *cipactli*, 3 *toxcatl* – that is, the eighth day of the group of thirteen days which begins with 1 *ocelotl*, which is at the same time the third day of the fifth month *toxcatl*.

The divinatory year of 260 days split up naturally into 20 groups of 13, each of which began with the figure 1 with a different sign appropriated to it: 1 *cipactli*, 1 *ocelotl*, 1 *mazatl*, etc., and so on until the last, 1 *tochtli*.[32] Each of these groups was considered as a whole fortunate, unfortunate or indifferent, according to the sense of its first day; but besides this each of the days might be good, bad or neutral according to its distinguishing number and sign. The days which had the numbers 7, 10, 11, 12 and 13 were held to be generally favourable, and those with the figure 9 unfavourable. But the influence of the figures had to be combined with that of the signs, and the divinatory calendar was in fact made up of a table of 260 special cases.

Furthermore, each group of thirteen was assigned to one or to two gods: the sun and the moon for the group 1 *miquiztli*, Patecatl, god of drink and drunkenness, for the group 1 *quiauitl*; the planet Venus and the god of the dead for the group 1 *coatl*, etc. Finally, nine deities, 'the lords of the night', made up a series parallel with that of the signs and running in an uninterrupted sequence beside them: their particular influence had certainly to be taken into account in the soothsayer's appreciation of any given day.

It was also necessary to reckon with the influence peculiar to the year itself, and likewise that which the cardinal points of space might have upon the signs. For the Mexicans thought of the world as a kind of Maltese cross,[33] the east uppermost, the north on the right, the west below and the south on the left. The twenty signs for days were divided into four sets of five, each ruled by one of the cardinal points: for example, the signs *cipactli* and *acatl* belonged to the east, *ocelotl* and *tecpatl* to the north, *mazatl* and *calli* to the west, and *xochitl* and *tochtli* to the south.[34]

After this, each cardinal point in succession ruled one day, following the order east, north, west, south; and also one year, also following the order *acatl* (east), *tecpatl* (north), *calli* (west) and *tochtli* (south). Because of this the day or the year was imbued with the qualities ascribed to each quarter – fertility and abundance to the east, barren aridity to the north, falling-off, old age and death to the west (setting sun), and a neutral character to the south. As for the groups of thirteen, they too underwent the influence of the cardinal points, and in the same order; for the first belonged to the east, the second to the north, the third to the west, the fourth to the south, and so on continuously.

Thus the spatial influences which ruled time fitted into one another like so many hollow wooden Russian dolls: or rather it may be said that Mexican philosophy did not conceive one abstract space and one abstract time, homogeneous and separate media, but rather on the other hand concrete multiplicities of time and space, single points and happenings, disparate and unique. The qualities peculiar to each of these 'moment-loci', expressed by the sign which indicated the days in the *tonalpoualli*, follow one another cyclically in an abrupt, total change according to a determinate rhythm, in conformity with an everlasting order.

When the Duality decides that a man shall be born or 'come down' (*temo*) he consequently finds himself inserted automatically into this order and in the grasp of the omnipotent machine. The sign of the day of his birth will govern him until the day of his death – it will even decide his death and so his after-life: it will decide whether he is to die as a sacrifice and thus join the splendid retinue of the sun, or to be drowned and so inhabit the unendingly happy Tlalocan, or to be consigned to the void in the shadowy hereafter of Mictlan. His whole fate is subjected to the strictest predestination.

There were certainly attempts at correcting fate, however. If a child were born under an unfortunate sign, some days were allowed to go by before naming him, until a fortunate sign should come. It was also conceded that by dint of penance, privation and self-control a man might escape the evil influences which doomed him, for example, to drunkenness, gambling and debauchery. But it does not seem that there was ever much hope of avoiding the inexorable operation of the signs. They were at the base of everything, the fate of individuals and the fate of communities; and the gods themselves were not free – it was because the sign I *acatl* ruled the destiny of Quetzalcoatl that he had to appear in the east in the shape of the morning star.[35]

Consequently the life of the Mexican was dominated by the portents drawn from the *tonalamatl*. The merchants waited for the day I *coatl* to begin their journey towards the remote countries of the south, because this sign promised them success and prosperity. Those who were born in the group 1 *ocelotl* would die as prisoners of war. Painters and scribes and weaving-women particularly honoured the sign 7 *xochitl*, which was favourable to them.

He who was born under the sign 2 *tochtli* would be a drunkard, and he who was born under the sign 4 *itzcuintli* would be prosperous and rich even if he never did anything. 1 *miquiztli* was favourable for slaves; 4 *eecatl* for wizards and black magic; 1 *calli* for doctors and midwives. On the day 4 *ollin* the dignitaries sacrificed birds to the sun: on 1 *acatl* they offered flowers, incense and tobacco to Quetzalcoatl. It would not be too much to say that no Aztec, whatever his state or calling, could do without the services of the diviners, or undertake any enterprise without knowing the signs.

Minds that were so very much under the dominion of fate could not but be uncommonly sensitive to omens, whether they were drawn from little everyday happenings or from extraordinary phenomena. An unaccustomed noise in the mountains, the cry of an owl, a rabbit running into a house or a wolf crossing the road foretold disaster.[36]

The night, so favourable to ghosts, filled itself with fantastic monsters, dwarfish women with flowing hair, death's-heads that ran after travellers, footless, headless creatures that moaned as they rolled upon the ground, 'and those who saw them were persuaded or were convinced that they would be killed in war or would presently die of an illness, or that some misfortune was about to fall upon them'.[37]

Other portents foretold wars or defeats. These omens were those extraordinary kind of events that the Romans called *portenta* and the Aztecs *tetzauitl*. On the eve of the battle which ended in the victory of the Mexicans a dog spoke to tell its master, an old man of Tlatelolco, of the misfortunes that were about to descend upon his town. The angry old man having killed his dog, a *uexolotl*, or turkey, which was spreading its tail in the courtyard of his house, opened its beak and spoke. The old man of Tlatelolco

grew angrier still, and crying 'You shall not be my omen
(*amonotinotetzauh*)' cut the bird's head off. Then a mask for
dancing that he kept hanging on the wall in his house spoke
out, and the old man, disturbed by these three prodigies,
went to tell the king Moquiuixtli. 'You are drunk, are you
not?' said the king. But a little while later the king was
struck down on the steps of his temple by the soldiers of
Axayacatl.[38]

One day the fowlers of the Mexican lake brought
Motecuhzoma II a strange bird that they had just caught.
'In the middle of its head this bird had a round mirror,
which showed the sky and the stars . . . When Motecuhzoma
looked into this mirror he saw a host of men, all armed and
mounted on horses. He sent for his soothsayers and asked
them "Do you know what I have seen? Here is a crowd of
people coming." But before the soothsayers could reply
the bird vanished.'[39]

The *Codex Telleriano-Remensis* depicts an immense
streamer of light leaping from the earth to the stars, under
the year 4 *calli*, or 1509. This phenomenon, which may
have been the zodiacal light, was afterwards thought to have
heralded the coming of the conquistadores. 'For many
nights,' says Ixtlilxochitl, 'there appeared a great brightness
that rose from the eastern horizon and reached the heavens;
it was shaped like a pyramid, and it flamed . . . and the king
of Texcoco, being extremely learned in all the sciences of
the ancients, and particularly in astrology . . . concluded
from this that his rule and his realm amounted to little; and
at this time he ordered his captains and the commanders of
his armies to put an end to the wars that they were waging.'[40]

Comets and earthquakes, which were always carefully
marked down each year in the hieroglyphic manuscripts,
were always considered omens of misfortune. So was the
lightning that struck a temple, or waves on the lake, there
being no wind to cause them, or again the voice of a woman,
such as that which was heard in the air a little before the
invasion, moaning and wailing.[41]

Indeed, man had but an insignificant place in the Mexican
vision of the world. He was governed by predestination;

neither his life nor his after-life were in his own hands, and
determinism ruled every phase of his short stay on earth.
He was crushed under the weight of the gods and the stars:
he was the prisoner of the omnipotent signs. The very
world in which he made his brief struggle was no more than
an ephemeral shape, one experiment among others, and
like them doomed to catastrophe. Horror and horrifying
monsters surrounded him on all sides: ghosts and apparitions
made their dark signals of despair.

The moral climate of ancient Mexico was soaked in
pessimism. The poems of the great king Nezaualcoyotl are
haunted by the idea of death and annihilation; and even
when other poets celebrate the beauties of tropical nature
one feels that the obsession is there and that 'it takes them
by the throat even amidst the flowers'. Religion, and the
art that expresses religion through sculpture, and even
the manuscripts whose glyphs enclose the wisdom of this
ancient people, everything crushes man with the harshness
of a fate that is beyond his control.

But their nobility resided in this, that they accepted the
world as they saw it. Theirs was an active pessimism; it
did not result in a discouraged idleness but in a fiery zeal
for the sacred war, in ardent service of the gods, in the
building of cities and the conquest of empires. Brought
face to face with a pitiless universe, the Mexican did not
attempt to veil it with illusions, but eked out the precarious
scrap of life that the gods had granted him with an un-
tamable strength, with labour and with blood.

AN IMPERIAL RELIGION

The Aztec civilisation, still young and still in its first
flowering, had hardly begun when the European invasion
cut short both its growth and the development and building-
up of its religious philosophy.

Such as it was at the eve of the catastrophe, or such as we
understand it to have been, it seems to us both complicated
and contradictory, made up of different contributions which
had not yet been assimilated and merged into a coherent
system.

The Mexican was a receptive religion. The conquering Aztecs were only too happy to seize not only the provinces, but also the provincial gods. All foreign gods were welcome within the precincts of the great *teocalli*, and the priests of Tenochtitlan, eager for knowledge and curious of ritual, willingly adopted the myths and practices of the distant countries that the armies had traversed.

This was the basis of the great misunderstanding between the Mexicans and the Spaniards. The first worshipped a great many gods and were willing to set up among them whatever the newcomers should bring: the second were the votaries of a closed religion whose churches could rise only upon the ruins of the former temples.

The complexity of Mexican religion is explained by the complexity of society and the state. If it is a reflection of the world, if it explains the world, still above all it reflects the complex society of which it is the expression.

Then again, it had become the religion not only of a city but of a very widely spread and diversified confederation. We have little knowledge of the form that the piety of the peasants and plebeians took. There is evidence of the belief of the old agricultural nations such as the Otomí[42] in the primordial junction of sun and earth (father and mother) and this is found again among the Nahuatl Mexicans in the form of the primordial couple, the Lord and the Lady of the Duality, as well as in the invocations which are invariably addressed to the sun-father and the earth-mother.

We also know that there were deities for districts and guilds, such as Yacatecuhtli, god of the merchants, Coyotlinaual, god of the feather-workers, Uixtociuatl, goddess of the salters, Atlaua, god of the fowlers on the lake. The stellar gods of the nomads from the north had combined with the gods of rain and agriculture which the settled tribes had worshipped since before the Christian era. And in the course of time Huaxtec gods like Tlazolteotl or Yopi gods like Xipe Totec had been brought in, together with all the little gods of drink and the harvest known as the *Centzon Totochtin*, or the Four Hundred Rabbits.

In this many-sided pantheon were assembled the beliefs

and the aspirations of different social classes and of various peoples. The myth-cycle of the sun is pre-eminently the religion of the warriors devoted to battle and sacrifice. Quetzalcoatl is the ideal of priests yearning for holiness. Tlaloc is the great god of the peasants. Mixcoatl, the god of the northern peoples, had his devotees as well as Xipe Totec, 'lord of the coast', and the plumed serpent of the Toltecs, and the carnal goddess of the eastern nations.

Each step of the social ladder had its god or gods, and each subdivision of living-place or work, and each village or city. It is the imperial religion of a great state that is in the process of formation, but that is still no more than a confederation of many little highly individual states, each with its own history and traditions and often its own language.

Just as the political institutions at the summit tended to grow stronger and to find the formation necessary for an imperial state, so the meditation of the priests tended to bring order into this theological chaos. A syncretism was coming into being, but unhappily through the confused, obscure accounts we can apprehend only a few aspects of it.

Some gods had risen above the crowd, and through them the Mexican thinkers attempted to bring about the religious synthesis that was essential to them: this they did by endowing the great gods with multiple attributes, by stating that many of the divine names were synonyms for these gods, and by postulating genealogies to link them together. Tezcatlipoca, in particular, seems to have been becoming the guiding principle in the world of gods.

According to one of the traditions, the first pair begot four sons, who were the creators of the other gods and of the world: the red Tezcatlipoca, identified with Xipe Totec and Camaxtli or Mixcoatl; the black Tezcatlipoca, who was the Tezcatlipoca usually worshipped under that name; the blue Tezcatlipoca, who was no other than Uitzilopochtli; and finally Quetzalcoatl. Thus the positions of a whole series of divine persons are fixed in relation to the four great directions in space and at the same time the number of persons is reduced to two, Tezcatlipoca and Quetzalcoatl: Uitzilopochtli, a parvenu, a newcomer with his tribe, is integrated; so is Xipe Totec, a foreign god.

There is a comparable work of synthesis apparent in books like the Borgia and Cospiano manuscripts, which probably come from the regions of Puebla, Tepeaca, Tehuacán and Tlaxcala.[43] Some distant towns, such as Teotitlán on the frontier of Oaxaca, were well known for the wisdom and the meditations of their priests.

Quetzalcoatl, who was particularly venerated at Cholula in this same region of Puebla, was also one of those whose stature rose high above that of the ordinary run of gods. As we have seen, one tradition made him the equal of Tezcatlipoca. He was the Toltec god, the god of the settled civilised people of the high plateau, the inventor of the arts, of writing and of the calendar; he was the expression of everything that makes life kinder and more lovely, as well as that of the planet Venus, with its message of resurrection. It was right, therefore, to set up against him the sombre northern god of the night sky, of war and magic. For the legend of Tula told how Tezcatlipoca the wizard had turned the beneficent god-king out of his town and condemned the plumed serpent to exile.

So, at least in some circles, in the *calmecac* where the erudite priests studied the many-coloured manuscripts or watched the march of the stars by night, a new conception arose – that of a divine world dominated by a small number of beings, or mythical personalities, each with many aspects.

Some went further. The pious king Nezaualcoyotl erected a temple dedicated to 'the unknown god, creator of all things' who was called Tloque Nahuaque, 'he of the immediate vicinity' or Ipalnemohuani, 'he by whom we live'. On the top of this temple was a tower with nine storeys 'which stood for nine heavens, and the tenth, which finished these nine storeys, was painted black and studded with stars outside, while the inside was adorned with gold, gems and precious feathers'. And this god, whom no man 'had either known or seen up to that time' was not represented by any statue or idol.[44]

This cult in no way hindered Nezaualcoyotl from worshipping a great many other gods at the same time. There was no monotheism here, but rather a belief in a supreme god raised above all the others, nameless (since the words which designate him are no more than epithets), with no history in myth, and faceless.

It is very likely that these philosophical and theological speculations were confined to a small circle of people high in the state and the church. The villagers of the high plateau or the tropical lands would certainly never have admitted that their local gods were inferior to any great deity, and the people of the various districts of the capital no doubt preferred the gods of their little temples, near to them and attached to them by tradition, to the abstract divinities of the priests.

In any case, one thing is certain, and that is that this religion, with its scrupulous and exacting ritual and the profusion of its myths, penetrated, in all its aspects, deeply into the everyday life of men. Continuously and totally, it moulded the existence of the Mexican nation.

Everything was under its domination: public life and private life; each stage of each person's progress from birth to death; the rhythm of time; the arts and even games – nothing escaped. It was this religion which, like a powerful frame, upheld the whole edifice of Mexican civilisation: so, when once this frame was broken by the invaders, it was not surprising that the entirety should have fallen in ruins.

CHAPTER FOUR

A MEXICAN'S DAY

The house, furniture and gardens. Different kinds of house: mats, chests, seats, various pieces of furniture: heating and lighting: the hearth, centre of the house: the splendour of the gardens—Getting up, washing and dressing, clothes. Personal cleanliness and baths: hairdressing: women's beauty and its care: men's and women's clothes: sandals: luxury in clothes and ornaments—Business, work, ceremonies. Farming work: state business and public service: the priests: law-suits: holidays and rites: various trades—Meals. The time of meals: Mexican cooking and its natural resources: banquets: tobacco and narcotics: alcohol and drunkenness.—Games and amusements. Hunting: the ball-game: gambling—The Rhythm of day and night. Measurement of time in a clockless civilisation: intervals marked by priestly instruments: nocturnal activity.

THE HOUSE, FURNITURE AND GARDENS

The sky above the volcanoes grows pale. The morning star shines with the brilliance of a gem and to greet it the wooden gongs beat on the temple-tops and the conchs wail. There are still wafts of mist over the water, in the icy air of this altitude, but they dissolve in the first rays of the sun. Day has begun. People are waking up in all the houses, great and small, from one end of the city to the other and in the lakeside villages and solitary huts.

With their wicker fans the women blow on the fire that smoulders between the hearth-stones, and then, kneeling before the *metlatl* of volcanic stone they begin grinding the maize. The work of the day begins with this dull rumble of the grinder: it has begun like this for thousands of years. A little later comes the rhythmic slapping of the women gently flattening the maize-dough between their hands to make the pancake-like tortillas or *tlaxcalli*.

In the gardens and courtyards there are the gobbling turkeys busily picking about: naked or sandalled feet pad along the earth roads: paddles stir the water of the canals. Everyone hurries towards the day's work. Very soon the men are all gone, to the city or into the fields, often carrying their *itacatl* (luncheon) in a bag; and the women stay at home.

In a town like Mexico there were naturally great differences between the various kinds of house, according to the rank, the wealth or the profession of the people who lived in them. At the one extreme stood the palaces of the emperor and the dignitaries, huge constructions with both a public and private character and with many rooms, and at the other the peasants' huts in the suburbs, made of mud and wattle, with grass roofs.

Most of the houses were made of sun-dried brick: the more modest constructions had only one main room – the kitchen would be a little separate building in the courtyard. The number of rooms increased with the family's wealth: an average type of house had a kitchen, a room where the whole family slept, and a little domestic shrine: the bathroom (*temazcalli*) was always built separately. If it was possible, the number of rooms was increased; and there was a tendency to reserve one or more for the women.

Craftsmen had their workshops and traders their warehouses. The site upon which each house was built was rarely completely covered by the buildings: there was an inner courtyard, a garden where the children could play in the perpetually spring-like weather of Tenochtitlan, and the women could weave and spin. Most of these plots were bordered on at least one side by a canal and each family had its own landing-place: it was thus that the merchants could come by night to store their goods without being seen.[1]

The houses, grand or simple, hardly differed at all in their furnishing. This was reduced, as it is in the East, to a point that would mean discomfort to us. The beds were no more than mats, many or few, finer or coarser: a sort of bed-curtain might be set up over them, as in the case of the beds the Spaniards were given in Axayacatl's palace. 'However great a lord he might be, no one had any bed other than this kind,' says Bernal Díaz.[2] And this was in a royal palace. Among the common people a single mat answered the purpose, and during the daytime it was a seat.

In fact it was a mat (*petlatl*) set upon a low platform made of earth or, for more solemn occasions, of wood, that was the seat, not only in private houses but everywhere – in law-courts, for example. The word *petlatl* was even used to mean a court or an office of the administration. A more highly-evolved chair existed, however – the *icpalli* made of wood or wickerwork and with a back – and in the manuscripts emperors and dignitaries are often shown sitting in them.[3]

They were low chairs, without feet: the cushion upon which one sat cross-legged rested directly on the ground. The back, which leaned backwards a little, came somewhat higher than the sitter's head. These *icpalli* were made particularly at Cuauhtitlán, which had to supply four thousand a year and as many mats, by way of tax.[4] The furniture meant for the emperor was covered with cloth or skins, and adorned with gold.[5]

A family's clothes, pieces of cloth and jewels were kept in wickerwork chests called *petlacalli*,[6] a word which also means the state treasure and is found in the name of the official, the *petlacalcatl*, in charge of the finances of the empire. These frail coffers, which were only covered baskets, offered no real resistance to thieves; nor did the lockless doors, and from this arose the extreme severity of the laws against theft. When it was desired to protect things very thoroughly they were closed in behind a false[7] wall in the house: Motecuhzoma did this to hide the treasure of Axayacatl. Mats, chests and a few seats, and all these woven out of reeds or rushes, that was the furniture of an Aztec house, rich or poor. In the emperor's palace, and no doubt among the dignitaries, there were also a few low tables and richly-ornamented wooden screens which served to keep off the excessive heat of the fire or to cut off a part of the room for a time. 'If it was cold,' says Díaz,[8] 'they made (for Motecuhzoma) a great fire of embers with bark that made no smoke and that smelt very pleasant; and so that these embers should not give more heat than he wanted, they put before the fire a kind of plank [sic] adorned with gold and having representations of idols upon it . . . and when he began to eat, a wooden door all decorated with gold was put in front of him, so that he should not be seen eating.'

In passing, one may observe the worthy Díaz' difficulty at this point, for he had obviously never seen a screen at home, in Spain. It is also clear from this description that even among the great men there was no dining-room: meals were eaten anywhere at all.

Thus furnished, or rather thus devoid of furniture, these houses must have appeared naked and cold, with their floors of beaten earth or flags and their whitewashed walls. It is probable, however, that the walls of the richer houses were decorated with frescoes or were hung with coloured cloth or skins. When guests were invited, the inside of the house was ornamented with flowers and branches. For heating there were wood fires – the importance of wood as a fuel is emphasised by the frequent mention of it in litera- ture – or braziers: they were not really very efficient methods of heating, and although the Mexican climate does not run to extremes of cold, the Aztecs must have shivered on their mats on those winter nights when the temperature fell suddenly. Yet the Aztecs were happier than the Romans, whose system of heating was not much better; for at least they were sure of being able to get warm again in the sun, when the day was come, for the winter is the dry season in Mexico. As for the lighting, it was no less primitive: resinous torches of pine-wood (ocotl) were used indoors, and outside links and huge braziers piled with resinous wood served for public lighting when circumstances – a religious ceremony, for example – called for it.[9]

In the middle of every house, particularly the most un- assuming, there was the hearth, the image and the incarnation of the 'Old God' the god of fire. The three stones between which the logs were burnt or upon which the pots rested had therefore a sacred character: the mysterious power of the god was within them, and anyone who offended the fire by walking on the hearth-stones was sure to die very soon.[10]

Fire was held in particular veneration by the merchants: during the night before the departure of a caravan they would gather at the house of one of their number, and standing before his hearth they would sacrifice birds, burn incense and throw magic figures cut out of paper into the flames. On their return they gave the fire its share of the feast with which they celebrated the fortunate outcome of their voyage.[11]

The luxury of the great houses did not reside in their furnishing, whose simplicity has been described, nor in their comfort, which was hardly better than that of the simplest dwellings, but in the size and number of their rooms and perhaps even more in the variety and splendour of their gardens.

The palace of king Nezaualcoyotl at Texcoco was a rectangle more than a thousand yards long by some eight hundred wide.[12] Part of this space was occupied by public buildings – council chambers, courts, offices, armouries – and part by private – the king's apartments, the harem, the apartments intended for the sovereigns of Mexico and Tlacopan: in all they amounted to more than three hundred rooms. The rest was given over to the gardens 'with many fountains, ponds and canals, many fish and birds, and the whole planted with more than two thousand pines . . . and there were several mazes, according to where the king bathed; and once a man was in he could not find the way out . . . and farther on, beside the temples, there was the bird-house, where the king kept all the kinds and varieties of birds, animals, reptiles and serpents that they brought him from every part of New Spain; and those which were not to be had were represented in gold and precious stones – which was also the case with the fish, both those of the sea and those that lived in the rivers and lakes. So no bird, fish or animal of the whole country was wanting here: they were there either alive or figured in gold and gems.'

Besides his palace at Texcoco the same king had had gardens planted in other places, particularly at Tetzcotzinco. 'These parks and gardens were adorned with rich and sumptuously ornamented alcázars[13] with their fountains,

their irrigation channels, their canals, their lakes and their
bathing-places and wonderful mazes, where he had had a
great variety of flowers planted and trees of all kinds,
foreign and brought from distant parts . . . and the water
intended for the fountains, pools and channels for watering
the flowers and the trees in this park came from its spring:
to bring it, it had been necessary to build strong, high,
cemented walls of unbelievable size, going from one
mountain to the other with an aqueduct on top which came
out at the highest part of the park.' The water accumulated
first in a reservoir beautified with historical bas-reliefs
'which the first bishop of Mexico, brother Juan de Zumárraga, had broken, because he believed that they had to do
with idolatry', and thence it flowed off by two principal
canals, the one to the north, the other to the south, running
through the gardens and filling basins, where sculptured
stelæ were reflected in the surface. Coming out of one of
these basins, the water 'leapt and dashed itself to pieces on
the rocks, falling into a garden planted with all the scented
flowers of the Hot Lands, and in this garden it seemed to
rain, so very violently was the water shattered upon these
rocks. Beyond this garden there were the bathing-places, cut
in the living rock . . . and beyond them the castle that the
king had in this park and in which still other rooms and
halls were seen, and many of them; one was a very large
hall with a court in front of it, and it was there that he
received the kings of Mexico and Tlacopan and other
great lords when they came to enjoy themselves with him:
the dances and the other spectacles and delights took place
in this court . . . The whole of the rest of this park was
planted, as I have said, with all kinds of trees and scented
flowers, and there were all kinds of birds apart from those
that the king had brought from various parts in cages: all
these birds sang harmoniously and to such degree that one
could not hear oneself speak. Outside the gardens and
beyond a wall the country began, full of deer, rabbits and
hares.'[14]

Has the hispanified Indian chronicler Ixtlilxochitl, himself descended from Nezaualcoyotl, let himself be carried

away by pride in the dynasty? The remaining traces of the gardens of Tetzcotzinco, alas, give but a faint idea of their former splendour; but they confirm Ixtlilxochitl in the essentials. The cascades, the sheets of water and the flower-beds have vanished, but the empty reservoirs are still to be seen cut in the rock; the aqueduct, the steps and the terraces are still there.[15]

Besides, the conquerors saw comparable marvels from the time they first came into the valley of Mexico. They passed the night before their entry into the capital at Iztapalapan: Díaz was entranced by the palace in which they stayed – 'so large and well-built in the best kind of stone, with the roof-timbers made of cedar and other sweet-smelling woods – very big rooms, and what was particularly worth seeing, patios covered over with cotton awnings. When we had looked through all this, we went into the garden; it was delightful to walk in it, and I was never weary of observing the variety of the plants and their perfumes, the flower-beds, many fruit-trees and roses [*sic*] of the country, and a pool of sweet water. There was another extraordinary thing: large boats could come right into this orchard from the lake.' And the old Spanish soldier, writing his memoirs many years later, adds sadly, '*Ahora todo está por el suelo, perdido, que no hay cosa.*' Now all that is fallen, lost: nothing is left any more.[16]

And this was only a *tecuhtli's* palace. What then must have been the emperor's country seats and pleasure-houses? Cortés wrote to Charles V, 'He (Motecuhzoma) had many pleasure-houses, both in the city and outside it . . . in one of them there was a magnificent garden and in it there rose belvederes made of marble, floored with exquisitely-worked jasper . . . There were ten lakes there where there were kept all the many and varied kinds of water-birds that live in that country . . . There were salt-water lakes for the birds of the seashore, and fresh-water for those of the rivers. From time to time these lakes were emptied for cleaning and then they were refilled by means of the canals: each kind of bird had the sort of food that was appropriate for it in its natural state. Thus those which ate fish were given fish, those which ate worms were given worms, those which ate maize were given maize . . . and I assure your Majesty that the fish-eating birds alone were given ten *arrobas* a day (about 264 lb). Three hundred men took care of these birds and did nothing else; others were solely occupied with looking after sick birds. There were corridors and places for watching above each of these lakes, where Motecuhzoma would stand to amuse himself by looking at them.'[17] And this was not all, for, the conquistador goes on, the Mexican emperor also kept freaks, and particularly albinoes, 'white from birth, in face, body, hair, eyelashes and eyelids'; also dwarfs, hunchbacks and other malformed people; birds of prey, in cages which were partly roofed to keep them from the rain and partly open for the sun and air; pumas, jaguars, coyotes, foxes and wild cats. Hundreds of attendants looked after each of the kinds of men or animals that made up this garden museum.

If the testimony of Cortés were insufficient, it is corroborated by that of his fellow-adventurers. Andrés de Tapia[18] uses almost the same words in listing the many kinds of birds, wild beasts and freaks that Motecuhzoma kept for his amusement. 'In very big jars and pots in this house,' he adds, 'there were quite large numbers of snakes and vipers. And all this purely with a view to magnificence.' Bernal Díaz confirms this detail, speaking of 'many snakes and venomous serpents which have a kind of sounding rattle on their tails: these are the most dangerous vipers of all. They are kept in jars and large pots, with a great many feathers, and it is there that they lay their eggs and bring up their little serpents . . . and when the tigers and the lions roared, and the wolves and the foxes howled, and the serpents hissed, it was dreadful to hear, and one would have thought oneself in hell.'[19]

However, we will not linger over our chronicler's reactions, for they are, after all, only those of a provincial who finds himself for the first time in his life in a zoological garden, that typical element of a civilised town. The undoubted fact is the care with which the rulers of ancient Mexico gathered around them all the animals and plants of their country. The Aztecs had a positive passion for flowers: the whole of their lyric poetry is a hymn to flowers, 'which intoxicate' by their loveliness and their scent.

The first Motecuhzoma, when he had conquered Oaxtepec in the Hot Lands of the west, decided to make a garden there where all the tropical species should be cultivated. Imperial messengers traversed the provinces in search of flowering shrubs, which were dug up with care to preserve their roots unbroken, and wrapped in mats. Forty Indian families, who came from the parts where these plants were found, were installed at Oaxtepec, and the emperor himself solemnly opened the gardens.[20]

All the Mexicans, though naturally on a more modest scale, shared this love of gardens. The citizens of Mexico grew flowers[21] in their courtyards and on their roofs, and the lake-side suburb Xochimilco, 'the place of the fields of flowers', was then, as it is now, the garden which supplied the whole valley. Each family also had its household animals: the turkey, that farmyard bird which Mexico has given to the world; some tame rabbits;[22] dogs, some at least being for eating, and fattened for that purpose; sometimes bees, and very often parrots or macaws. Life was led much more out of doors than in, under the most sunlit sky in the world; and the city, still near to its original earth, mixed innumerable splashes of green and the delicate mosaic of flowers with the dazzling whiteness of the temples.

GETTING UP, WASHING AND DRESSING, CLOTHES

The Mexican slept on a mat, without a nightshirt and indeed almost naked except for his loincloth, with his cloak or his blankets (if he had any) over him. At daybreak he had only to put on his sandals and tie his cloak on his shoulders, and he was ready to go to his work. At least, this was the case with the plebeians: the dignity of the officials called for more considerable preparation. Everybody got up very early: the law-courts, for example, opened at dawn, and the judges took their seats in the earliest half-light.[23]

But for all that a love of cleanliness seems to have been general throughout the population. No doubt the members of the ruling class gave up more of their time and attention to it than ordinary citizens – Motecuhzoma 'washed his body twice a day' says Andrés de Tapia, not without astonishment.[24] But everybody 'bathed often, and many of them every day' in the rivers, lakes or pools.[25]

The young men were accustomed to this by their education: they were often obliged to get up at night to bathe in the cold water of the lake, or in a spring. The Aztecs did not make soap, but there were two vegetable products which served instead, the fruit of the *copalxocotl*, called the soap-tree by the Spaniards, and the root of the *saponaria americana*. Either of them would give a lather which could be used not only for washing but also for the laundry.[26] The fact that habits of cleanliness were very thoroughly established is proved by the exceptions – in some cases hair went unsoaped and the body unwashed: merchants, for example, when they left for a long and dangerous expedition, would vow not to bathe until their return, which for them was a very real sacrifice. During the month *Atemoztli*, as a penance people did not use soap.[27]

Bathing was not only an act of cleanliness; it was also very often a ritual ablution. The prisoners who were to be sacrificed to Uitzilopochtli during the festivities of the month *Panquetzaliztli* underwent a ritual bath. 'The old men of the *calpulli* procured the water at Uitzilopochco, in a cave', and the victims were called *tlaaltiltin*, 'those who have been bathed'.[28] The baths that the priests took in the waters of the lake during the month *Etzalqualiztli*[29] also had an obviously ceremonial character.

To some degree the same applied to the typically Mexican steam-bath, the *temazcalli*. This very characteristic practice, which still goes on in the Nahuatl villages, was so general in the days before the Spaniards that the greater part of the houses had close by them a little hemispherical building made of stones and cement which was used for having a steam-bath.

The fireplace was built outside the *temazcalli* itself, and it had a common wall with it, made of porous stone: this wall was brought to a glowing heat by a fire of wood. When it was ready the Indian who intended to bathe crept into the *temazcalli* by a little low door and threw water on the red-hot wall. He was then enveloped in steam, and he switched himself violently with grasses. Often there would be another person there, particularly if the bather were an invalid, to massage him; and after the massage the bather would lie upon a mat to let the bath have its effect.[30] Clearly, the bath was expected to have two effects; on the one hand it was thought of as an act of cleanliness and as a form of medical treatment, and on the other as an act of purification. Women who had had babies went to the *temazcalli* before taking up ordinary life again – a practice that still prevails.[31] The *Codex of* 1576 records that in the year *ce acatl*, or 1363, 'the wives of the Mexicans had their children at Zoquipan and bathed themselves at Temazcaltitlan (the place of the steam-baths)'.[32]

Nature, in giving the Indians a sparse and meagre beard, has spared them the problems and wretchedness that afflicted the Greeks and the Romans and which afflict the Europeans now. They did not shave. In their old age their chins were adorned by a beard rather like those which one sees on Chinese sages in the painting and sculpture of the Far East; and in this case too it was a mark of wisdom. Hair was generally worn cut short across the forehead and long elsewhere; but certain ranks and professions had their own kind of haircut. The priests shaved the front and the sides of their head, but let the hair on the top alone; while the young warriors wore a long lock which they cut off when they had accomplished their first feat of arms.

Female beauty looked after itself in Mexico with resources not unlike those which are to be found in the Old World: looking-glasses made of obsidian or pyrites, carefully polished,[33] ointments, creams and scent. The women, who were naturally bronze-brown, tried to give their skins a light yellow tint – they are often depicted in manuscripts with this colour, in contrast to the men.[34] They succeeded by using an ointment called *axin*, or a yellow earth, *tecozauitl*, which was so much in request that some provinces supplied it as tribute. The custom of staining one's teeth black or red was general among the Huaxtecs and the Otomí,[35] and some Mexican women had taken to it. As for their hair, the prevailing fashion at the time of the conquest required that it should be raised on the head so as to form two loops above the forehead, like little horns: this is particularly to be seen in the *Codex Azcatitlan*.[36]

Women's fashions in Mexico tended to react against the barbarous delight in ornamentation which was general among the neighbouring peoples. The Otomí women, not content with making themselves up and staining their teeth, went so far as to cover their bosoms and arms with tattooing, 'in a very delicate blue pattern, dyed into the very flesh with little knives'.[37] At Tenochtitlan a woman of the ruling class was supposed to rely upon cleanliness alone to enhance her charms.

In the morning 'wash your face, wash your hands, clean your mouth . . .' said a father to his daughter. 'Listen to me, child: never make up your face nor paint it; never put red on your mouth to look beautiful. Make-up and paint are things that light women use – shameless creatures. If you want your husband to love you, dress well, wash yourself and wash your clothes.'[38]

It was the *auianime*, the courtesans who accompanied the young warriors, who used these aids to beauty. The courtesan 'grooms herself and dresses with such care that when she is thoroughly ready she looks like a flower. And to make herself ready she first looks in her glass, she bathes, washes and freshens herself in order to please. She makes up her face with a yellow cream called *axin*, which gives her a dazzling complexion; and sometimes, being a loose, lost woman, she puts on rouge. She has also the habit of dyeing her teeth (red) with cochineal and of wearing her hair loose for more beauty . . . She perfumes herself with an odoriferous censer, and in walking about she chews *tzictli*,[39] making a clacking noise with her teeth like castanets.'[40]

The man's chief garment, which was kept on at night, was the loin-cloth, *maxtlatl*, which went round his waist and between his legs, to be tied in front; the two ends, often fringed and embroidered, fell before and behind. The loin-cloth, whether in its simplest form of a plain length of material or in the utmost elaboration of ornament, is to be found among the Olmecs and the Mayas in the highest antiquity.[41] In the sixteenth century all the civilised nations of Mexico wore it, except the Tarascas in the west and the Huaxtecs in the north-east,[42] a fact that somewhat scandalised the Mexicans of the centre.

A man of the people wore nothing else when he was working on the land or carrying burdens. But the use of the cloak, the *tilmatli*, had become quite general: it was made of agave-fibre for ordinary people and of cotton for others; or sometimes of rabbit-hair that might be threaded through or reinforced with feathers for the winter.[43] It was a simple, rectangular piece of cloth, and it was tied over the right shoulder or the chest: buttons, hooks and brooches were unknown to the Aztecs. A man, on sitting down, would slide the cloak round so as to bring it all forward and cover his body and legs.[44]

An Indian crowd in the Mexican streets must have looked quite like a crowd of Athenians, with their cloaks: the Indians wore them in the same way as our forefathers in classical antiquity. But the piece of cloth that they covered themselves with, which was white and unornamented among the ordinary people, could show an extraordinary wealth of colour and pattern among the dignitaries. The weaving-women's art – for it was women who made these splendid clothes – seems to have come from the east, from the Hot Lands where the cotton grew, and where the material seemed to copy the iridescent plumage of the tropical birds.

In Aztec times it was still admitted that the most beautiful materials and the most brilliantly coloured embroideries came from the Totonac and Huaxtec countries. The tribute brought thousands of loads of the splendid cloaks, loin-cloths and skirts woven in the eastern provinces, Tochpan, Quauhtochco, Cuetlaxtlan and Tochtepec, to Mexico. The weaving-women of the capital itself were held to be particularly favoured by Xochiquetzal, the goddess of flowers, youth and love: and it was said that women born under the sign *ce xochitl*, one – flower, would be both skilful weavers and generous with their favours.[45]

The *Codex Magliabecchiano*[46] reproduces many styles of *tilmatli* decorated with patterns in which there is a most charming combination of imagination, dignity and measure. The most usual themes are suns, stylised shells, jewels, fish, abstract geometrical shapes, cacti, feathers, skins of tigers and snakes, rabbits and butterflies.

There are others to be found in the various manuscripts:[47] Sahagún[48] lists and describes certain varieties – for example, that which was called *coaxayacayo tilmatli* (literally 'cloak with snakes' faces'). 'The whole cloak was tawny, and it had the face of a monster or a demon on a red background in a silver circle. It was entirely decorated with these circles and these faces, and all round it there was a fringe.' Another cloak 'was woven with designs that represented sea-shells, which were made of rabbit-hair dyed red on a background of pale-blue whirlpools. These designs were framed in blue, one half light blue, the other dark; and they also had a border of white feathers. The fringe was made of rabbit-hair, and its colour was red.' Still others 'had a tawny background, and scattered upon it butterflies woven from white feathers'. One can imagine the fantastic effect that these brilliantly-coloured clothes must have had under the blazing Mexican sun, when the crowd of nobles and warriors thronged round the emperor.

The priest's *tilmatli* was black or very dark green, and it was often embroidered with skulls and human bones. The emperor's – and he alone had the right to wear this equivalent of the Roman purple – was coloured with the blue-green of the turquoise; and indeed it was called *xiuhtilmatli*, 'the turquoise cloak'.

Maxtlatl and *tilmatli*, loin-cloth and cloak, these were the essentials of the masculine costume. There are a very great many pictures in the manuscripts – quite apart from the details supplied by a study of the sculpture – and among these, although they are post-cortesian, may be cited those which are to be found in the Bibliothèque Nationale at Paris, and which are attributed to Ixtlilxochitl.[49]

They represent Indian nobles, and there is in particular a very charming portrait of the young Nezaualpilli, king of

Texcoco, wearing a loin-cloth and a magnificent cloak, both of them woven with geometrical patterns, and carrying a bunch of flowers in his left hand, while his right has a feather fan or fly-whisk. Although they are basically so simple, one cannot help admiring the grace, the dignity and the splendour of these clothes.

Nevertheless it is clear from the texts and the iconography of the subject that there were also other garments in general use. A kind of triangular apron could prolong the loin-cloth from hip to upper thigh: this is to be seen as early as the warrior-caryatids in the ancient Toltec city of Tula,[50] as well as in the figure of the emperor Tizoc in the bas-reliefs of the monument that commemorates him.[51] Sometimes the priests and the warriors wore, under their cloaks or instead of them, a very short-sleeved tunic, the *xicolli*, which opened in front and which could be closed by tying a ribbon.[52] Another version of the *xicolli* had no opening, but had to be pulled over one's head like a shirt[53] or like the blouse (*huipilli*) that the women wore. This tunic could either cover the trunk only, like a waistcoat or a short jacket, or it could fall over the loin-cloth as far as the knees.

Then there are two other facts that should be pointed out: the first is that those who could would put on two or three cloaks one on top of the other; the second, that although ordinarily the Mexican wore loose clothes, in time of war, on the other hand, he had close-fitting garments. The 'uniforms' of the tiger-knights,[54] for example, entirely conformed to the shape of their bodies, as do the mechanic's or airman's overalls; the blouse finished in a helmet that covered the head, and the trousers went down as far as the ankles. The traditional armour of the Aztec warrior, the *ichcahuipilli* or 'cotton blouse', was a close-fitting garment so stuffed or wadded that it could turn an arrow. Thus the ancient Mexicans had at the same time both the loose and fitting, the two great divisions that the costume of the world falls into, and of which each nation usually chooses only one.

The basis of the Mexican woman's costume, as the *maxtlatl* was the basis of the man's, was the *cueitl* or skirt, made of a length of cloth wrapped round the lower part of the body, tied at the waist by an embroidered belt, and falling almost to the ankles. Among the lower classes and in the country the women often left their bosoms uncovered, but in the town and among the women of the middle class or the better sort a kind of blouse called a *huipilli* was worn outside the skirt: it was embroidered at the neck. Everyday clothes were plain and white, but ceremonial or holiday clothes displayed a great variety of colours and patterns.

All witnesses emphasise the brilliance and the splendour of the blouses and the skirts worn by the women of noble families and those who took part in the ritual dances. In the dances of the month *Uey tecuilhuitl*, the women, especially the *auianime*, danced with the soldiers 'and they were all well dressed, and they wore ornaments, and beautiful skirts and blouses. Some of their skirts were decorated with hearts, others with a braided pattern like the bosoms of birds, others with the patterns of blankets, or with spirals or leaves; and others again were of plain cloth. They were bordered and fringed: they all had (embroidered) hems. As for their blouses, some had flowing brown designs, others (patterns representing) smoke, others black ribbons; others were decorated with houses, others with fishes . . . The collars were all broad and the (embroidered) edges were also wide and full.'[55] King Uitziliuitl's two favourites are shown dressed in white blouses embroidered at the neck and waist, and in white skirts with broad embroidered hems.[56]

In this case too, it was from the east that the art of embroidering in many colours and the taste for embroidery and splendid materials came to influence the dwellers on the high plateau. The eastern goddesses, such as Tlazolteotl, always appear in the pages of the figured manuscripts with a cotton scarf wound round their heads, with spindles stuck in it. The women of the Huaxtecs and the Totonacs of the slopes of the Sierra Madre, and the old nations like the Otomí who had long been in contact with their eastern neighbours, were particularly eager for style and brilliance. 'Their (the Huaxtecs') clothes are elegant and distinguished, for it is in their country that are made the cloaks called *centzontilmatli* or *centzonquachtli*, which means "cloaks of a thousand colours". The cloaks decorated with monsters' heads or painted, and those which have whirlpools are brought from those parts; and the (Huaxtec) weavers surpass themselves in the making of these materials and many others like them . . . The women take great care of their appearance; they are very well dressed and they go about looking very fine.'[57]

As for the Totonacs, 'their women gaze at themselves in their looking-glasses. They wear skirts and blouses with woven patterns and they know very well how to dress themselves. So their skirts were called *intlalapalcue*, many-coloured skirts . . . the noblewomen were magnificently dressed in these; the ordinary women in skirts of blue. All of them threaded feathers into their hair, dyed different colours: they walked about gracefully adorned with flowers.'[58] It was the same with the people who lived on the shores of the Gulf: 'the women are excellent weavers, very expert at working in cloth; and this is quite natural, since they belong to such a good, rich country.'[59] As for the Otomí women, they were perfectly happy to take any fashions that pleased them from the neighbouring tribes, and 'whatever they saw in the line of clothes, that they put on.'[60]

It was no doubt through them that the habit of wearing that typically eastern garment the *quexquemitl* was introduced into central Mexico: this was a graceful lozenge-shaped pelerine or mantle, richly decorated and embroidered. In the pre-cortesian era the many-coloured *quexquemitl* belonged particularly to the women of the Totonacs,[61] but Aztec sculpture shows certain goddesses with their bosoms covered by this fringed cloak.[62] At the present time the Indian women belonging to the various tribes of the eastern slopes or the high plateau (Totonacs, Nahua, Otomí) still weave this traditional garment for themselves.[63]

No doubt fashion at Tenochtitlan accentuated simplicity in contrast to the showy medley sought after by the provincials; but even so a procession of women going to a temple must have been a remarkably colourful sight and remarkably varied, for although the cut of the blouses and the skirts may have been the same, still the multicoloured stuffs, the infinite diversity of pattern, and the brilliance of the jewels and feathers made the brown-faced, brown-armed women look like the marvellous birds of the tropics.[64]

This tendency towards luxury in clothes, although it was restrained by regard for a certain traditional austerity, increased with increasing technical development, particularly with that of cloth-making. The nomadic people of the north and no doubt the Aztecs themselves to begin with, dressed in skins; the long-established settled people of the high plateau wove the fibre of the agave, *ixtle*. At the date of which we are speaking the plebeian's loin-cloth and *tilmatli* were still made of this cloth, which was considered suitable for the common people; besides, the spinners had attained such skill that they could draw an extremely fine thread from the agave fibre, and it was possible to weave very supple cloth, as some Indians still do today.[65] Some other vegetable fibres, such as those which were used for making paper, were also used for cloth. But cotton, a native of the Hot Lands of the east and of the west, soon became very much sought after by the Aztecs and was considered the essential textile staple, *inichcatl intetechmonequi*, 'the indispensable cotton'.

When, at the end of the fourteenth century, the king Uitziliuitl wished to marry a daughter of the lord of Cuauhnahuac (Cuernavaca, which has a semi-tropical climate) his prime motive seems to have been to provide his city with cotton. 'King Uitziliuitl asked for the hand of a princess of Cuauhnahuac named Miahuaxihuitl, daughter of this same Ozomatzin, who ruled over Cuauhnahuac. And the old men said that the lord Ozomatzin had all the peasants of Cuauhnahuac at his command and that they brought him the indispensable cotton and all the fruits that grow in those parts: and of all these things nothing came to Mexico; this cotton did not reach the Mexicans, and for this reason they were very wretched.'[66]

The traders and then the warriors who came into the rich tropical lands from the plateaux were chiefly in search of cotton: trade and tribute brought immense quantities of it to Mexico, either as the raw fibre or as manufactured cloth.[67]

The men and women of Mexico, particularly those of the working-class, often went barefoot; but as they rose in the social scale they might put on *cactli*, sandals with fibre or hide soles, which were kept on by interlacing straps and which had a heel-piece.[68] In the more elaborate kinds other straps were wrapped cross-wise up the wearer's shins as far as his knees, forming a greave (*cozehuatl*): this was the typical footwear of the warriors.

Motecuhzoma's sandals were heavily ornamented with gold:[69] it is clear from the native iconography, from the Mayan bas-reliefs, through the figured manuscripts to the sculpture of the Aztecs, that the sandal (which has survived to our time in the form of the everyday *huaracha* of the Mexican Indians) could assume a great many varieties of shape and decoration. The precious metals, gems, skins of wild animals, such as jaguars, and the feathers of tropical birds could all enter into its composition.

The clothes and the footwear of the ancient Mexicans may have been relatively plain, but on the other hand nothing can give any idea of the overflowing variety or the baroque wealth of their jewels and their head-dresses. The women wore earrings, necklaces and bracelets on their arms and ankles. The men had the same ornaments, but in addition they pierced the septum of their nose to hold gem or metal jewels; they also made holes in the skin beneath their lower lip so as to wear chin-ornaments of crystal, shell, amber, turquoise or gold; and they placed huge and splendid structures of feathers upon their heads or their backs.

In this display of rank and of luxury everything was strictly regulated in conformity with the hierarchic order. Only the emperor might wear the turquoise nose-ornament -- the division between his nostrils was perforated with great ceremony after his election[70] – and only warriors of a certain rank had the right to wear such and such a jewel, whose kind and shape was exactly laid down.[71] The 'emblems' or feather ornaments, dazzlingly coloured head-dresses, bronze-green plumes of *quetzal*-feathers, immense butterflies, cones

138

made of feathers or gold, cloth or feather-mosaic banners to
be fixed to the shoulders of chiefs, decorated shields – all
these were reserved for those who had won the right to
them by their exploits, and death was the punishment for
any man who should presume to attribute to himself one of
these marks of honour.[72]

The Indians of Mexico and Central America have, since
the remotest antiquity, (as may be seen in the Mayan
frescoes of Bonampak[73]) literally worshipped feathers – the
long, splendid green plumes of the *quetzal*, the red and yellow
of the parrots. They formed one of the most important
articles to be delivered up to the tax-collectors under the
Aztec empire. The huge feather-ornaments, together with
the jewels of gold and turquoise, raised the warrior, the
dignitary and the emperor high above ordinary humanity.
On the one side, in its simplicity Mexican costume touched
the classical antiquity of the white-robed Mediterraneans:
on the other, the Redskin world of the American native,
but with a delicacy unknown to the rude inhabitants of the
prairie.

We have a precise idea, from bas-reliefs and manuscripts,
of the magnificent ornaments that could make of a man
something greater than a man, almost a divine being,
hieratic and filled with splendour. When, to the hollow
scream of conchs, the beat of gongs and the harsh cry of
trumpets, there suddenly appeared to the people crowded
on the central square the emperor, rigid beneath the gold
and turquoise diadem, amidst the brilliance of green plumes,
while the armour, the emblems and the banners of the great
men formed a mosaic of a thousand colours around him,
who would not have thought that here was the chosen of
Tezcatlipoca, 'the ruler of the world', 'the father and
mother of the people'? In that society, with its very marked
graduations, ornaments and jewels, gold and feathers, were
the symbols of power and of the ability to govern.

BUSINESS, WORK, CEREMONIES

There we have the inhabitants of Tenochtitlan, suitably
dressed, shod, brushed and made fine: and, as we have

seen, at work since dawn. Many of them were still country-
men, although they lived in the city; but unfortunately it is
impossible to say what proportion they bore to the others.
They either grew maize, vegetables and flowers in their
gardens on the islands, upon *chinampas* or on the lake-shore,
or else they went in pursuit of the wildfowl or the fish of the
lake. Their tools and their weapons were simple: a digging-
stick broadening into a spade for the workers on the land,
a net, a bow and arrows, a spear-thrower and a net game-bag
for the fowlers and fishermen.

The head of a noble family said to his sons, 'Never forget
that you descend from noble forefathers: never forget that
you do not descend from gardeners or wood-cutters. What
are you going to be? Would you like to be traders, walking
with a stick in your hand and a load on your back? Would
you like to be farmers or labourers? Would you like to be
gardeners or wood-cutters? I will tell you what you must
do. Listen to me and remember what I say. (First) pay
great attention to dancing, to the drum and the bells and to
singing . . . (then) take pains to learn an honourable craft,
like that of making things with feathers, or other handicrafts,
because that will give you your bread in time of need; and
above all learn about farming, for farming is nourished by
the earth . . . Your ancestors could do all those things, for
although they were noble and of high descent, they always
saw to it that their lands and their inheritance were cultivated. Because if you think of nothing but your descent
and your nobility, how will you maintain your family? What
will you live on yourself? Nobody has ever seen anybody
live on nobility alone.'[74]

In this down-to-earth lesson one can also very clearly see
how a nobleman of Tenochtitlan regarded the vocations,
and what order he put them in. First come the rites, for it
is the rites that he means when he speaks of song and music:
this same father makes it certain, for, says he, 'in doing this
you will be pleasant to our lord god who is in all places
(Tezcatlipoca) and you will put your hand into the bosom
of his treasures'; then come the honourable crafts, such as
those of the artist-craftsmen who worked in feathers, gold

and gem-stones; and above all agriculture. Of course there was no question of a Mexican noble working on the land like 'a labourer or a gardener'; the suggestion is that he should direct the exploitation of his estate.

The notion of high blood which certainly exists here, in spite of the disillusioned warning 'Nobody has ever seen a man live on nobility alone', does not follow the same boundaries as it did in our own feudal society, for example. The noble can work with his hands: but he may not become a plain peasant, nor a trader.

As we have seen, the estates that members of the ruling class controlled were many and extensive, often far, and sometimes very far, from Mexico. Although in theory the land belonged to the state, these people had in fact a tenancy that was becoming more and more like downright ownership: they therefore devoted a considerable portion of their time to visiting their estates and seeing to their proper cultivation. They might, however, be replaced by majordomos, *calpixque*, some of whom were trustworthy slaves who at length succeeded in growing wealthy and who often freed themselves.

It must be realised that the household of a great Aztec lord, with its fields and woods, lakes and rivers, its workshops with many women spinning and weaving, and with craftsmen working for the master himself, formed a considerable economic entity which was partially self-supporting and which was a producer of food and clothing. On the other hand, there is no doubt that the unceasing wars and the increasing labour of administration prevented the high officials from giving their own affairs anything but the most general supervision. The gentleman-farmer was becoming more and more an officer, a judge, a courtier or a statesman, and the most important part of the work had passed into the hands of stewards.

The business of the state and of the 'high command', *tlatocayotl*, took up the energies of the ruling class to an ever-increasing extent. In the first place there was the war, for which all the young men had trained themselves from their childhood, being so anxious to rise to be *tequiuaque*, and, if they could, to be promoted to the higher ranks. Then there were the innumerable public offices, which required industry, integrity and conscientiousness in those who filled them. For example, there were the *achcacauhtin*, the officers of the law who were charged with carrying out the sentences of the courts; there were the judges who sat from dawn until two hours before sunset with only a break for a light meal and a short siesta[75] and who were liable to the death sentence if they accepted a bribe;[76] tax-gatherers who were obliged to go on arduous and dangerous voyages and who were also sentenced to death if they embezzled any part of the tribute;[77] ambassadors who were sent with an ultimatum from the emperor to distant cities and who often escaped only with great difficulty; all these, and many others, such as the teachers who saw to the education of the boys in the local schools, owed their whole time and their whole energy to the service of the state.

The Mexicans had a lofty conception of public service and of the authority that went with it: the greatest lord was bound to obey the orders of a simple messenger bearing the commands of a court of law.[78] But at the same time the laws and customs were terribly severe: woe to the drunken judge, the over-accommodating judge; woe to the dishonest civil servant. The sentence of the king of Texcoco was always quoted as an example – he, hearing that one of his judges had favoured a noble against a *maceualli*, had the unrighteous justice hanged.[79] If the power was very great, the duties were very heavy.

The higher a man rose in rank, the less time he had for himself. The accounts of the conquerors describe Motecuhzoma's palace continually filled with a crowd of officials and warriors[80] who passed their whole day there. And one may cite those general sessions called *nappualtlatolli*[81] ('the eighty days' speaking') which took place at the end of each period of four months by the native calendar, during which all outstanding political or judicial business was dealt with, the sittings lasting from dawn until night. Still more, one may cite the councils – the *Tlatocan* at Mexico and the four great councils at Texcoco – which, to judge by the accounts that have come down to us, were a positive endurance test,

with their uncountable speeches full of stylised eloquence
and loaded with traditional figures. The Mexican upper
class was, by definition, that part of the nation which
devoted itself to public life; but public life laid very heavy
burdens upon them, and took up by far the greater share of
their time and energies.

As for the priests, who together with the civil or military
officials made up a great proportion of this upper class,
their entire life was out of their personal control, since their
religious duties occupied them both day and night and since
unfaithfulness to their vows brought upon them the severest
kind of punishment. The tenth statute of Nezaualcoyotl[82]
punished the lecherous or drunken priest with death. It
may be observed, in passing, that the gravity of the sentence
always increased in proportion with the rank of the culprit:
the punishment for a plebeian who was drunk in public was
a severe admonition and the shame of having his head
shaven; for a noble, it was death.[83] It was also death for a
noble who had robbed his father, whereas a *maceualli* guilty
of the same crime got off with penal slavery.[84] Duty,
responsibility and danger increased with power and wealth.

Judges and law-courts have often been referred to: it
appears that law and court cases had a large place in everyday
life. The Indians were of a litigious nature, and they kept
the lawyers busy. In the towns and villages of the provinces
there were courts of first instance, whose judges pronounced
upon relatively unimportant cases. Above them, at Mexico
and Texcoco, there were judges, natives of each region, for
the cases that were sent up to them from those regions.

The court of appeal for the whole empire sat at Texcoco:
it was made up of twelve judges, and it sat every twelve days
under the presidency of the king of Texcoco to decide the
most difficult cases. No case could last for more than eighty
days, for the whole object of the general sessions was to
wind up all unconcluded business.

It was a most uncommonly expeditious system. Each
trial brought into being a file, kept by an official of the court
who noted down in pictographic writing all the testimonies
and the sentence, which was immediately put into force.

It may be added that this mediaeval Mexico had no knowledge of judicial torture, of the 'question' and the rack which was only suppressed in France in the eighteenth century.[85]

The degree to which the members of the ruling class were taken up by their duties is surprising; but one is positively astonished when one tries to count up the time that they had to devote to worship and to ceremonies. Of course everybody in Mexico took part in the innumerable holidays, or rather holy days, and in the complicated rites which took place on them; but here again it was the dignitaries who bore the brunt.

Their presence was very often called for in the sacrifices, dances, singing, processions and parades not only in the town, but more than once right round the lake. The solar year was divided into eighteen months of twenty days (plus the five intercalary days of evil omen, during which all activity was reduced to a minimum) and a fresh set of rites and ceremonies belonged to each of these months.[86] Some at least of these called for a very great effort from a very large number of people, an immense amount of organisation and a very considerable expense.

It was not the priests alone who celebrated the rites, but on the contrary some part or other of the population, according to the month: it might be the young men, the girls, the warriors, the dignitaries, certain guilds like that of the *pochteca* or the goldsmiths; or often it might be the whole nation that took an active part.

During the seven first days of the month called 'the great feast of the lords'[87] the emperor had the whole population served with food and drink 'in order to show his good-will towards the humble people (*maceualtzintli*)'. Every evening, at sunset, the songs and the dances began, in the light of torches and braziers, 'and sometimes Motecuhzoma came out to dance'. For long hours on end the warriors and the women, holding hands, came and went between the rows of braziers and torch-holders; the dancing and the rhythmic chanting did not stop until well on into the night.

On the tenth day there began the series of sad and cruel ceremonies in which the central rôle was played by a woman dressed and adorned to represent the goddess of the young maize, Xilonen. Her face was painted yellow and red; she wore a head-dress of *quetzal*-plumes, a turquoise necklace with a golden disk hanging from it, embroidered clothes and red sandals. In her hand she carried a shield and a magic rattle, the *chicauaztli*. In the night before the sacrifice 'everybody stayed up, nobody slept, and the women sang the hymns of Xilonen. And at dawn the dances began. All the men, indeed, the war-chiefs, the young men, the officers, everybody carried the maize-stalks that they called *totopantli* ('bird-flags'); and the women danced also, going with Xilonen.' Everybody, dancing and singing, advanced in procession through the twilight and the dawn towards the temple of the maize, Cinteopan, while the priestesses beat the two-toned gongs and the priests sounded their horns and conchs. The procession surrounded the woman who for a few hours was the incarnation of the goddess, and it carried her forward with it towards her fate: she had scarcely entered the Cinteopan before the officiating priest stepped forward, with his gold-hilted flint knife in his hand; and the headless Xilonen became a goddess in her death.

'Then, for the first time, they ate the cakes of young maize'; the women and 'the maidens who had never looked at any man'; danced and each person made maize-cakes and offered them to the gods.

The fifth month, *Panquetzaliztli*, began with songs and dances, which took place each evening from sunset to midnight. Nine days before the great feast of Uitzilopochtli, the preparation of the sacrificial victims began; they were ritually bathed, and everybody, the captives and the captors, danced the 'dance of the serpent' together during part of the night.

On the twentieth day the captives went to take their leave of their masters, singing 'as if their voices were going to break, as if they were hoarse', and dipping their hands in ochre or blue paint they left the marks of them upon the lintel or the jambs of the door. Then they began to put on the ornaments that had been got ready for them. At dawn there began the great procession of Paynal, the little

messenger-god who represented Uitzilpochtli: it went from
the centre of the capital to Tlatelolco, from there to the
villages of the shore, Popotlan, Chapultepec, and as far as
the outskirts of Coyoacán. Now and then the procession
stopped and some victims were sacrificed. When Paynal,
having made this long circuit, reappeared at Tenochtitlan
and entered the sacred precinct, the conchs sounded, and
one by one the captives were sacrificed upon the stone,
before the gate of Uitzilopochtli's temple.

Other customs had a character not unlike that of the
popular merriment at the time of our Carnival. During the
first days of the month *Atemoztli*, the priests and the young
warriors formed themselves into opposing bands and fought
with twigs and reeds. If the warriors captured a priest 'they
rubbed him with agave leaves, which caused him to itch
and to burn; and if one of the young warriors were taken
the priests scratched his ears, arms, chest and legs with a
thorn until he cried out. And if the priests managed to
chase one of the young men into the palace, they pillaged it,
carrying off all the mats, the carpets made of rope, the seats
with backs, the beds and the stools. If they found any
gongs or drums they took them too; they carried off everything. And if the young warriors pursued the priests into
their monastery (*calmecac*), they too sacked it, and carried
off the mats, the conchs and the chairs.'

This same element of antagonism, and the same temporary
permitting of acts that would at other times be severely
punished, is also found in the month *Tititl*. This time it
was the little boys who were armed with bolster-like bags
filled with paper or leaves and who attacked the girls and
the women. They had sticks or branches to defend themselves: but the urchins did their best to take them by
surprise – they would hide their sacks and surround an
unsuspecting woman, and then suddenly banging her with
bags they would all bawl out 'Here is a bag, lady.' After this
they would run away, laughing.[88]

These ceremonies, whether they were terrible or beautiful,
or as horrifying as the *Tlacaxipeualiztli*, which finished in a
dance of the priests dressed in human skins, or as happy as

that of *Tlaxochimaco*, in which avalanches of flowers ran in all the temples, necessarily took up a considerable part of the time, the labour and the resources of the community. They were both very frequent and very long, most scrupulously observed – each detail was laid down with extraordinary care – and all the more numerous and absorbing in that Mexico, the capital of the empire, participated in every cult and worshipped every god.

For this reason the Mexicans had the reputation, even among their near neighbours – those of Texcoco, for example – of being so religious that it was impossible to know how many gods they honoured.[89] But in order to have a clear idea of what this continual religious activity meant to them, it is necessary for us to redefine the words 'rite' and 'ceremony', and to strip them of the conventional attributes that they have acquired in our civilisation.

For the ancient Mexicans there was nothing more vitally important than these motions, these songs, dances, sacrifices and traditional actions, because as they saw it, these things assured the regular succession of the seasons, the coming of the rains, the springing of the plants upon which they lived, and the resurrection of the sun. The Mexican nation, and above all the priests and the dignitaries, was engaged day after day in a continually renewed white-magic operation, a perpetual collective effort without which nature itself would be destroyed. It was therefore the gravest of life's occupations, the most imperative of duties.

Nevertheless, this great preoccupation with religious ceremony did not prevent either the guilds or the people from following their ordinary callings. In their workshops the craftsmen cast and chiselled the gold, and at the same time the *pochteca* made ready for their voyages or sold the goods that they had brought back from the distant provinces. Commerce, in all its forms, spread through the markets and in the streets: a host of minor trades provided those who worked at them with at least something to help towards their family's maintenance. Women sold those maize cakes called tamales to passers-by, as well as *atolli*, a maize porridge, cocoa ready for drinking, dishes seasoned with peppers and tomatoes, and cooked meat. But it was men who displayed maize, calabash-seeds, oil-seeds, honey, saucepans and mats.[90] No doubt they all did their best to attract clients by praising their wares and crying them with those traditional cries that give a street its life. The hurried lawyer hastening to the court, like the official going to his office or the countryman spending a day in the town to sell his produce, would stop for a moment and eat a snack before going on. The timber-carriers, panting as they trotted under their heavy load, would come down from the mountains; and some would go in relays so as not to fail under the weight of the beams and rafters. Elsewhere a team of labourers called out by the local authority would be repairing an aqueduct under the orders of an official.

The system of the *tequitl*, or requisitioned collective labour, to which the plebeians were liable, provided for the execution of public works. In this manner the authorities had very considerable quantities of labour at their disposal; and it was thus, for example, that the great dike called 'the old water-wall' (*ueue atenamitl*) was built in the time of Motecuhzoma I, by workmen called up from all parts.[91] By the same system, too, Indians from Texcoco, Atzcapotzalco, Tlacopan, Coyoacán, Xochimilco and four other towns cut the canal to bring the water from a spring to Mexico, under the reign of Auitzotl.[92] 'An ant-hill, one would have said,' observes the chronicler; and indeed it is exactly an ant-hill that one thinks of at the spectacle of the quiet, efficient, orderly work that fills all the industrious length of the day.

MEALS

The Mexican of former times was the same frugal being that he is today. Most of the time he was satisfied with a sparse and meagre diet, primarily composed of maize in the shape of cakes, pottage or tamales, and of beans and *huauhtli*, or amaranth, seeds and *chian*, or sage. However, for all that, it is but justice to admit that the diet of the precolumbian plebeian was more varied than the diet of his equivalent today, for it included some plants, both cultivated (like the *huauhtli*[93]) and wild, and batrachians and insects, all of which are much less used today, if not totally forgotten. The upper classes, of course, were able to enjoy a much more advanced kind of cookery.

At dawn, the time of rising, there was no meal, no breakfast: this happened only at about ten o'clock, after some hours of work, and it nearly always consisted of a bowl of *atolli*,[94] a maize porridge, thick or thin as the case might be, and either sweetened with honey or seasoned with pimento. Rich men and dignitaries could drink cocoa, a luxury imported from the Hot Lands, sweetened with vanilla-scented honey or mixed with green maize, with *octli* (fermented agave sap) or with pimento.[95]

The main meal was in the middle of the day, for everybody, during the hottest hours; and those that could, followed it with a short siesta. For the common people it was but a brief affair – maize-cakes, beans, pimento or tomato sauce and sometimes tamales; rarely any meat, such as game, venison or poultry (turkey). Water was their drink. A family, squatting round the hearth on their mats, would eat their frugal meal without spending long over it: the man of the house would often be obliged by his work to be away at noon, and he would eat his lunch, his *itacatl*, from a bag prepared by his wife in the morning.

But in rich men's houses dinner was a matter of many and varied dishes. Every day more than three hundred were prepared for Motecuhzoma, and a thousand for the inhabitants of the palace. Before eating, the emperor chose whatever pleased him among the day's dishes – turkeys, pheasants, partridges, crows, wild or tame ducks, deer, wild boars, pigeons, hares, rabbits. Then he sat down, alone, on an *icpalli*, and a low table was put in front of him, with a white tablecloth and white napkins.

'Four very handsome, very clean women gave him water for his hands in the deep finger-bowls that are called *xicales* (calabashes); other plate-like vessels were held under his hands, and they gave him towels; then two other women brought maize-cakes.'[96] From time to time the sovereign was pleased to honour one of the dignitaries of his suite by giving him one of the dishes that he liked. When he had finished the first and chief course they brought him fruit 'of all the kinds that grow in the country; but he only ate a very little fruit, and that at long intervals.'[97] After this he drank cocoa and washed his hands as he had at the beginning of the meal. Dwarf or hunchbacked buffoons produced their tricks and their jokes: Motecuhzoma took one of the painted, gilded pipes that had been placed within his reach, smoked for a short while, and went to sleep.

In the emperor's palace at Mexico, and no doubt in the palaces of the allied kings and the great men in the provinces, enough food was made ready to supply the personal suite, the officials, the priests, etc. 'When the sovereign had eaten, he bade his pages or his servants serve all the lords and ambassadors who had come from the various towns, and also the palace guards: there were also fed those who brought up the young men, who are called *tepuchtlatoque*, as well as the priests of the idols, and the singers and the servants and all those who belonged to the palace and also the workmen, the goldsmiths, the feather-workers, the lapidaries and those who make mosaics, and those who make the splendid shoes for the dignitaries, and the hairdressers who cut their hair.'[98] They were also given cocoa prepared in various ways: Sahagún lists some ten different recipes.

The skill of the Aztec chefs was shown by a comparable variety in their dishes: the same historian gives seven kinds of maize-cake, six of tamales, many kinds of roast or seethed meat, some twenty made-dishes of poultry, fish, batrachians or insects, and an infinite variety of vegetable, pulse, sweet-potato, pimento and tomato dishes.

Among the dishes that the rulers particularly liked may be mentioned tamales stuffed with meat, snails or fruit – the last being served with clear poultry soup; frogs with pimento sauce; white fish (*iztac michi*) with red pepper and tomatoes; axolotls, a kind of newt peculiar to Mexico and considered a great delicacy, with yellow peppers; fish served with a sauce made of crushed calabash-seeds; other fish with a sharp fruit not unlike our cherries; winged ants; agave worms (*meocuilin*); maize and *huauhtli* pottages, salted or sugared, with pimento or honey; French beans (*exotl*); and various kinds of roots, including the *camotli*, or sweet potato.[99]

As the ancient Mexicans had neither fat nor oil, they could not fry; everything was either grilled or more often boiled and very highly peppered and seasoned. As they had no cattle either, the meat part of their diet came solely from game and the two domesticated creatures, the turkey and the dog.

Central Mexico, at that time, was very rich in game – rabbits, hares, deer, wild pigs (peccaries), birds such as pheasants, crows, doves, and above all the innumerable species of wildfowl that filled the lakes. This wealth in the lakes and the marshes had been a happy compensation for the wretchedness of the Aztecs in the early days, and in the sixteenth century the people still drew a considerable share of their food from these birds, which, at given seasons, arrived in hosts to settle on the water and make their nests in the reeds and the rushes.[100]

Furthermore – and this was no doubt something that had persisted from the days when the tribe had barely managed to keep itself in the marshes – the Mexicans ate a wide variety of things that came from the water – frogs, axolotls, tadpoles (*atepocatl*), fresh-water shrimps (*acociltin*), little water-flies (*amoyotl*), aquatic larvæ (*aneneztli*), white worms (*ocuiliztac*) and even the eggs that a water-fly, the *axayacatl*, laid in enormous quantities upon the water and which were eaten as a sort of caviar under the name of *ahuauhtli*. Poor people and the lakeside peasants skimmed a floating substance from the surface which was called *tecuitlatl* ('stone dung'); it was something like cheese, and they squeezed it into cakes; they also ate the spongy nests of water-fly larvæ.

Those things were the meat of poverty, which the tribe had been happy enough to find, no doubt, when it was lowly and poor, and by the sixteenth century they were no more than supplements in the diet of the humblest people. But even the rich and the lords themselves did not scorn batrachians, some reptiles, such as the iguana (*quauhcuetzpalin*), and some ants, nor the agave-worms, which are still thought of as a great delicacy in Mexico today. And then, since the empire had stretched to reach both the oceans, they had learnt the delights of sea-fish, turtles, crabs and oysters.[101]

The turkey (*totolin:* the male was called *uexolotl*, from which comes the present *guajulote*) was a native of Mexico, and it had been domesticated there from the earliest times. The Spaniards often called it 'the chicken of the country'. It the was chief inhabitant of the farm-yard or poultry-run, and each family had some in its garden, next to the house. The poorer people ate turkey only on great occasions, however.

As for the dog, it was a particular hairless kind which was fattened for eating. Its flesh was no doubt less esteemed than that of the turkey, for Sahagún tells us that 'in dishes the turkey-meat was put on top, and the dog underneath, to make it seem more (*para hacer bulto*)'.[102] However, a great many of these creatures were reared, and the chronicler Muñoz Camargo states that he had some of them himself well after the conquest.[103] The custom died out because of the introduction of European cattle, and also, it appears, because the killing of the dogs was inextricably mixed with certain pagan ceremonies and it was opposed by the Spanish authorities.

For the same kind of reason the Spanish clergy and missionaries laboured against the growing of the amaranth (*huauhtli*). From the point of view of the material well-being of the Mexicans they had only too much success; but in their eyes this plant, which gave a considerable harvest, was too closely bound to the native religion.[104] It is known, however, that the ancient Mexican thought of their four food-plants as almost equally valuable: they were maize (*centli*) which was revered above all as the essential source of life, the bean (*etl*), amaranth and sage.

The *Codex Mendoza* shows that the cities that were subject to tribute were obliged to furnish the Aztec collectors with considerable quantities of these four commodities each year. The seeds of the last two could be made into *tzoalli* and *chianpinolli*, refreshing and nourishing gruel; and an oil not unlike linseed oil was extracted from the seeds of sage and used for paint.

The period between the two harvests, the time in June and July when ends would barely meet, was a time of anxiety and extreme hunger for the Indians of those days, as it still is for those who live in the remote country or the infertile parts. 'Then men were hungry indeed; then the grains of maize cost a great deal; and then was the time of great dearth.'[105]

In Mexico the government tried to remedy this situation by distributing victuals to the people during the month *Uey tecuilhuitl*. The emperor 'showed his good-will towards the common people' by causing them all to be given tamales and maize-porridge. Elsewhere people were obliged to revert to gathering wild plants, in the manner of those who lived before agriculture. The Aztecs may have reproached the Otomí with stooping so low as to eat unclean animals, such as snakes, rats and lizards,[106] but they themselves were obliged to seek the edible wild plants, the *quilitl* (*quelites* in modern Hispano-Mexican); and they could distinguish the use and appearance of a wonderful variety of them. Sahagún describes a great many species,[107] including the *huauhquilitl* or wild amaranth, which was particularly valued. The peasant women sold them in the markets: the mother of the emperor Itzcoatl himself had sold *quilitl* in the market-place of Atzcapotzalco.[108]

In spite of its apparent abundance, nature was hard on men in Mexico. Famines often occurred; every year there was the threat of shortage, and agricultural techniques were too primitive to be able to contend with uncommon emergencies, such as swarms of locusts, sudden multitudes of rodents, excessive falls of rain or snow. One of the chief tasks of the native government was the accumulation of sufficient reserves in the granaries to cope with these disasters: in 1450 the three rulers of the allied cities distributed the saved-up stores of grain of ten years and more.[109] But still there was always the need for stop-gap foods, animal or vegetable, in an emergency; and the primitive nomad, living by hunting and gathering, continually shows through the settled farmer. In time of dearth the peasants of the central plateau would slip back through many centuries.

As we have seen, the Mexicans breakfasted in the middle of the morning and dined at the beginning of the afternoon. The second meal was also the last, for most of them, unless they should happen to take a gruel (thirst-quenching and nourishing at the same time) made of maize, amaranth or sage before going to bed. But those who stayed up, dignitaries or merchants giving a feast or a banquet, would sup abundantly, and often all night long.

Stores had to be procured in advance for one of these banquets – maize, beans, pulses, peppers, tomatoes, eighty or a hundred turkeys, a score of dogs, twenty loads of cocoa. The guests came towards midnight. 'When they had all come, they were given water for washing their hands and then the meal was served. Once this was done with, they washed their hands again and their mouths and then cocoa and pipes were handed about. Lastly the guests were given cloaks and flowers as presents.'110 Here one is concerned with a gathering of rich merchants. The feasts went on until the dawn, with dances and songs, and the party broke up only in the morning, after a last cup of scented cocoa, redolent of honey and vanilla.

Tobacco, as it has already been pointed out, had a great place. Guests, at least among the ruling class and the merchants, were given pipes ready for smoking at the end of the meal. These were cylindrical tubes, with no separate bowl, and they were made of reed, or perhaps sometimes of baked clay; they were highly decorated, and they were charged with a mixture of tobacco, charcoal and liquid-ambar.111 One thus had a kind of large aromatic cigar; and its taste must have been rather unlike that which is expected in a cigar today. There was not very much smoking between meals. Strolling about with a pipe in one's hand was a mark of nobility and elegance.

Tobacco was widely used in medicine and in religious ceremonies. It was thought to have pharmaceutical virtues and a religious value, and in some ceremonies the priests carried a calabash filled with tobacco on their back. The use of the plant among the laity in the pre-cortesian period does not seem to have spread to the common people.

Other far more efficacious narcotics or intoxicants were also in use; and the users of them sought either consolation or prophetic visions. The authors[112] particularly mention the *peyotl*, a little cactus which is a native of northern Mexico and which brings about coloured hallucinations. 'Those who eat it,' says Sahagún, 'have horrifying or comic visions, and this drunkenness lasts two or three days before going off. This plant is used as a food by the Chichimecs; it sustains them and gives them courage to fear neither battle nor thirst nor hunger; and they say that it preserves them from all danger.'

Peyotl still plays a great part in the religious life of the Indians of the north-west of Mexico and the south of the United States.[113] Other plants, whose effects have not yet been studied, appear to have been used as narcotics; among them were the vegetative parts of the *tlapatl*, one of the solanaceæ, and the seeds of the *mixitl*. But the one most often referred to in literature was a fungus, the *teonanacatl* ('sacred fungus'), which was served to the guests at the beginning of a banquet. 'The first thing that was eaten at this feast was a little black fungus which makes men drunk and gives them visions: it also inclines them to lechery. They ate it before sunrise . . . with honey; and when they began to grow warm, they started to dance. Some sang, some wept, so drunk were they by reason of these funguses; and others did not sing, but sat quiet in the room, thinking. Some saw they that were going to die, and wept; some saw themselves devoured by a wild beast; some saw themselves taking prisoners upon a battlefield, or else growing rich, or the masters of many slaves. Others saw that they would be convicted of adultery and that by reason of this crime their heads would be crushed; others saw that they would steal and be killed; and there were many other visions. When the drunkenness caused by these funguses had died away, they talked to one another about the visions that they had.'[114]

Perhaps the most surprising point for us in all these descriptions is that there is never at any time any question of alcoholic drinks. Yet the Indians were perfectly well acquainted with an alcoholic drink – *octli* (now called *pulque*), which is obtained by fermenting the sap of the agave, and which is quite like cider. The importance of *octli* is proved by the very important rôle played in religion by the gods of drink and drunkenness, those who were called the *Centzon Totochtin* ('the Four Hundred [innumerable] Rabbits'), the lunar and terrestrial gods of plenty and of the harvest, as well as Mayauel, the goddess of the agave.[115]

But the ancient Mexicans were perfectly well aware of the danger for them and for their civilisation that alcoholic intoxication implied. Perhaps no culture in history has ever set up more rigid barriers against this danger. 'That drink which is called *octli*,' said the emperor in his address to the people after his election, 'is the root and the origin of all evil and of all perdition; for *octli* and drunkenness are the cause of all the discords and of all the dissensions, of all revolt and of all troubles in cities and in realms. It is like the whirlwind that destroys and tears down everything. It is like a malignant storm that brings all evil with it. Before adultery, rape, debauching of girls, incest, theft, crime, cursing and bearing false-witness, murmuring, calumny, riots and brawling, there is always drunkenness. All those things are caused by *octli* and by drunkenness.'[116]

When one studies the literature upon the subject, one has the feeling that the Indians were very clearly aware of their strong natural inclination to alcoholism, and that they were quite determined to work against this evil, and to control themselves, by practising an extraordinarily severe policy of repression. 'Nobody drank wine (*octli*) excepting only those who were already aged, and they drank a little in secret, without becoming drunk. If a drunk man showed himself in public, or if he were caught drinking, or if he were found speechless in the street, or if he wandered about singing or in the company of other drunkards, he was punished, if he were a plebeian, by being beaten to death, or else he was strangled before the young men (of the district) by way of an example and to make them shun drunkenness. If the drunkard were noble, he was strangled in private.'[117]

There were ferocious laws against public drunkenness. The statutes of Nezaualcoyotl punished the priest taken in drunkenness with death; and death was the punishment for the drunken dignitary, official or ambassador if he were found in the palace: the dignitary who had got drunk without scandal was still punished, but only by the loss of his office and his titles.[118] The drunken plebeian got off the first time with no more than having his head shaved in public, while the crowd jeered at him; but the backslider was punished with death, as the nobles were for their first offence.[119]

Here we have an exceedingly violent case of socially defensive reaction against an equally violent tendency, whose existence has been historically proved, for when the conquest had destroyed the moral and judicial underpinning of Mexican civilisation, alcoholism spread among the Indians to an extraordinary degree.

However, even so severe a system as this had to have some kind of safety-valve. *Octli* was not entirely prohibited. Old men and women were allowed to drink, particularly on certain holidays, and it was even conceded that they might get drunk. For example, when the 'baptism' or rather name-giving of a child was celebrated, 'at night the old men and the old women gathered to drink *pulque* and to get drunk. In order that they should get drunk a large jar of *pulque* was put before them, and the person who served it poured the drink into calabashes and gave each one a drink in turn. . . And the server, when he saw that the guests were not yet drunk, began serving them again in the reverse order, beginning at the left side by the lower end. Once they were drunk, they would sing . . . some did not sing, but held forth, laughing and making jokes; and when they heard anything funny they would roar with laughter.'[120] All this was as though the Mexicans, wishing to cut their losses, allowed the pleasures of drink only to those whose active life was over, while at the same time they set up a barrier of terrible punishments against indulgence by young people or middle-aged men.

GAMES AND AMUSEMENTS

We have already touched upon the realm of games and

amusement in speaking of banquets. No doubt these great feasts always had some relation to a religious festival or to a religious ceremony; but, like our wedding-breakfasts or Christmas Eve parties, they were also occasions for being merry with one's friends and relations. Those who had the means, and foremost among them the emperor, loved, as they ate or smoked, taking their cocoa at the end of the meal, to hear poems recited or sung to the accompaniment of flutes, drums and two-toned gongs (*teponaztli*). The guests themselves danced to the sound of these instruments, after the feast.

One of the most valued delights was that of hunting. The common people may have hunted for the pot or to sell their game, but the nobles hunted for the pleasure of it. In their gardens and their parks, and in the game-filled countryside, they went after birds with their blow-pipes. 'Motecuhzoma, wishing to amuse himself, went with twenty-five of the most important Mexicans to a palace which he had at Atlacuhuayan, which is now called Tacubaya. He went into the garden alone to divert himself with killing birds with a blow-pipe.'[121] This is the blow-pipe that shoots baked-clay balls, and it had been known for a very long time throughout Mexico and Central America: it is the blow-pipe of the Quiché demi-gods in the *Popol Vuh*, and the same as that which is shown in the reliefs on a vase from Teotihuacán.[122]

There were also great battues, which took place particularly in the fourteenth month of the year, *Quecholli*, which was sacred to Uitzilopochtli, the god of war, and to the god of hunting, Mixcoatl. On the tenth day of this month all the warriors of Mexico and Tlatelolco met on the wooded slopes of Zacatepetl, and spent the night there in huts they had made from branches. At dawn the next day they ranged themselves in a long line 'like a single length of rope', and they drove the deer, coyotes, rabbits and hares forward before leaping in to attack the surrounded creatures. Those who killed a deer or a coyote were given a present by the emperor, who also provided food and drink for everybody. In the evening the hunters returned to the city, carrying as trophies the heads of the animals that had been killed.[123]

The Mexicans were passionately addicted to gambling; and there were two games that fascinated them to such a pitch that some Indians finished by losing all their belongings and even their liberty, for they would come to the point of selling themselves as slaves:[124] these were *tlachtli* and *patolli*.

Tlachtli, the ball game, had been played in Mexico from the remotest antiquity: courts have been found in cities dating from the height of the Mayan civilisation, El Tajín and at Tula; the one at Chichén-Itzá in Yucatán is among the most splendid monuments in all Central America. Courts are often represented in the native manuscripts, and their plan is shown as a double T.[125] Two sides faced one another, one on each side of a central line, and the game consisted of causing a heavy rubber ball to pass into the other part of the court.

In the side-walls there were two carved stone rings, and if one of the sides managed to throw the ball through either of them, that side won the game out of hand: this was an uncommon and a difficult feat, however; and it was made all the more so by the fact that the players were not allowed to touch the ball with either their hands or their feet, but only with their knees and their hips. The players threw themselves to the ground to get at the ball, and they received the full impact of it on their bodies when it was in flight; so, like modern Rugby or baseball players, they were padded and provided with knee-caps and leather aprons, and even with chin-pieces and half-masks covering their cheeks. They also wore leather gloves to protect their hands from the continual scraping on the ground. But in spite of all these precautions accidents were not uncommon: some players, hit in the stomach or the belly, fell never to rise again; and after the game most of them had to have incisions made in their buttocks to let out the extravasated blood.[126] For all that, the game was played with very great enthusiasm. Only the ruling class was allowed to play.

Tlachtli certainly had a mythological and religious significance: it was thought that the court represented the world and the ball a heavenly body, the sun or the moon. The sky was a sacred *tlachtli* in which divine beings played with the stars as their ball. But in the everyday life of the laity the game was the pretext for huge bets, in which great quantities of clothes, feathers, gold and slaves changed hands: it was essentially a game for great men; and for some of them it ended in ruin and slavery.

Ixtlilxochitl tells how the emperor Axayacatl played against the lord of Xochimilco and laid the market-place of Mexico against a garden belonging to this lord. He lost. The next day Mexican soldiers appeared at the palace of the fortunate winner and 'while they saluted him and made him presents they threw a garland of flowers about his neck with a thong hidden in it, and so killed him.'127

Patolli was a game with dice, not unlike our game of ludo. The *Codex Magliabecchiano* shows four players sitting on the ground or on mats round a table shaped like a cross and divided into squares. At one side there is the god Macuilxochitl, tutelary deity of dancing, music and gambling, watching over them.

For dice the players used beans marked with a certain number of pips; and according to the figures obtained at each throw they moved small coloured stones from square to square on the board. The winner of the game and the stakes was the one who first came back to the square he had started from.

Patolli, like *tlachtli*, had a hidden inner meaning. There were fifty-two squares on the board, that is, the same number of years that are contained by the combined divinatory and solar cycles. *Patolli* is still played: or at least it was still played twenty years ago, among the Nahua and Totonac Indians of the Sierra de Puebla.128 Unlike the aristocratic ball game it was the most generally played game in all classes, and in it the Indians' passion for gambling could run unchecked. It is a curious fact that the Aztecs, although they were so puritanical about drinking and although their sex-life was so restrained, never seem to have tried to curb gambling. The divinatory books go no farther than warning those who were born under certain signs such as *ce calli*, for example, 'one – house', that they would be great gamblers, and that in gambling they would lose all their possessions.[129]

THE RHYTHM OF DAY AND NIGHT

The Mexicans, having neither clocks nor clepsydras, nor sundials either, could not divide their days with any precision. However, a life of intense social and ritual activity presupposes the existence of certain fixed points, those which Muñoz Camargo calls the 'hours and moments (fixed) for the government of the republic'. If we are to accept what this chronicler says, the trumpets and conchs were sounded from the top of the temples of Tlaxcala six times every twenty-four hours, to wit, at the rising of Venus, in the middle of the morning, at noon, in the middle of the afternoon, at the beginning of night, and at midnight.[130] Still, expressions such as 'the middle of the morning' or 'the middle of the afternoon' are, in the absence of a time-measuring machine, necessarily uncertain; yet it is true that the priests knew how to make observations of the heavenly bodies, of the sun's course and of the movement of certain stars. They were therefore able to fix the intermediary points between the east and the zenith and between the zenith and the west with a reasonable degree of accuracy. At night, they watched Venus and the Pleiades.

According to Sahagún, the temple drums and conchs marked nine divisions in the twenty-four hours: four during the day – at sunrise, the middle of the morning, noon and sunset – and five during the night – the beginning of night (the end of the twilight), the hour for going to bed, the hour when the priests were to get up to pray, 'a little after midnight', and 'a little before dawn'.[131] Some of these divisions were therefore quite long, the equivalent of three or four hours; and others were very short.

The notion of an abstract time, susceptible of division and calculation, never seems to have arisen. But the days and nights had their rhythm; and this rhythm originated from the temple-tops, the towers of the gods and of the ritual that dominated the countryside and regulated human existence. By day, above the noise of the moving city, or in the silence of the night, there would come the sudden harsh cry of the conchs and the melancholy roll of drums to mark the stages of the sun or the stars; and at each of these stages the priests offered up incense to the sun or to the lords of the shadows. It is very likely that these fixed points were used to determine the time for meetings, to call councils and to open or close judicial hearings. The temple instruments ordered the day as the church bells might in a Christian community.

One might have supposed that a civilisation that was almost without artificial light must have found its activities cut short by the fall of night; but this was not so. There were the priests who got up several times in the night to pray and chant, the youths from the local schools who were sent to bathe in the icy water of the lake or the springs, the lords and the merchants who feasted, the furtive traders who glided over the lake with their canoes loaded with wealth, sorcerers going to their sinister assignations – a night-life that animated the darkened city. And the night, too, was pierced here and there by the glowing hearths of the temples and the glare of resinous torches.

The dark hours of the dreaded yet alluring night offered their cover for the most sacred rites, the most important visits, the loves of the warriors and the courtesans. Often the emperor would rise, to offer his blood in the darkness and to pray. A watcher with preternaturally acute senses, gazing over the whole valley from the top of one of the volcanoes, might have seen here and there the flickering of the flames and have heard the music at the banquets, the beat of the dancing, the voices of the singers; and then, at intervals, the roll of the *teponaztli* and the scream of the conchs. So the night would pass away; but at no time was the dark vault of the sky without its human observer – the anxious watch for a tomorrow that might never come. Then the dawn came and above the rumble of the waking town the triumphant cry of the sacred trumpets rose towards the sun, the 'turquoise prince, the soaring eagle'. A new day was beginning.

CHAPTER FIVE

FROM BIRTH TO DEATH

Baptism. The reading of the omens: giving the name—Child-
hood and youth, education. Infancy: the two systems of
public education—Marriage, family life. Leaving school:
rôle of the marriage-brokers: weddings: chief and secondary
wives: the polygamous family: woman's status in Aztec
society: adultery and divorce: birth of a child: apotheosis of
women dying in childbirth—Sickness and old age. Physicians
and healing-women: accepted opinions on sickness: charms and
spells: medicinal plants: place of the old in society: the rite
and the significance of confession—Death and the hereafter.
The funeral rites.

BAPTISM

When a child was born into a Mexican family, the midwife
who had taken care of the delivery acted as priest and saw
to the fulfilment of the rites. It was she who addressed the
baby and welcomed it, saluting it with the names of 'precious
stone, *quetzal*-feather', and at the same time warning it of
the uncertainty and the sorrows of this life – 'Here you are,
come into this world where your parents live in toil and
weariness, where there is over-much heat, and cold and
wind . . . we cannot tell if you will live long among us . . .
we cannot tell what kind of fate will be yours.'[1] All these
traditional themes were to be repeated an indefinite number
of times in the ceremonies that followed.

The midwife cut the baby's umbilical cord; but not
without haranguing him at length. If it were a boy, she said
to him, 'Dear son . . . you must understand that your home
is not here where you have been born, for you are a warrior,
you are a *quecholli* bird, and this house where you have just
been born is only a nest . . . your mission is to give the sun
the blood of enemies to drink and to feed Tlaltecuhtli,

163

the earth, with their bodies. Your country, your inheritance and your father are in the house of the sun, in the sky.' And to a girl she would say, 'As the heart stays in the body, so you must stay in the house; you must never go out of the house . . . you must be like the embers in the hearth.'[2] Thus from the first moment the man was devoted to the fate of a warrior and the woman to that of a Cinderella seated by the fireside.

Then the midwife washed the child, praying to Chalchiuhtlicue, the goddess of water, 'Goddess, be pleased that his heart and his life may be purified, that the water may carry away all stain, for this child puts himself in your hands, oh Chalchiuhtlicue, mother and sister of gods.'

As soon as the birth was known in the family and the locality, or even for the great families as far off as in other cities, the complex ceremonial of the 'salutations' began. The old women of the family thanked the midwife solemnly, and she answered in a speech full of imagery. Chosen orators, usually old men, went to greet the new-born child, and other old men appointed for the purpose, answered with long discourses.[3]

The Aztecs' taste for rhetoric found satisfaction in endless pompous dissertations upon the favour of the gods and the mysteries of fate. Times beyond number the baby was compared to a necklace, to a jewel of precious stones, to a rare feather. The child's mother was extolled, she 'who was the peer of the goddess Ciuacoatl Quilaztli'. They boasted about the glorious history of the family. If the father were a dignitary or a lawyer he was reminded of 'his office and its great importance and its great weight in the courts and in the government of the state'. 'Lord,' they said to him, 'it is truly your image, your likeness: you have a scion – you have flowered!' From time to time (and this was one of the obligatory figures in fine language) the orator would excuse himself for going on too long. 'I am afraid of wearying you and of giving you pains in your heads and your stomachs.' Then he would go on with renewed vigour. Those who spoke on behalf of the family would return thanks in an equally garrulous manner. At last those who had come to greet the baby gave their presents: there would be an many as twenty or forty cloaks or suits of clothes among people of the ruling class; but among the plebeians the presents would only be food and drink.

During these festivities, the father would send for the *tonalpouhqui*, or soothsayer, a specialist in the study of the sacred books. This person, who was offered a meal, as well as his fee of cloth and turkeys, began by asking the exact moment of the birth, so that he might decide what sign the child was born under. He then consulted his *tonalamatl* to find the sign of the day of the birth and the set of thirteen days to which it belonged.

If the sign of the day were considered good and fortunate, he could say 'Your son is born under a good sign. He will be a lord or a senator, rich, brave, pugnacious; he will be courageous and he will shine in war; he will reach high rank among the commanders of armies.' And then one could go on to the naming of the child the next day. But if the sign of the day proved to be calamitous, then the *tonalpouhqui* exercised his wit to find a better sign in the same set of thirteen, as nearly as possible in the four following days. 'The child is not born under a good sign,' he would say, 'but in this series there is another, a reasonable sign that will diminish and correct the unfortunate influence of the principal sign.' This was usually possible, since the signs that carried figures greater than ten were always favourable, as well as those that had the figure seven.[4] At a pinch, it was possible to delay the baptism for more than the ordinarily allowed four days.

The naming itself was carried out not by the soothsayer, nor by a priest, but by the midwife. The ceremony had two parts, the ritual washing of the child and the actual naming.

They began by getting ready a great deal of food and drink for the family feast that would follow the baptism; they also made a little shield, a bow with four arrows, each corresponding to one of the cardinal points, if the child were a boy, and little spindles, a shuttle and a box if it were a girl. All the relatives and friends gathered in the mother's house before sunrise.

As soon as day broke they arranged the symbolic objects in the inner courtyard or in the garden. The midwife, provided with a full water-jar, addressed the baby, saying 'Eagle, jaguar, valiant warrior, oh my grandson! Here you are come into this world, sent by your father and mother, the great god and the great goddess. You have been made and begotten in your own place, among the almighty gods, the great god and the great goddess who live above the nine heavens. It is Quetzalcoatl, who is in all places, who has done you this kindness. Now be joined to your mother the goddess of the water, Chalchiuhtlicue, Chalchiuhtlatonac.' With her wet fingers she set some drops of water on his mouth. 'Take and receive this, for it is with this water that you will live upon earth, and grow and grow green again; it is by water that we have what we must have to live upon this earth. Receive this water.'

After this she touched the baby's chest with her wet hand and said, 'Here is the heavenly water, the very pure water that washes and cleans your heart and that takes away all stain.' Then she threw some drops on his head. 'Let this water enter into your body, and may it live there, this heavenly water, the blue celestial water.' Lastly she washed the child's whole body, saying the formula meant to keep off evil. 'Wherever you may be, you who might do this child a mischief, leave him, go off, go away from him; for now this child is born again – he is new-born and new-formed by our mother Chalchiuhtlicue.'

After the four water-rites, the midwife presented the child four times to the sky, invoking the sun and the astral gods. In this way the traditional gestures were regulated by the holy number. The last formula also invoked the earth, the divine spouse of the sun. And, taking the shield and the arrows, the midwife begged the gods that the boy might become a courageous warrior, 'so that he may go into your palace of delights where the brave who die in battle rest and rejoice'.

The ceremony for naming the girls was similar, but the baby was not presented to the sun, which was the god of men and warriors: after the ritual washing the midwife and the relatives, in a touching ceremony, spoke to the cradle in which the little girl would lie, calling it Yoalticitl, 'the healer by night', and saying, 'You who are her mother, take her, old goddess. Do her no harm; watch over her kindly.'⁵

When these rites were over, the name of the child was chosen and announced. The ancient Mexicans had no surnames, but some names were often handed down from grandfather to grandson in the same family. The birthday was also taken into consideration: a child who was born during the set of thirteen days that was ruled by the sign *ce miquiztli*, under the influence of Tezcatlipoca, received one of the appellations of this god.⁶

In some tribes, and particularly among the Mixtecs, each person was called by the day of his birth, usually followed by a nickname; for example 'seven – flower, eagle's feather' or 'four – rabbit, garland of flowers'.⁷ There was a very great variety in Mexican personal names. Taking them at random from the texts one finds such names as Acamapichtli (handful of reeds), Chimalpopoca (smoking shield), Itzcoatl (obsidian snake), Xiuhcozcatl (turquoise necklace), Quauhcoatl (eagle-snake), Citlalcoatl (snake of stars), Tlacateotl (godlike man), and Quauhtlatoa (speaking eagle). Women were given charming names like Matlalxochitl (green flower), Quiauhxochitl (rain-flower), Miahuaxiuitl (turquoise-maize-flower) and Atototl (water-bird). All these names, like those of villages, mountains, etc., could be represented by pictograms in the manuscript records.⁸

The ceremony closed with a family banquet, at the end of which the old men and women might give themselves up to the pleasures of drink.

CHILDHOOD AND YOUTH, EDUCATION

In the *Codex Mendoza* there is a series of pictures divided into two columns (the one on the left for the boys, the one on the right for the girls) which shows the stages in the education of a Mexican child. This education seems to have been one of the parents' chief cares, and to have been carried out with a great deal of concern and firmness. At the same time this table shows the rations that each child

167

was allowed – half a cake of maize at each meal for a three-year-old, one cake at four and five years, a cake and a half from six to twelve years and two cakes from thirteen onwards. These rations were the same for both sexes.

To judge by this manuscript, the education of a boy was entrusted to his father between the age of three and fifteen years, and that of a girl to her mother; this very probably means that such was the case in families in modest circumstances, for judges and important officials obviously did not have the necessary time for educating their children personally – besides, as it will be seen later, the family's part in education usually ceased much earlier.

The pictures in the *Codex Mendoza* also show how the children were dressed. On occasion the boys up to the age of thirteen wore a small cloak tied at the shoulder, but they did not wear the *maxtlatl;* it was only after thirteen, at the beginning of man's estate, that they appeared in a loincloth. The little girls, on the other hand, wore the usual blouse from the beginning, and a skirt which, although it began short, very soon descended to their ankles.

During the first years the parents' teaching was limited to good advice (a blue scroll, the colour of the precious stone, is shown coming from their lips) and to showing them how to do little domestic tasks. The boy learnt to carry water and wood, and to go to the market-place with his father and pick up the maize scattered on the ground. The little girl watched her mother spinning, but did not begin to handle the spindle herself until she was six. From seven to fourteen the boys learnt to fish and to manage boats on the lake, while the girls spun cotton, swept the house, ground the maize on the *metlatl* and at last began to learn the use of the loom, a very delicate instrument in precolumbian Mexico.

It was an essentially practical education, and a very severe one: punishments rained down upon an idle child, whose parents would scratch him with agave-thorns or compel him to breathe the acrid fumes of a fire in which red peppers were burning. Mexican teachers seem to have been very much in favour of the iron hand.

Still according to the *Codex Mendoza*, it was at fifteen
that the youths might enter either the *calmecac*, a temple or
monastery in which they were entrusted to priests, or the
school called the *telpochcalli*, 'the house of the young men',
which was run by masters chosen from among the experienced warriors. But here the document is in disagreement
with the most authoritative texts. It seems sure that education at home stopped much earlier. Some fathers sent their
children to the *calmecac* as soon as they could walk; and in
any case they went to school between six and nine years of
age.[9]

As we have seen, there were two possibilities open to a
family, the *calmecac* and the *telpochcalli*. In theory the
calmecac was kept for the sons and daughters of the dignitaries, but the children of the trading class[10] were also
admitted, and there is a passage in Sahagún[11] which seems
to say that the children of plebeian families could also go
there. This supposition is strengthened by the fact that
the high priests were 'chosen without any regard to their
family, but only to their morals, their practices, their
knowledge of doctrine and the purity of their lives';[12] yet
it was obligatory for a priest to have been brought up in a
calmecac.

There were several *calmecac* in Mexico, each attached to a
given temple. The *Mexicatl teohuatzin*, the 'vicar-general'
of the Mexican church, was in charge of their administration
and of the education of the boys and girls in them.[13] Each
district, on the other hand, had several *telpochcalli*, which
were administered by the *telpochtlatoque*, the 'masters of
the young men', or for the girls by the *ichpochtlatoque*,
'mistresses of the girls', who were not religious but lay
officials.[14]

In general, the higher education given in the *calmecac*
prepared the pupils either for the priesthood or for the high
offices of the state: it was rigid and severe. The *telpochcalli*
produced ordinary citizens, although this did not prevent
some of them from reaching the highest rank, and its pupils
had much more freedom and were much less harshly
treated than those in the religious school.

There was no night of uninterrupted sleep for the scholars of the *calmecac*. They had to get up in the darkness to go into the mountains, each by himself, to offer incense to the gods and draw blood from their ears and legs with agave-thorns. They were obliged to undergo frequent and rigorous fasts. They had to work hard on the temple's land, and they were severely punished for the least fault.

The whole emphasis of this education was upon sacrifice and abnegation. 'Listen, my son,' said a father to a boy about to enter a *calmecac*, 'you are not going to be honoured, nor obeyed, nor esteemed. You are going to be looked down upon, humiliated and despised. Every day you will cut agave-thorns for penance, and you will draw blood from your body with these spines and you will bathe at night even when it is very cold... Harden your body to the cold... and when the time comes for fasting do not go and break your fast, but put a good face upon both fasting and penance.'[15] Above all it was a school of self-control and of firmness towards oneself. The pupils were also taught 'to speak well, to make proper salutations and to bow', and lastly '(the priests) taught the young men all the songs that are called holy, which were written in their books by means of their characters, as well as the astrology of the Indians, the interpretation of dreams and the reckoning of the years.'[16]

Girls were consecrated to the temple from their earliest days, either to stay there for a given number of years or until they should be married. They were under the direction and the instruction of elderly priestesses, and they lived chastely, growing expert in the working of beautifully embroidered materials, taking part in the ritual and offering incense to the gods several times a night. They had the title of priestesses.[17]

How very different and how very much less austere was the life of the other young people. It is true that the boy who went to the *telpochcalli* had many disagreeable and commonplace tasks, such as the sweeping of the communal house; and he went with the others, in bands, to cut wood for the school or to take part in public works – the repairing of ditches and canals and the cultivation of the common land. But at sunset, 'all the youths went to sing and dance in a house called *cuicacalco* ('the house of singing') and the boys danced with the other young men . . . until after midnight . . . and those that had mistresses went off to sleep with them.'[18]

There was little room in their education for the religious exercises, the fasts and the penances which had so much importance in that of the pupils of the *calmecac*. Everything was done to prepare them for war; from their earliest age they associated only with experienced warriors, whose exploits they admired and dreamed of rivalling. So long as they were bachelors they lived a communal existence, enlivened by dancing and songs, and by the company of the young women, the *auianime*, who were officially allowed them, as courtesans.

Indeed, these two systems of education were so different that from certain points of view they seem opposed and even hostile. Sahagún, making himself the mouthpiece of the nobles, the former pupils of the *calmecac*, says that the young men of the *telpochcalli* 'did not lead a good life, for they had mistresses; they presumed to utter light and ironic words, and spoke with pride and temerity.'[19] This antagonism showed itself, and burst out with the consent of public opinion in certain circumstances – during the month *Atemoztli*, for example, when the youths of the *calmecac* and those of the *telpochcalli* threw themselves upon one another in mock battles.[20]

Underlying this contrast is the contrast between the gods who presided over the two branches of education. The god of the *calmecac* was Quetzalcoatl, the priests' own god, the god of self-sacrifice and penance, of books, the calendar and the arts, the symbol of abnegation and of culture. The young men's god was Tezcatlipoca, who was also called Telpochtli, 'the young man', and Yaotl, 'the warrior', Quetzalcoatl's old enemy who had expelled him from the earthly paradise of Tula long ago by his enchantments.

To send a boy to the *calmecac* was to devote him to Quetzalcoatl; to send him to the *telpochcalli* was to pledge him to Tezcatlipoca.[21] Beneath the mask of these divine persons two different concepts of life are set one against the other: on the one hand there is the priestly ideal of self-denial, the study of the stars and the signs, contemplative knowledge and chastity; on the other, the ideal of the warriors, with the emphasis deliberately set upon action, battle, the collective life and the fleeting pleasures of youth. It is by no means the least curious feature of Aztec civilisation that a society so passionately given to war should have chosen the teaching of Quetzalcoatl to mould its rulers, and that it should have left that of Tezcatlipoca to the more numerous, but the less honoured, class.

A deeper study of this society would no doubt bring to light profound contradictions which in their turn would explain those internal tensions that the community sublimated from time to time by forms of ritual. The origin of these contradictions would have to be sought in the super-imposition and mixture of the differing cultures, that of the Toltecs, passed on by the settled inhabitants of the valley, and that of the nomadic tribes to which the Aztecs had belonged, which together made up the Mexican civil-isation as it was at the time of its discovery by the Europeans. Native thought was dominated by dualism – in this case that which set up Quetzalcoatl against Tezcatlipoca – and this dualism is also found in the education itself.

However that may be, this education functioned: it prepared governors, priests, warriors and women who knew their future work. It was only in the *calmecac* that what may properly be called intellectual teaching had a considerable place; but there all the knowledge of the time and the country was taught – reading and writing in the pictographic characters, divination, chronology, poetry and rhetoric.

It should also be remembered that the songs which were learnt by heart often concerned the history of the cities, of former reigns and wars, and in this way the young people came to know their own past. In the *telpochcalli*, however, the songs and the dances and the music did not provide the future warriors with any excessive load of learning.

In a general manner, Mexican education in both its forms hoped to produce strength of mind and of body, and a character devoted to the public good. The stoicism with which the Aztecs were able to meet the most terrible ordeals proves that this education attained its end.

Lastly, although their system was divided into two markedly distinct branches, it is evident that this separation did not bring into being an impassable barrier against the rise of boys of poor or lowly family, since the highest offices, such as that of *tlacochcalcatl*, were sometimes held by plebeians who had been at a *telpochcalli*. And then in their turn the sons of these promoted plebeians might go to the *calmecac*.

It is well worth noting that in that age and upon that continent an American native race practised compulsory education for all[22] and that no Mexican child of the sixteenth century, whatever his social origin, was deprived of schooling. One has but to compare this state of affairs with what is known of our own classical antiquity or middle ages to realise the care that the native civilisation of Mexico, for all its limitations, devoted to the training of its young people and to the moulding of its citizens.

MARRIAGE, FAMILY LIFE

Once he was twenty a young man might marry, and most Mexicans did so between this age and twenty-two. Only the high dignitaries and the rulers could live for years with concubines before being officially married – the king of Texcoco, Nezaualcoyotl, was an example of this.[23] Marriage was considered as primarily a matter for the families and by no means for the individuals; at least, this was the traditional view of it. But it is likely that the young people could offer suggestions to their parents, if no more.

But before passing from the celibate to the married state, that is, before reaching full adult status, it was necessary to be free of the *calmecac* or the *telpochcalli* and to gain the consent of those who had been the young man's masters for so many years. This permission was asked for at a banquet given by the young man's family.

The *telpochtlatoque* were asked to a feast as magnificent as the family's means would allow: there would be tamales, different kinds of ragout and cocoa. The masters, having relished the dishes, smoked the pipes that they were given; and then, in the happy atmosphere of well-being that comes after a good meal, the young man's father, the elders on the paternal side and the local councillors brought a polished stone axe with great ceremony, and turning to the masters, addressed them in the following words: 'Lords, and masters of the young men, here present, do not be wounded if your brother, our son, desires to leave your company. At this time he wishes to take a wife. Behold this axe: it is the sign that this young man is going to leave you, according to the custom of the Mexicans. Take it and set free our son.' To this a *telpochtlato* replied, 'We have all heard, we and the young men with whom your son has been brought up, that now you intend to marry him and that from now on he will leave us for ever: let it be as you wish it to be.' Then the masters took the axe, a symbolic gesture of acquiescence in the young man's withdrawal, and ceremoniously left the house.[24]

Of course, everything had been known in advance, the feast, the request and the reply; but this occasion was ruled, as were so many others, by the Indian love of form and of traditional words and actions. According to Motolinía[25] the *telpochtlato* did not let his pupils go without a homily, 'exhorting them to behave like worthy servants of the gods and not to forget all they had learnt at school; and, since they were going to take a wife and set up house, to work like men and feed and maintain their family . . . He also told them that in time of war they should conduct themselves like brave and courageous soldiers.' As for the girls, 'they too were not left without advice or good teaching, but on the contrary, they were admonished at length, particularly the daughters of the lords and dignitaries.' They were told that three precepts above all others should guide their lives: they should serve the gods, they should be chaste, and they should love, serve and look up to their husbands. 'Although they were heathens,' adds the missionary, 'the Mexicans were not without good customs.'

When the relatives of the young man had decided upon the choice of his future wife, which was not before they had consulted the soothsayers to know what omens were to be drawn from the signs under which both the parties were born, they then called in the *cihuatlanque*, the old women who acted as go-betweens; for no advance was to be made directly. These women went to see the girl's parents, and 'with a great deal of rhetoric and fine language'[26] they explained the purpose of their visit. Good manners required that the first time they should be answered with a humble excuse and a civil refusal. The girl was not yet old enough to marry; she was not worthy of the person who asked for her.

However, everybody knew how to take this, and the next day, or some days later, the matrons came back and finally the parents went so far as to say, 'We do not know how this young man can have made such a mistake, for our daughter is of no value, and indeed she is rather stupid. But still, seeing that you seem to set so much store by it, we will have to speak to the girl's uncles and aunts, and all her other relatives. So come back again tomorrow, and we will settle the matter.'

When they had had their family council and when all the relatives had given their consent, the girl's parents told the young man's parents, and then there was no more to arrange but the day of the wedding. For this the soothsayers were consulted again, in order to set the marriage under a favour-able sign, such as *acatl* (reed), *ozomatli* (monkey), *cipactli* (water-monster), *quauhtli* (eagle), or *calli* (house). It was also necessary to prepare the dishes, the cocoa, the flowers and the pipes for the marriage-feast. 'They made tamales all night and all day for two or three days, and hardly slept at all' during the time of getting ready.[27] If the family had the least degree of wealth or the smallest claim to standing, the marriage was a most important business. All the relations and friends were invited, as well as the young man's former masters and the considerable people of the district or the town.

The marriage-ceremony itself took place at the young man's house at nightfall. The day before there was feasting at the bride's house: at a midday banquet the old men drank *octli* and the married women brought their gifts. In the afternoon the bride had a bath and washed her hair: her legs and arms were decorated with red feathers and her face was made up with the light yellow of *tecozauitl*. Thus adorned, she sat near the fire on a dais covered with mats, and the elders of the young man's family came to offer her the ceremonial greeting. 'My daughter,' they said, 'you honour us, the old men and old women who are your relations. You are now counted among the women; you are no longer a child; you have started to be a grown-up person. Poor child! You must leave your father and your mother. Daughter, we welcome you and wish you happiness.'

One can imagine the bride, decorated with feathers and flowers, made up, dressed in many-coloured embroideries, moved and somewhat trembling though accustomed by her education to hide her feelings, compelling herself to be calm as she answered, 'Your hearts have been good to me; I feel that the words that you have spoken are precious. You have spoken to me and advised me like true fathers and mothers. I am grateful for all the kindness that you have shown me.'

At night, a procession conducted the bride to her new home. The young man's relations went in front, 'many respectable old women and matrons', then came the bride: an old woman carried her on her back; or if she were of good family it was in a litter that she went to her new house, on the shoulders of two porters. She was accompanied by two lines of girls, relations and unmarried friends, holding torches in their hands.[28]

The happy procession wound along the streets amid songs and shouts and through the crowds of onlookers who cried out 'Happy girl!' until it reached the bridegroom's house. He came forward to receive her; in his hand he had a censer, and when the bride reached the threshold she was given another. As a sign of mutual respect each censed the other, and everybody went into the house, singing and dancing.

The marriage-rite took place before the hearth. To begin with, the two young people, seated beside one another upon two mats, were given their presents. The bride's mother gave her future son-in-law men's clothes; the bridegroom's mother gave the bride a blouse and a skirt. Then the *cihuatlanque* tied the young man's cloak and the girl's blouse together, and from that moment they were married: the first thing that they did was to share a dish of tamales, each giving the other the little maize-cakes by hand.

At this stage the happiness of the wedding-party broke out into songs and dances; then the guests set upon the heaps of food and those whose age allowed them became exceedingly drunk. The married pair, however, who had gone off to the marriage-chamber, stayed there in prayer for four days, without consummating their marriage. During all this time they did not come out of their room except to offer incense at the family altar at noon and at midnight. On the fourth night there was a bed made for them, a pile of mats among which were placed feathers and a piece of jade: these were probably symbols of the children who were to be born, they always being called 'rich plumes', and 'precious stones'. On the fifth day they bathed themselves in the *temazcalli*, and a priest came to bless them by scattering a little consecrated water over them.

In great families the ceremony of the fifth day was almost as elaborate as that of the marriage itself: the relatives blessed the newly-wedded pair four times with water and four times with *octli*. The bride adorned her head with white feathers and her arms and legs with coloured plumes; there was another exchange of presents and at another banquet the two families and their friends had another opportunity of dancing, singing and drinking. Among the plebeians these festivities were quieter and less costly, but their general plan was the same as that which has just been described.

This, at any rate, was the ideal that everybody tried to accomplish. Yet in practice it happened that amorous young couples did not ask their parents' consent, but went off together privately. It seems that these were usually plebeians who did not want to have to wait until they had accumulated all the things that were necessary for the presents, the feasts, etc. 'At the end of a certain time, when he had saved up enough to invite their families, the young man went to see his wife's parents and said, 'I admit my fault . . . we were wrong to be joined without your consent . . . You must have been quite astonished not to see your daughter any more (sic). But we both agreed to live together like married people, and now we would like to live properly and work for ourselves and our children: forgive us, and give us your consent.' The parents agreed, 'and they then went through the ceremonies and what festivities their poor means would allow.'[29]

It was in this manner and according to these rites that a man married his principal wife, and he could only marry in this way with one woman; but he could have as many secondary wives as he liked. The Mexican marriage-system seems to be a compromise between monogamy and polygamy – one 'legitimate' spouse (this is the term generally used by the chroniclers), she with whom a man was married with all the ceremonies that have been described, but an in-definite number of officially-recognised concubines who had their place in the house, and whose status was in no way the subject of sniggering or contempt.

The historian Oviedo recounts a conversation that he says he had with the Spaniard Juan Cano, the third husband of Doña Isabel Montezuma, the daughter of the emperor Motecuhzoma II, as follows –

'Question. I have been told that Montezuma had a hundred and fifty sons and daughters . . . How can you maintain that Doña Isabel, your wife, is a legitimate daughter of Montezuma, and how did your father-in-law manage to tell his legitimate children from the bastards, and his real wives from his concubines?

Answer of Don Juan Cano. The Mexicans observed the following custom when they married a legitimate wife . . . They took the flap of the bride's blouse and tied it with the cotton cloak that the bridegroom wore . . . And those who were married without this ceremony were not held to be really married, and the children born of the union were not considered legitimate and did not inherit.'[30]

The Aztec chronicler Pomar[31] states, 'The king (of Texcoco) had as many wives as he chose, and of every kind of descent, high or low; but only one legitimate wife among them all.' The texts are unanimous upon this point: for example, Ixtlilxochitl says that the custom of the rulers was 'to have one legitimate wife who could be the mother of their successor'.[32] The anonymous conquistador also says that 'the Indians have many wives – as many as they can feed, like the Moors . . . but there is one who is above all the others and whose children inherit to the detriment of their half-brothers'.[33] Muñoz Camargo states that the legitimate wife gave orders to her husband's concubines, and indeed that it was she who adorned and beautified the one whom her husband chose 'in order to sleep with her'.[34]

There is no doubt that the half-barbarous tribes which came from the north were monogamous, as all the descriptions of their manner of life demonstrate. Polygamy must have remained customary among the settled inhabitants, the former Toltecs, of the central valley, and as the standard of living rose it became more and more usual, particularly in the ruling class and among the sovereigns. The latter numbered their secondary wives by hundreds or by thousands (Nezaualpilli of Texcoco had more than two thousand[35]) and there was an established custom of ratifying the alliances between cities by the exchange of wives of the various dynasties.

One should not be led astray by the expressions 'legitimate' and 'illegitimate' which were used after the Spanish conquest because of the influence of European ideas: the condition of the secondary wives and of their children was in no way a shameful one. Perhaps in theory only the sons of the principal wife succeeded, but the authorities abound in examples to the contrary: one has but to mention the most famous of them all, that of the emperor Itzcoatl, who was the son of a concubine of the most humble origin. In any case, the children of secondary wives were always considered *pilli*, and if they were worthy of them, they could reach the highest offices in the state. It would be totally erroneous to think of them as 'natural children' or 'bastards', with the connotations that these words have in our world.

Yet if in theory the polygamous family was accepted without question, in fact the jealousy between a man's wives and the rivalry between their children caused a very great deal of trouble. Sometimes the concubines would plot to sow discord between the husband and his children by the principal wife: it was in this way that a favourite of king Nezaualcoyotl succeeeded in bringing disaster upon the head of the young prince Tetzauhpiltzintli, 'the wonderful child'.

Tetzauhpiltzintli, the son of the king and his chief wife, 'rejoiced in all the gifts that nature can bestow upon an illustrious prince. He had an excellent disposition, and although his tutors and masters never had to take pains with him he became a widely accomplished person, a considerable philosopher, a poet and soldier of the first order, and he was even deeply versed in nearly all the mechanical arts . . . Another prince, the son of the king and a concubine, carved a precious stone in the form of a bird in so lifelike a manner that the bird seemed to be living, and he gave this jewel as a present to his father. His father was delighted with the aspect of the jewel, and he wished it to be given to his son Tetzauhpiltzintli, for he loved him exceedingly.'

Who could have believed that this charming family scene could develop into a tragedy? This, however, was the case. For the concubine's son, following his mother's counsels, went to the king and told him that the prince had made a most ungracious reply, which made him suspect that he meant to revolt against his father: that he had said that he did not care for the mechanical arts which preoccupied the prince who had carved the jewel, but only for military affairs and that he was determined to rule the world, and, if possible, to become a greater man than his father; and that while he spoke in this way he had showed his half-brother an arsenal filled with weapons.

The king was very much moved at this news, and sent a confidential servant to visit his son; and in fact the messenger observed that the palace which had been given to the prince had its walls covered with arms. Nezaualcoyotl consulted with his allies, the rulers of Mexico and Tlacopan, and begged them to see his son and to reproach him, so that he might return to his duty. But the two other monarchs, who were perhaps not at all sorry to weaken the neighbouring dynasty, 'went to the prince's palace under the pretence of visiting him to see some building that he was having done; and certain officers who accompanied them, feigning to put a garland of flowers about his neck, strangled him . . . When the king heard of the death of the prince, whom he loved dearly, he wept bitterly, bewailing the hardness of the two kings' hearts . . . For several days he stayed in the woods, sad and afflicted, lamenting his unhappiness, for he had no other legitimate son to succeed him at the head of the kingdom, although by his concubines he had had sixty sons and fifty-seven daughters. Most of the sons had become famous soldiers, and the daughters had married lords of his court or else of Mexico or Tlacopan; and to all these he had given many estates, villages and lands.'[36]

It seems that the royal house of Texcoco was marked out for a tragic fate: Nezaualpilli, Nezaualcoyotl's successor, was also responsible for his own son's death. Huexotzincatzin, his eldest son, 'was an outstanding philosopher and poet, as well having other gifts and natural graces, and so he composed a satire addressed to the lady of Tula, his father's favourite concubine. She, too, was an excellent poet, and they took to exchanging poetic blows. The prince was suspected of making advances to the favourite. The matter was brought before the court, and as, according to the law, it was a case of treason towards the king which carried the death-penalty, it was necessary to carry out the sentence, although his father loved him beyond measure.'[37]

In passing, it may be noticed that this palace-drama was

one of the remote causes of the fall of the Mexican empire: for, Nezaualpilli's heir dying in these circumstances, the succession to the throne of Texcoco was furiously disputed by several of his half-brothers, and one of them, Ixtlilxochitl, went over to the Spanish side with his supporters and his army.

This 'lady of Tula' who was, perhaps against her will, the cause of the tragic death of Huexotzincatzin, may be held up as a finished type of the Mexican magnate's favourite. Although she was only the daughter of a person engaged in commerce she was as cultivated as she was beautiful – she could compete with the king and the great men in knowledge and in poetry. She had a kind of private court and she lived in a palace that had been built for her; and 'she kept the king very submissive to her will'.[38]

It appears that all these wives, principal and secondary, had a great many children, and the polygamous families became exceedingly numerous. Nezaualpilli had a hundred and forty-four sons and daughters, of whom eleven were by his chief wife.[39] The *Crónica Mexicayotl* lists twenty-two children of Axayacatl, twenty of Auitzotl and nineteen of Motecuhzoma. The *Ciuacoatl* Tlacaeleltzin, a great imperial dignitary under Motecuhzoma I, first married a noblewoman, a girl from Amecameca, by whom he had five children, then twelve secondary wives, each of whom had a son or a daughter; but, adds the text, 'other Mexicans say that the elder Tlacaeleltzin, the *Ciuacoatl*, begot eighty-three children'.[40]

Clearly, only dignitaries and wealthy men could contend with the expense of families such as these. Even though it was limited to the upper strata, polygamy hastened the progress of demographic evolution and helped to compensate the effects of frequent war. Many men died on the battlefield or as sacrifices before they had been able to marry or, in any case, before they had had time to beget many children. In the lists of names that are to be found in some chronicles the annotations 'killed in fighting against Uexotzinco' or 'killed in battle at Atlixco' continually recur, like a funereal leitmotiv.[41] The widows could either stay by themselves and then remarry – and it often happened that a widow married one of her husband's slaves and made him her steward[42] – or else become a secondary wife to one of the dead man's brothers.[43]

The man was the unquestioned head of the family, and the atmosphere of the family was decidedly patriarchal. He was supposed to treat all his wives as equals, but a bad husband would sometimes make one of them, particularly the principal wife, undergo all kinds of miseries. Public opinion was very much against this. Moquiuixtli, the ruler of Tlatelolco, had married a sister of the Mexican emperor Axayacatl, the princess Chalchiuhnenetzin: but apart from the fact that her breath smelt, she 'was skinny, and she had no flesh, and because of this her husband never wished to see her. He took all the presents that her brother Axayacatl sent her and gave them to his secondary wives. The princess Chalchiuhnenetzin suffered much: she was made to sleep in a corner against the wall, by the *metlatl*, and she only had a coarse cloak to cover herself with, and that all in rags. And king Moquiuixtli would not sleep with her: he spent his nights only with his concubines, very lovely women, for the noble Chalchiuhnenetzin was but a meagre creature – she had no flesh, and her bosom was no more than bone. So Moquiuixtli did not love her, and he used her ill. All this came to be known and the emperor Axayacatl grew furious: it was for this reason that the war (between Mexico and Tlatelolco) began. And this is how it can be said that Tlatelolco perished because of the concubines.'[44]

Nevertheless, the Mexican woman must not be thought of as a kind of perpetual minor: although she lived in a society dominated by men she was by no means as subjugated as might be supposed at first. In former times women had held the supreme power, as at Tula, for example;[45] and it even appears that a woman, Ilancueitl,[46] was at the origin of the royal power in Mexico. At least in the beginning, the royal blood ran through the female side, and Ilancueitl brought the Toltec lineage of Colhuacán to Mexico, thus allowing the Aztec dynasty to lay claim to descent from the famous line of Quetzalcoatl.[47]

At a later period, there is the example of a plebeian of the humblest origin becoming the *tlatoani* of a province because of his marriage with a daughter of the emperor Itzcoatl.[48] There is no doubt that as time went on the power of the men grew greater, and that there was a continually-increasing tendency to shut the woman up between the four walls of the house. But she retained her own property, and she could do business, entrusting her goods to itinerant traders,[49] or exercise certain professions, such as those of priestess, midwife or healer, in which she enjoyed a high degree of independence. The profession of the *auianime*, whom the Spanish chroniclers tend to treat as whores although at the same time they state that 'they gave their bodies for nothing',[50] was not only recognised, but valued; they had their own place reserved for them, beside the young warriors whose companions they were, in the ceremonies of religion.[51]

Some customs betray a certain antagonism between the sexes: sometimes it was the boys and the young men who attacked the women in the street with pillows, occasionally getting more than they bargained for in return, and sometimes it was the girls who jeered at the uncouth young warriors and insulted them bitterly.

During the festivities of the month *Uey Tozoztli*, the girls went in procession, with their faces painted and their arms and legs decorated with feathers, carrying the consecrated ears of maize; and if a boy ventured to say anything to them, they would turn on him, shouting 'Really, here is a long-haired creature (that is, one who has not yet been in battle) that is talking. But what have you got to say? You had better go and do something so that you can have your hair cut, hairy. Or perhaps you are really only a woman like me?' Then the boys would try to put a good face on it by replying with an assumed coarseness, 'Go and cover your belly with mud. Go and drag yourself about in the dust.' But among themselves the discomfited young men would say 'The words of the women are piercing and cruel; they wound our hearts. Let us go and volunteer for the war. Perhaps then, my friends, we shall have a reward.'[52]

The old women who had outlived the time when they had
to be submissive to their husbands, or who had outlived the
husbands, had a great deal of independence; they were much
respected, and, like the old men, they were allowed to drink
their *octli* from time to time. In reading the texts one sees
them hurrying to help their daughters or their relations, or
devoutly attending the innumerable ceremonies in which
they had a part to play. They were matrons and they were
matchmakers, and they were always there when there was a
family feast, at which they would have their place at table
and the right to make long speeches. In a country in which
age in itself confers privileges, an old woman is among those
whose advice is asked for and listened to, even if it is only
by those of her immediate neighbourhood.

The Mexican woman, during her life as a wife and a
mother, or from about her twentieth year to her fiftieth, had
a great deal to do. Perhaps the kings' favourites could
cultivate poetry, but the ordinary Indian woman, with her
children, her cooking, her weaving and the countless duties
of a housewife, had little time to spare. In the country, she
also shared in the work on the land; and even in the towns
she looked after the poultry.

It is difficult to say whether there was very much adultery.
The extremely rigorous repression and the frequent references
to the execution of adulterers in literature seem to show
that the community was aware of a serious danger and that
it reacted violently against it, in something of the same
manner that it did against drunkenness. The punishment
was death for both. They were killed by having their heads
crushed by a stone: the women, however, were strangled
first.[53] Not even the highest dignitaries could escape this
punishment. But although the law was so severe, it insisted
that the crime should be thoroughly proved, and the
testimony of the husband alone counted for nothing:
impartial witnesses were necessary to confirm his evidence,
and the husband who killed his wife, even if he found her
in the very act, was also liable to the death-penalty.[54]

Perhaps the best known and the most dramatic example
of adultery in the history of ancient Mexico also comes from

the chronicles of the royal house of Texcoco. Among the secondary wives of king Nezaualpilli was a daughter of Axayacatl, the Aztec emperor. This princess, although she was little more than a child, 'was so vicious and so devilish that if she found herself alone in her apartments and surrounded by those who served her (elsewhere Ixtlilxochitl says that there were no fewer than two thousand of them) and who, because of the splendour of her name, respected her, she would indulge in a thousand extravagances. This reached such a point that if she saw a handsome and well-shaped young man whose form agreed with her tastes and inclinations, she would give secret orders that he should enjoy her charms. When she had satisfied her desires, she would have him killed and a statue made in his likeness. She would adorn this statue with gorgeous clothes and jewels of gold and precious stones, and she would have it put in the room in which she usually passed her time. There were enough of these statues to go almost round the walls. When the king went to see her and asked her what these statues were for, she replied that they were her gods. For his part, he believed her, knowing how religious the Mexicans were, and how deeply attached to their false gods.'

But something happened to betray the Aztec princess's secret. She was so imprudent as to give one of her lovers (he being still alive) a jewel that her husband had given her. Nezaualpilli, filled with suspicion, arrived one night at the young woman's apartments. 'The women and the servants told him that she was asleep, hoping that the king would go away, as he had done before. But distrusting them, he went into the bedroom to awake her. He found nothing there but a statue, stretched on the bed and crowned with a wig.' During this time the princess was making merry with three young men, of excellent family.

All four were condemned to death and executed, as well as a great number of her accomplices in adultery and assassination, in the presence of an immense crowd. These events contributed not a little towards the embittering of the relations between the house of Texcoco and the imperial family of Mexico, which, although it hid its resentment,

never forgave the allied king for the punishment that the
Aztec princess had suffered.[55]

There was little question of divorce in ancient Mexico.
Desertion of the conjugal domicile by either the husband
or the wife constituted grounds for the dissolution of the
marriage. The courts could authorise a man to repudiate
his wife if he proved that she was sterile or unconscionably
neglectful of her household duties. On her side, the wife
could complain against her husband and have judgment in
her favour if he were convicted of beating her, for example,
or of not maintaining her or of abandoning the children: in
this case the court gave her custody of the children, and the
conjugal property was equally divided between the two
former spouses. The divorced woman was free to marry
again whenever she chose.[56]

Marriage, whether it was calm or troubled, marked the
entry of the Mexican into adult society. 'From the time
that they (the young people) were married, they were
registered with the other households . . . and, although the
country was full of people, and indeed overflowed with
them, they were all taken into account.'[57] A married man
had a right to a piece of the land that belonged to his *calpulli*
and to the occasional distributions of victuals or clothes.
He was a fully-privileged citizen, and the reputation that he
had in his neighbourhood depended largely upon the
decency of his family life and the care with which he brought
up his children.

There is no doubt that the Mexicans, behind the stiff
formalism of their family relationships, loved their children
tenderly. *Nopiltze, nocuzque, noquetzale,* 'sweet son, my
jewel, my precious feather' – this is a father speaking to his
boy.[58] When a woman was pregnant the news was a matter
for great joy in both the families, and for festivities to which
the relations and the great men of the neighbourhood or the
village were invited.

After a banquet, and while the guests smoked their pipes,
an elder would speak in the name of the future father, and
addressing the important men he would say, 'Relations and
my lords, I would like to say a few boorish and clumsy

words, since you have all come together here, by the will of our god Yoalli Eecatl ('the night wind', Tezcatlipoca), who is in all places. It is he who has given you life up to this time, to you who are our shelter and our protection, you who are like the *pochotl*, which gives so much shade, and the *ahuehuetl*, which shelters the animals under its branches. In the same way you, my lords, you are the protectors and the preservers of the small and humble people who dwell in the mountains and upon the plains. You look after the poor soldiers and warlike men, who look upon you as their prop and their comfort. No doubt you have your anxieties and cares, and that we cause you pain and distress . . . Listen, my lords who are here, and all of you old men and old women with whitened heads: you must know that our god in his mercy has granted . . . (here the name of the pregnant woman) recently married, a precious stone, a splendid feather.'

The orator still had a long course to run, in which he would call dead forebears to memory, 'who are at rest in the caves, in the waters, in the underworld'. Then in succession would come a second orator in the names of the relatives; then one of the important guests, who would address himself particularly to the young woman, comparing her to a piece of jade and to a sapphire, and reminding her that the life that she carried within her came from the holy pair Ometecuhtli-Omeciuatl; then the young woman's father and mother, and lastly she herself, to thank those who had come and to ask whether she deserved the happiness of having a child. In the words that she was to say, in the conventional phrases, one detects that uncertain note, that anxiety in the face of what is to come, which sounds so often in the expression of the Aztec mind.[59]

A pregnant woman was under the protection of the goddesses of fertility and of health, of Teteoinnan, the mother of the gods, patroness of the midwives, who was also called Temazcalteci, 'the grandmother of the steambath', and of Ayopechtli or Ayopechcatl, the little feminine deity of childbed. We know the text of a prayer, a true magical formula, which was sung to invoke the last-named goddess.

'Down there, where Ayopechcatl lives, the jewel is born, a child has come into the world.

'Down there, where Ayopechcatl lives, the jewel is born, a child has come into the world. It is down there, in her own place, that the children are born.

'Come, come here, new-born child, come here.

'Come, come here, jewel-child, come here.'[60]

For a long time before the birth of the child, the young woman, at least in the better sort of families, received attentive care. A midwife was chosen for her, and the old relations went to engage her, with great ceremony, to look after the future mother. As soon as she had agreed, though not without first objecting that she was only an 'unfortunate, stupid, unintelligent old woman', the midwife went to her patient's house and lit the fire for a steam-bath. She and the young woman went into the *temazcalli*, taking great care that the bath was not too hot, and she palpated her client's belly to find out how the baby lay.

Then she gave her advice: the woman was to abstain from chewing *tzictli*, for fear that the baby's palate and gums should swell, which would prevent it from feeding; she was neither to let herself grow angry nor to be frightened, and the household was told to give her anything that she longed for. If she were to look at red objects, the child would be born askew. If she went out at night, she was to put a little ash in her blouse or her belt, otherwise she might be terrified by ghosts. If she were to look at the sky during an eclipse the child would be born with a hare-lip, unless the mother had taken the precaution of carrying an obsidian knife under her clothes, against the skin. It was also said that if the father, going out at night, were to see a phantom, the child would have a heart-disease.[61] In short, a whole network of prohibitions and traditional precepts surrounded the mother during the entire period before the birth, and even the father too, in order, as they thought, to protect the child.

The midwife alone had the management of the lying-in: she took charge of the household, prepared the food and the baths, and massaged the patient's belly. If the birth was delayed, the woman was given a draught made from *ciuapatli*[62] (*Montanoa tomentosa*), which, taken as an infusion, causes strong contractions: if this did not answer, then they turned to the last resort, a drink made of water in which a piece of the tail of a *tlaquatzin*, or opossum, had been mixed. This brew was thought to bring about an immediate and even violent delivery.[63]

If baths, massage and medicines had no effect, the midwife shut herself into a room with the patient. She invoked the goddesses, particularly Ciuacoatl and Quilaztli. If she saw that the child was dead within its mother, she took a flint knife and cut the foetus to pieces.[64]

It was clearly understood that a woman who died in childbirth was upon the same footing as a warrior who died in battle or as a sacrifice. 'After her death, her body was cleaned; her head and her hair were washed with soap and they dressed her in her best new clothes. And her husband carried her on his back to the place where she was to be buried. The dead woman's hair was left loose and untied. All the midwives and the old women gathered to go with the body; they carried shields and swords, and as they went they made the cries of warriors about to attack. The young men called *telpopochtin* (these were the inmates of the *telpochcalli*) came out to meet them and struggled to take the woman's body away from them . . .

'The dead woman was buried at sunset . . . in the courtyard of the temple dedicated to the goddesses called the heavenly women or *ciuapipiltin* (princesses) . . . and her husband and his friends guarded her four nights running to prevent anyone from stealing the body. The young warriors watched to see if they might steal it, for they considered it as something holy or divine; and if, in fighting with the midwives, they succeeded in getting it, then at once, and in front of these very women, they would cut off the middle finger of the left hand. And if they could steal the corpse by night, they would cut off this same finger and the hair, and keep them as relics. The reason why the warriors tried to take the finger and the hair of the dead woman was this: when they went to war they put this hair or this finger in their shields, and they said that because of it they would be brave and valiant . . . that the hair and the finger would give them strength and that they blinded the eyes of their enemies.

'It was said that the woman (dead in childbed) did not go to the underworld but into the palace of the sun, and that the sun took her with him because of her courage . . . The women who are killed in war or who die at their first lying-in, are called *mociuaquetzque* (valiant women), and they are numbered among those who die in battle. They all go to the sun, and they live in the western part of the heavens; and that is why the old people called the occident *ciuatlampa* (the women's side) . . . The women welcomed the sun at the zenith and went down with him as far as the west, carrying him on a litter made of *quetzal*-plumes. They marched before him, shouting with joy, fighting, making much of him. They left him in the place where the sun goes down, and there those of the lower world came to receive him.'[65]

The destiny of the 'valiant woman' in the hereafter was therefore exactly the equivalent, the counterpart, of that of the warriors who died in battle or upon the sacrificial stone. The warriors accompanied the sun from its rising to its height, and the women from the zenith to its setting. The women had become goddesses, and therefore they were called the *ciuateteo* 'the divine women'. Their sufferings and their death earned them apotheosis. They were the formidable deities of the twilight, and on certain nights they appeared at the crossroads and struck those that met them with paralysis.[66] They were identified both with the occidental goddesses of Tamoanchan, the western paradise, and with the monsters of the end of the world.

SICKNESS AND OLD AGE

The ancient Mexicans' ideas on sickness and medicine and their practices were an inextricable mixture of religion, magic and science. There was religion, for certain deities were held either to send illnesses or to heal them; there was magic, for generally the illness was attributed to the black magic of some sorcerer, and it was by magic that the remedy was sought; and there was science, for Aztec medicine had in some respects a curiously modern appearance, with its knowledge of the properties of plants and minerals and the use of bleeding and of baths. There is no doubt, however, that of these three factors, the first two were by far the most important; and of these two, magic predominated over religion. The physician (*ticitl*), either man or woman, was above all a sorcerer, but a benign sorcerer, accepted and approved by the community; whereas the caster of spells, the black magician, was condemned.

Among the Nahua Indians of the present day in the Sierra de Orizaba, sickness is attributed to four possible causes: the introduction of a foreign body into the person of the sufferer by black magic; injuries or death inflicted upon the sufferer's totem, his animal double or *naualli*, by an enemy or a malignant wizard; the loss of the *tonalli*, a term which is used for the soul and the vital breath, as well as the sign under which the patient was born and thus his fate or destiny; and lastly the 'airs' – in Spanish *aires* and in Nahuatl *ehecatl cocoliztle*, 'airs of sickness' – the invisible and baleful influences that float about mankind, particularly at night.[67]

These ideas descend directly from those which were current in the days before the Spaniards came. The belief in the introduction of a foreign body by magic to cause illness was very widely spread, and the healing-women were called *tetlacuicuilique*, 'they who draw out stones (from the body)', *tetlanocuilanque*, 'those who draw out worms from the teeth', and *teixocuilanque*, 'those who draw out worms from the eyes.'[68]

Although the Nahuatl expression in its present sense is probably a recent usage, formerly the term *tonalli* embraced the genius peculiar to each person, his good fortune and his 'star', in the sense of his predestination.[69] As to the malignant 'airs', they were formerly thought to originate with Tlaloc and the *Tlaloque*, the mountain gods. 'They (the Indians) believed that certain illnesses, which seem to be those which are caused by the cold, came from the mountains, or that these mountains had the power of healing them. Those who had these diseases made a vow to offer a feast or a sacrifice to some particular mountain in their neighbourhood or for which they felt a special devotion. Those who were in danger of death by drowning in the rivers or the sea made the same kind of vow. The diseases for which these vows were made were gout in the hands or the feet, or any other part of the body, palsy in a limb or the whole body, swelling of the neck or of some other part of the body, the withering of a limb or general stiffness . . . Those who were afflicted with these illnesses vowed to make images of the god of the wind, of the goddesses of the water and of the god of the rain.'[70]

Skin diseases, ulcers, leprosy and dropsy were also attributed to Tlaloc.[71] Convulsions and infantile paralysis were thought to come from those *ciuapipiltin* who were mentioned earlier. 'These goddesses go about in the air together, and when they choose they appear to those who live upon the earth, and they strike boys and girls with sickness by paralysing them and by getting into human bodies.'[72] The present belief in the 'airs' is only the same tradition, in an impersonal form.

Other deities, Tlazolteotl and her companions, who presided over carnal love, could also cause disease. It was believed that the man or woman who indulged in forbidden love spread about them, like a lasting evil spell, that which was called *tlazolmiquiztli*, 'the death (caused by) lust', and that because of this their children and relatives were afflicted with melancholy and consumption. It was like an uncleanliness that was both physical and moral; and one could only be cured by the steam-bath, the rite of purification, and by calling upon the *tlazolteteo*, the goddesses of love and desire.[73]

The god of youth, music and flowers, Xochipilli, who was also called Macuilxochitl, punished those who did not obey prohibitions – men and woman who lay together during fasts, for example – by sending them venereal diseases, piles and skin diseases. Xipe Totec was thought to be responsible for eye-diseases.[74]

If some gods caused sickness, others, or the same, could heal. The *Tlaloque* and Xochipilli might answer prayers and sacrifices and take away the maladies that they had sent. The fire-god helped women in labour,[75] as did the goddess Ciuacoatl also, who looked after those who took steam-baths. Another goddess, Tzapotlatenan, cured ulcers or eruptions on the scalp, chaps and hoarseness; and a little black-faced god, Ixtlilton, healed children. 'In his temple there were closed pots that held what was called his black water (*ixtlilauh*). When a child fell sick, it was taken to the temple of Ixtlilton; a jar was opened; the child was made to drink some of the black water, and it was cured.'[76]

When an Indian became unwell, the first thing to do was to find the reason for his illness, and the diagnosis was made by divination, not by any observation of his symptoms. To do this, the physician threw maize upon a piece of cloth or into a vase full of water, and he drew his conclusions from the manner in which the grains fell, in groups or separately, or how they floated or sank to the bottom.

To know whether a sick child had lost its *tonalli*, the healing-woman held it over a vessel filled with water and looked into it as into a mirror while she called upon the water-goddess. '*Tlacuel, tla xihuallauh, nonan chalchiuhe, chalchiuhtli ycue, chalchiuhtli ihuipil, xoxouhqui ycue, xoxouhqui ihuipil, iztaccihuatl.* (Listen, come, you my mother, stone of jade, you who have a jade skirt, you who have a jade blouse, green skirt, green blouse, white woman.)' If the child's face seemed darkened in the water-mirror, as if it were covered with a shadow, it meant that its *tonalli* had been stolen.[77]

In other cases the *ticitl* turned to the holy plant called *ololiuhqui*,[78] whose seed produced a kind of intoxication and visions. Sometimes *peyotl* or tobacco was used, being taken either by the doctor or the patient, or by a third person. The hallucinations that these plants induced were thought to bring revelations as to the cause of the disease, that is to say, as to the magic which caused it and the identity of the sorcerer. A man's denunciation by these oracles was never questioned; and from this cause arose much bitterness and many undying hatreds between the families of the sick people and the alleged sorcerers.[79]

Then there were other forms of diagnostic magic in use – the divination by strings, which was the speciality of the *mecatlapouhque* (fortune-tellers by the strings),[80] and the 'measurement of the arm', a rite in which the healer, having rubbed his hands with tobacco, 'measured' the left arm of the patient with the palm of his right hand.[81]

Once the nature and the cause of the malady had been decided, the treatment began. If it were an illness sent by a god, they tried to appease him with offerings. In other cases, the treatment including magical operations to a greater or a less degree – invocations, insufflations, laying on of hands, 'drawing out' of stones, worms, or pieces of paper that were supposed to have been put into the patient's body[82] – and medical treatment based upon positive knowledge – bleeding, baths, purges, dressings, plasters and the giving of extracts or infusions of plants.

Tobacco and vegetable incense (*copalli*) played a great part in all these practices. The tobacco was spoken to, as it was crushed or ground; and it was called 'he who has been struck nine times'. The healer's fingers were termed 'the five *tonalli*',[83] and generally speaking the language used in these magic formulae was very figurative and obscure. For example, this was the way in which a headache was treated: the *ticitl* firmly massaged the patient's head and said, 'You, the five *tonalli* who all look in the same direction, and you, the goddesses Quato and Caxoch, who is the powerful and venerable being who is destroying our *maceualli*? It is I who speak, I the priest, I the lord of spells. We will find him at the edge of the sacred water (the sea), and we will throw him into the sacred water'. Saying these words he pressed the patient's temples between his hands and blew on his head. Then he invoked the water in these terms, 'Listen to me, mother, you who have a jade skirt. Come here and give back his life to this *maceualli*, our god's servant'. As he spoke, he spread water over the patient's face and head. If this treatment did not answer, and if the head swelled, the healer applied tobacco mixed with a root called *chalalatli*, at the same time making this incantation: 'I the priest, I the lord of spells, (I ask) where is he who is destroying this bewitched head. Come, you who have been struck nine times and crushed nine times (tobacco), and we will cure this bewitched head with the red medicine (the root *chalalatli*). I call the cold wind that he may cure this bewitched head. Oh wind, I say to you, do you bring the cure for this bewitched head?'[84]

When the sickness was in a man's chest, they gave him a maize porridge mixed with the bark of *quanenepilli* (passion-flower),[85] and laid hands on him, saying, 'Come, you the five *tonalli*. I the priest, I the lord of spells, I seek the green pain, the tawny pain. Where is it hidden? Enchanted medicine, I say to you, I the lord of spells, that I wish to heal this sick flesh. So you must go into the seven caves (the lungs). Do not touch the yellow heart, enchanted medicine: I expel from this place the green pain, the tawny pain. Come, you the nine winds, expel the green pain, the tawny pain.'[86]

At the same time as these invocations and magic gestures, the Mexican physicians understood the use of treatment founded upon a certain knowledge of the human body – a knowledge that was no doubt quite widely spread in a country with such frequent human sacrifices – and of the properties of plants and minerals. They reduced fractures and they splinted broken limbs.[87] They were clever at bleeding patients with obsidian lancets.[88] They put softening plasters upon abscesses and finely-ground obsidian upon wounds – 'Ground like flour, this stone spread on recent wounds and sores, heals them very quickly.'[89]

Their pharmacopœia included certain minerals, the flesh of certain animals, and above all a very great number of plants. The good Father Sahagún goes so far as to warrant the virtues of some stones – 'There are also,' he writes, 'certain stones called *eztetl*, blood-stones, which have the power of stopping bleeding from the nose. I have tried the virtue of this stone myself, for I have a piece of it the size of a fist or a little less, and in that year of 1576, during the epidemic, I revived many people who were losing their

blood and their lives through their nostrils. It was enough
to take it in one's hand and to hold it for some moments,
to stop the bleeding, and the patients were cured of this
disease which killed and still does kill so many in New
Spain. And there are many witnesses of these facts in this
town of Santiago Tlatelolco.'[90]

The same historian reports that a certain stone called
quiauhteocuitlatl ('gold of rain') 'is good for those who are
terrified by a thunder-clap . . . and also for those who have
an inward heat (fever). This stone is found in the neighbourhood of Jalapa, Itztepec and Tlatlauhquitepec, and the
natives of these parts say that when it begins to thunder and
rain in the mountains, these stones fall from the clouds,
plunge into the earth, and so grow year by year; and the
Indians look for them . . . they dig the ground and bring
out these stones.'[91]

It is certain that fantastic properties were attributed to
stones, to animals (the opossum's tail that has already been
mentioned, for example) and to plants: but it is equally
certain that the Indians had been able to amass a considerable
amount of positive experimental knowledge of the plants
of their country, in the course of time. In this respect, if
their medicine is compared with that which raged in western
Europe at the same period, it may be asked whether that
of the Aztecs were not the more scientific: apart from the
magical trappings that the Mexican *ticitl* assumed, there
was without any doubt more true science in their usage of
medicinal plants than in the prescriptions of the European
Diafoirus of that time.

The conquistadores were certainly much impressed by the
efficacy of some of the native medicines. In 1570 Philip II
of Spain sent his doctor, Francisco Hernández, to Mexico;
and he, in seven years of strenuous labour, spending the
vast sum (for that age) of sixty thousand ducats, brought
together a considerable body of information upon the
medicinal plants of the country, and collected a magnificent
herbal. Unfortunately, he died before he could publish his
work, and part of his manuscripts was destroyed in the
burning of the Escurial in 1671: nevertheless, large extracts

were published in Mexico and Italy, and they give an idea of the extraordinary wealth of the Mexican materia medica in the sixteenth century: Hernández enumerated no less than some twelve hundred plants used in medicinal treatment.[92]

Sahagún devotes much of his eleventh book to herbs and healing plants, and modern research has shown that in many cases the Aztec physicians had very accurately, though empirically, distinguished the properties of the plants which they used as purges, emetics, diuretics, sedatives, febrifuges, etc.

Among others may be mentioned Peruvian balm, jalap, sarsaparilla, *iztacpatli* (*psoralea pentaphylla L.*), which was successfully used against fever, *chichiquauitl* (*garrya laurifolia Hartw.*) effective against dysentery, *iztacoanenepilli*, a diuretic, *nixtamalaxochitl*, a counter-irritant, valerian, which they used as an anti-spasmodic, and *matlalitztic* (*commelina pallida*) an antihaemorrhagic; but the field is still largely unexplored, and there is a great deal that remains to be done in the way of identifying the countless species mentioned in the texts and verifying their curative properties.[93]

The Mexican who managed to escape death from war and from illness (and from doctors) and who reached a sufficiently advanced age to be counted among the *ueuetque*, the elders who played so important a part in family and political life, could look forward to a peaceable and honoured existence in his last years.

If he had served the state as a soldier or as an official, he would be a pensioner, and as such he would receive his lodging and his maintenance.[94] Even if he were only a simple *maceualli* he would take his place in the local council. If he could speak at all he could indulge himself in magniloquent harangues upon all those occasions (and they were many) when custom and etiquette required them. Respected by all, he would admonish, advise and warn. He could at last allow himself, at banquets and family meals, to indulge fearlessly in *octli*, even to the point of inebriation, with the men and women of his own generation.

Death approached. In preparing themselves for it, those

who had committed some grave crime, some hidden sin such as adultery, during their lives, thought of confession. The effect of confession was not only the absolution of the sinner: it also removed him from the reach of the law. But confession could happen only once in a lifetime, and so most people never called for a confessor until as late as possible.

Two deities presided over confession – Tezcatlipoca, because he saw everything, being invisible and omnipresent, and Tlazolteotl, the goddess of lechery and unlawful love, who was also called Tlaelquani, 'she who eats filth (sin)' and thus 'she who gives absolution'. 'She was called Tlaelquani, because the penitent confessed to her and set out all his sins before her. He told her and he spread out before her eyes all his unclean doings, however grave and ugly, without hiding anything, even out of shame. When a man confessed before her, everything was shown.'

It was Tlazolteotl who inspired the most vicious desires, 'and, in the same way, it was she who forgave them. She took away the defilement; she cleaned, she washed . . . and thus she forgave.'

The penitent told a *tlapouhqui*, skilled in the reading and the interpretation of the sacred books, of his wish to confess, and the priest, consulting his books, fixed upon an auspicious date. If the penitent were a man of importance, the confession would take place at his house: if not, he would attend the priest upon the given day. The two of them sat on new mats, beside a fire. The *tlapouhqui* threw incense into the flames, and while the aromatic smoke spread about the room, he called upon the gods. 'Mother of the gods, father of the gods, oh you old god (the fire), behold a poor man who has come. He has come weeping, sad and anxious. Perhaps he has sinned. Perhaps, self-deluded, he has lived unchastely. He comes with a heavy heart, full of sorrow. Lord, our master, you who are near and who are far, make his trouble cease, pacify his heart.'

Then, addressing the penitent, he exhorted him to confess sincerely, to open all his secrets, not to be restrained by shame. The penitent swore that he would tell the whole truth: he touched the earth with a finger which he then put to his lips, and threw incense into the fire. He was thus bound by an oath to the earth and to the fire (or the sun), that is to say, to the supreme duality. Then he told his life at length, and recounted all his sins.

When he had finished, the priest set him a penance that would vary in severity: short or lengthy fasts, scarification of the tongue – it might be pierced through and have as many as eight hundred thorns or straws pushed through the wound – sacrifices to Tlazolteotl, and various austerities. Once the penance was done the man could 'no longer be punished upon this earth'. The priest was bound to the most absolute secrecy, 'for that which he had heard was not for him, but had been said, secretly, for the deity'.[95]

DEATH AND THE HEREAFTER

Two different sets of funerary rites were in use among the Aztecs: cremation and burial.

All those who died of drowning were buried, as well as those who had been killed by lightning and those who had died of leprosy, gout or dropsy – in short, all who had been marked out and withdrawn from this world by the gods of the water and of the rain.[96] The body of a drowned man, in particular, was regarded with the utmost religious awe, for it was believed that when an Indian was drowned in the lake he had been dragged to the bottom by the *auitzotl*, a fabulous creature. When the body came to the surface again, showing no wound, but with its eyes, nails and teeth gone – torn out by the *auitzotl* – nobody dared touch it. They went to tell the priests.

'It was said that the divine *Tlaloque* had sent the drowned man's soul to the earthly paradise, and because of this the body was carried with great respect upon a litter to be buried in one of the oratories that are called *ayauhcalco* (little temples of the water-gods, on the shore of the lake): the litter was decorated with reeds, and they played on the flute before the body.'[97]

And then, as we have seen, the women who died in labour and who were deified, were buried in the court of the temple of the *ciuapipiltin*. All other bodies were cremated. In the course of time all the civilised tribes of Mexico have used either the one form or the other: we need mention no more than the funerary chambers of the Mayas of Palenque and those of the Zapotecs and the Mixtecs of Monte Albán, and the famous pyre of Quetzalcoatl – for the tradition of the Toltecs was that of cremation.[98] The nomadic peoples of the north buried their dead, but adopted the Toltec custom: at least the chief families did so. King Ixtlilxochitl of Texcoco was the first ruler of that dynasty whose body was burnt 'according to the rites and ceremonies of the Toltecs'.[99] It is probable that the old settled nations of the plateau practised burial; and this would explain why the dead who had been marked out by Tlaloc and his fellows should have had this form of interment reserved for them.

In Aztec times the two kinds of ceremony existed side by side, and the family's choice was determined only by the manner of the death. Important people were solemnly buried in vaulted underground chambers.[100] The anonymous conquistador tells how he himself took part in the opening of a tomb in which they found a dead man seated upon a chair, with his shield, his sword and his jewels about him: the tomb contained gold to the value of three thousand *castellanos*.[101] Father Francesco di Bologna also describes an 'underground chapel' in which the body was seated upon an *icpalli*, splendidly dressed and surrounded by weapons and gems.[102]

When the dead man had been a very high dignitary or a ruler, some of his wives and servants were killed, 'those who, of their own free-will, wished to die with him';[103] and they were buried or cremated, as the case might be, so that they should be able to follow him in the hereafter.

When the cremation of a body was intended, it was dressed in its best clothes and fastened in a squatting position, with the knees drawn up to the chin; then the whole was wrapped in several layers of cloth kept in place by bands, so as to form a kind of funerary bundle or mummy. Dead kings are always shown like this in historical records.

This mummy was then carefully decorated with paper and feather ornaments, and a mask of carved stone or mosaic was fixed in the place of the face.[104] Rulers were adorned, like Uitzilopochtli, with royal and sacred ornaments, or with clothes bearing the great god's symbols.[105] Then, to the sound of the funeral chants, *miccacuicatl*, the corpse, watched over by the elders, was burnt upon a pyre. When the cremation was over, the ashes and the bones were collected and put into a jar, together with a piece of jade, the symbol of life; and this jar was buried in the house. The ashes of the emperors were preserved in the temple of Uitzilopochtli.

Some of the dead, as we have seen, had been chosen by the gods for a life beyond death: for the 'companions of the eagle' and for the 'valiant women' there was to be joy of the sun's palaces, full of light and sound; and for those beloved of Tlaloc an endless peaceful happiness, careless and idle, in the warm gardens of the east. But most of the dead were held to go under the earth, into the dark world of Mictlan. To help the dead man in the bitter trials that he would have to overcome, they gave him a companion, a dog which they killed and burnt together with him. There were also offerings burnt for him eighty days after the funeral, and again at the end of a year and again after two, three and four years. It was thought that when the four years had passed, the dead man would have arrived at the end of his journey among the shadows; for then he would have reached the 'ninth hell', the last region of Mictlan, the place of his eternal rest.[106]

CHAPTER SIX

WAR

War. The meaning of war in religious myth and its legal justification: casus belli: *chivalry in the negotiations leading to the declaration of war: conduct of war: negotiations for peace: why the Mexicans were overcome by the Spanish invaders.*

War (*yaoyotl*) was so important a preoccupation with the Aztecs and it held so great a place in the structure of their society and the life of their state that it seems necessary to treat it separately.

We have already seen the general idea of the nature of war and the religious and mythical connotations that it possessed. Sacred war was a cosmic duty: it was symbolised by the double glyph *atl-tlachinolli* ('water' – that is, 'blood' – and 'conflagration') which, like an obsession, continually recurs in all the bas-reliefs of the *teocalli* of Sacred War.[1] Men, by waging war, complied with what had been the will of the gods since the beginning of the world.

According to the legend, the Four Hundred Cloud-Serpents (*Centzon Mimixcoa*, the northern stars), which had been created by the higher gods to give food and drink to the sun, abandoned their duty. 'They took a jaguar and did not give it to the sun. They decked themselves with feathers; they went to bed with their feather-ornaments on; they slept with women and they became drunk with the wine of *tziuactli*.' So the sun spoke to the men, who were born after the *Mimixcoa*, and said to them, ' "My sons, you must now destroy the Four Hundred Cloud-Serpents, for they do not give anything either to our father or to our mother," . . . and it was thus that war began.'[2]

But as well as its mythico-religious aspect, war had another side: it was the imperialistic cities' means of conquest, and as such, it acquired a justificatory legal basis. The official version of the three allied cities, Mexico, Texcoco and Tlacopan, was founded upon two pseudo-historical claims: it was asserted that the three dynasties had succeeded the Toltecs, who had ruled over all central Mexico, by right; and at the same time that, thanks to the house of Texcoco, the descendants of the Chichimec conquerors, they had a kind of suzerainty over the whole country. 'The three rulers thought of themselves as lords and masters over all the others, basing themselves upon the right that they claimed to have over the whole country, which had belonged to the Toltecs, whose heirs and successors they were, and upon the fresh conquest of the land by the great Chichimec, Xolotl, their ancestor.'[3] From this point of view, any city that was independent and intended to stay independent, was a rebel.

In practice, a *casus belli* was needed to attack a city or a province. The most usual arose from attacks on the travelling *pochteca*, or traders. If they were robbed, pillaged and even perhaps massacred, then the military forces of the empire at once prepared to avenge them. The documents make it clear that a refusal to trade or the breaking-off of commercial relations was considered to be tantamount to a declaration of war. Ixtlilxochitl justifies the undertakings of the central cities by stating as the motive that the others 'had not agreed to trade or communicate with our people'.[4]

The Mexicans set out for the conquest of the isthmus of Tehuantepec after the inhabitants of several towns in that region had killed nearly all the members of a caravan of merchants.[5] The cause of the war between Mexico and the neighbouring city of Coyoacán was the rupture of the traditional trading relations. 'The Mexican women set off, carrying fish, frogs and ducks . . . to sell them at Coyoacán. Guards who had been placed on the roads thither took away everything that they had brought. They went back to Tenochtitlan weeping and moaning. . .' After this insult the Mexican women no longer went to the market at Coyoacán; and the chief of that city, seeing this, addressed

his dignitaries and said to them, 'Brothers, you see that the
Mexican women do not come to the market any more: this
is no doubt because of the insults that we have offered them.
Let us then get our weapons ready, our shields and our
swords . . . for soon we shall see the Mexicans coming, led
by the banner of the eagle and the tiger.'[6]

There were other accepted *casus belli*. A ruler, having
called his council to get it to take the final decision, was
required to show the reasons that appeared to him to
justify an expedition. 'If it was because merchants had
been killed, the council would answer that it was a good
reason and a just cause, meaning thereby that trade and
business are a natural right, like hospitality and welcome
for travellers, and that it was lawful to make war against
those who did not observe this rule. If it was a messenger
who had been killed, or if the ruler gave some other minor
reason, the council said to him, as many as three times,
"Why do you want to make war?" meaning thereby that that
was not a just nor a sufficient cause. But if the ruler called
them together several times, the council yielded in the end.'[7]

To judge by the Mexican chronicles, some wars broke out
solely for political reasons, that is, because one city dis-
trusted the undertakings of another and decided to attack
by way of defence. The people of Atzcapotzalco declared
war against Tenochtitlan the day after the election of
Itzcoatl, 'because of the hatred of the Mexicans that filled their
hearts'; and fearing no doubt that the new sovereign would
lead his tribe in a career of conquest, they determined to
crush the menace in its beginnings and to exterminate the
Mexicans.[8]

Fifty years later, the emperor Axayacatl decided to launch
an attack upon Tlatelolco, Mexico's twin city; for he was
persuaded that its ruler was trying to ally himself secretly
with the neighbouring cities in order to make war on
Tenochtitlan at the first opportunity. When there was a
high degree of tension and distrust between cities, the most
trivial incident could set off the conflict: in fact, it was
the scolding and the insults of the market-women of
Tlatelolco that began the war between these two.[9]

Generally speaking, however, the war, the fighting itself, only started after long and painful negotiations. When Atzcapotzalco, having decided to wipe out the Aztecs, began hostilities by pushing their forward posts to the outskirts of the city, several Mexican embassies were still able to cross the lines, with the enemy's permission, to try to negotiate peace.

These conversations broke down before the determination of the men of Atzcapotzalco to be done with this dangerous tribe; but up to the end the coming and going of the envoys and their interviews with the enemy sovereign were surrounded with the traditional ceremony. When at least it appeared that no possibility of peace remained, the *atempanecatl* Tlacaeleltzin[10] was charged with a last embassy to the ruler of Atzcapotzalco. He brought him the gifts of a cloak, a feather crown and some arrows. The enemy king thanked him and begged him carry his acknowledgments to Itzcoatl; then he gave him a shield, a sword and a splendid warrior's suit, 'desiring him to do his best to return to his place safe and sound.'[11] All this passed according to the rules of a courteous and chivalrous ceremonial, which required that enemies who were about to engage should treat one another with all the marks of esteem.

At the time when the alliance of the three cities was at the height of its power, it scrupulously observed complex rules before entering into a war. The idea that underlay their approach was that the city which was intended to be incorporated into the empire really already belonged to it by a certain kind of right – this was the official theory mentioned earlier on – and if the city accepted this, if it agreed without a struggle, then it was not even required to pay tribute – a voluntary 'gift' would be enough, and the Mexican state would not even send an official to collect it. Everything would be based upon a friendly agreement.[12]

Each of the three imperial cities had its own ambassadors, who played their successive parts in the proceedings which were intended to make the province in question submit without a war.

First the ambassadors of Tenochtitlan, the *quauhquauhnochtzin*,[13] presented themselves before the authorities of the place. They spoke in particular to the elders, dwelling upon the miseries that arise from war. Would it not be far more simple, they asked, if your sovereign were to accept 'the friendship and the protection of the empire'? All that was required was that the lord should give his word 'never to be an enemy to the empire, and to let the traders and their people come and go, buy and sell'.

The ambassadors also asked that the ruler should admit an image of Uitzilopochtli into his temple upon a footing of equality with that of the greatest local god,[14] and send a present to Mexico in the shape of gold, gems, feathers and cloaks. Before they withdrew, they gave the people with whom they had been speaking a certain number of shields and swords, 'so that it might never be said that they had been defeated by treachery'. They then left the town and went to camp at some place on the road, leaving the people of the province twenty days (one native month) to reach a decision.[15]

If there were no decision at the end of this time, or if the city would not agree, the ambassadors of Texcoco, the *achcacauhtzin*,[16] arrived. They gave the lord of the place and his dignitaries a solemn warning – 'If, after a fresh interval of twenty days, they did not submit, the lord would be punished with death, in conformity with the law that laid down that his head should be broken with a mace, unless he were killed in battle or taken prisoner and sacrificed to the gods. In the same way the other knights of his household and his court would be punished according to the wishes of the three heads of the empire. When this warning had been given to the lord and all the nobles of his province, if they submitted within twenty days, they would be made to give a yearly present to the three sovereigns, but not to a very great amount; and they were all admitted to the grace and friendship of the three sovereigns. If the (local) lord refused, then at once the ambassadors anointed his right arm and his head with a certain liquid that should allow him to withstand the furious attack of the army of the empire. They set a tuft of feathers, the *tecpillotl* ("sign of nobility"), fixed by a band of red leather, upon his head, and gave him a present of many shields, swords and other weapons.' After this they went to join the first ambassadors to wait until the end of the second respite.

If this new period of twenty days elapsed and the 'rebellious' city still would not submit, then a third embassy, sent this time by the king of Tlacopan, came to give a last warning. These envoys addressed the warriors of the city particularly, 'since it was they who would have to bear the brunt of the war'. They gave them a third and last respite, and stated that if they were to persist in their refusal, the imperial armies would devastate their province, that the prisoners would be carried off as slaves and the city reduced to the condition of a dependency. Before withdrawing they gave swords and shields to the officers and men, and then they joined the two earlier embassies.

When the last period of twenty days had expired, the city and the empire were *ipso facto* in a state of war. Yet even then they waited, if it were possible, for the augurs to point out a favourable date for the opening of the campaign – one of the thirteen signs beginning with *ce itzcuintli*, 'one – dog', for example, the series consecrated to the god of the fire and the sun.[17]

The Mexicans, then, knowingly deprived themselves of the advantage of surprise. Not only did they leave their opponents all the time necessary to prepare their defence, but they even supplied them with arms, even if it were no more than a symbolic quantity of them. This whole behaviour, these embassies, speeches and gifts very clearly demonstrate the chivalrous ideal of the warrior in American antiquity.

It should also be recognised that underlying this there was the idea that war was truly a divine judgment, that in the long run it was the gods who decided the outcome, and that this decision should have its full value without being perverted in the very beginning, which would be the case if the struggle were too unequal or if the enemy were taken by surprise so that he could not fight.

At the same time, with that mixture of idealism and rude

common sense which is so often found among the Indians, they had no hesitation in using all the ruses of war. Before ever hostilities began they sent secret agents into the enemy territory; these men, who were called *quimichtin* (literally 'mice'), wore the clothes and the head-dress of the country and spoke its language. Disguised traders were also sent on these missions, and they returned to the provinces that they had formerly travelled through as itinerant merchants.[18]

These were dangerous missions, for the people of the cities were on their guard. In a country made up of little separate divisions in which everybody was known by his neighbours and in which costume, language and customs differed from one place to another, it was difficult to pass unnoticed; and the detected spy was put to death at once, together with his accomplices.[19] But if, on the other hand, the spy came safely home and gave an exact account 'of the peculiarities and the weaknesses of the place and of the negligence or the vigilance of the people' he was given lands as a reward.

Ruses of war were also much used in battle. Bodies of troops would pretend to flee in order to draw the enemy into an ambush: by night, warriors would dig trenches that they covered with foliage or straw and in which they would hide, only coming out when the hoodwinked enemy was unprepared to meet their attack[20] – the emperor Axayacatl won the battle of Cuapanoayan by just such a stratagem, and conquered the valley of Toluca.[21]

What would now be called the engineers were responsible for other kinds of operation: in 1511 the Aztecs took the fortified town of Icpatepec on the top of a precipitous mountain by climbing the cliffs with ladders that were made on the spot.[22] Villages on the lake islands were attacked by raft-borne commandoes; in the *Codex Nuttall* there is a picture of such an attack by three warriors standing in boats that almost sink under their weight, while beneath them swim fishes, crocodiles and serpents.[23]

The basic armament of the Mexican warrior was made up of the round shield, the *chimalli*, made of wood or reeds, and covered with feathers and mosaic or metal ornaments, and the wooden sword, the *macquauitl*, whose cutting-edges of obsidian could inflict terrible wounds. As missile weapons they had the bow, *tlauitolli*, and above all the spear-thrower, *atlatl*, with which they propelled darts (*mitl*) or javelins (*tlacochtli*).

Some nations, such as the Matlaltzinca of the valley of Toluca, used the sling; and the half-savage Chinantecs of the mountains of Oaxaca had long, stone-tipped lances. The Aztec warriors wore a kind of tunic stuffed with cotton, the *ichcahuipilli*, by way of armour, and helmets, more decorative than functional, made of wood, feathers or paper, loaded with ornaments and plumes. Each chief could be distinguished in the turmoil of battle by a flag or an emblem: these precious and fragile constructions of reeds and feathers, gems and gold, were fixed to their shoulders; and each had its own particular name. Only those whose rank and exploits entitled them to it might use one of these ensigns.[24]

When a set battle was on the point of beginning, the warriors uttered deafening cries, increased by the dismal howling of conchs and the piercing noise of bone whistles.[25] These instruments not only raised the courage of the troops, but also served as signals: some chiefs hung a little drum about their necks and struck it to give their orders.[26] The archers and the javelin-throwers first discharged their weapons and then the warriors rushed forward with sword and shield, using much the same tactics as the Romans did, with their *pilum* and sword. But when the hand-to-hand fighting began the battle took on an aspect completely unlike anything known in our ancient world; for here it was not so much a matter of killing the enemy as of capturing him for sacrifice. Specialists with ropes followed the fighting-men in order to bind those who had been over-thrown before they could recover consciousness.[27] The battle spread out into a great number of separate duels in which each tried less to kill his opponent than to gain possession of his person.

While the end and aim of each war was to capture an enemy, or several enemies, the general intention of operations was clearly to bring about the enemy's defeat. There was, however, a conventional notion of what constituted defeat: a city was beaten, and acknowledged itself to be beaten, when the attacking force succeeded in reaching the temple and burning the sanctuary of the tribal god. Thus the symbol for conquest in the native manuscripts is generally a blazing temple with an arrow sticking into it.[28]

The taking of the temple was the defeat of the local god and the victory of Uitzilopochtli: from that moment on, the gods had spoken, and all further resistance was useless. The defeat had the nature of a symbol, and it reflected a decision taken upon a more than human level – taken, indeed, by the gods. Mexican war, therefore, had no resemblance to the total wars which our civilisation has brought to such a fatal pitch of efficiency. The Aztecs' intention was not to force the enemy to yield by ruining the country or massacring the population, but to make manifest the will of Uitzilopochtli. As soon as his will had become obvious to everybody the war had no further object. Those who had presumed to resist the empire – that is, to resist the empire's god – had no possibility other than acknowledging their mistake and trying to obtain the least unfavourable conditions that they could.

For war, which began with talks, ended in negotiations. On the very field of battle, in the streets of the invaded city, while flames destroyed the sanctuary, an enemy delegation approached the Mexicans. The fighting stopped, and in this temporary armistice, this precarious truce, an astonishing bargaining began. In effect, the defeated said, 'We were wrong. We acknowledge our error. Spare us. We beg to be admitted to the protection of your gods and the emperor. Here is what we offer –' and the envoys would give the list of the victuals, merchandise, jewels and services that they proposed as tribute.

Generally the victors replied that these were not enough. 'No. You must expect no mercy. . . As well as this you must send us men every ten days to serve by turns in our palaces. . .' They bargained. The defeated would yield a little ground, literally and figuratively. 'We will give up our territory as far as Techco,' said the beaten Chalcas. At the end, the Aztecs said, 'Consider what you are pledging yourselves to very thoroughly. Do not come to us one day and say that you never made any such promises.'[29] In short, it was a question of a contract agreed to by both victors and vanquished, and which bound the one equally with the other.

The idea that underlay this negotiation was that the winner, as the favourite of the gods and their instrument, had all possible rights: if he wished, he could annihilate the conquered city, carry off all the inhabitants or massacre them, and pull down its sanctuary. But he renounced his total power for a consideration: this consideration, or compensation, was the tribute, the ransom, as it were, with which the vanquished bought the right to live. The Mexicans insisted that the city should acknowledge the supremacy of Uitzilopochtli and thus that of Tenochtitlan, that it should have no independent foreign policy, and that it should pay taxes. In exchange, it kept its institutions, its rites, its customs and its language. The city remained the essential nucleus, the centre of all political and cultural life. It was obliged to become a member of the confederation, but it was not in itself abolished. The empire was nothing more than a league of autonomous cities. There were only a very few towns in which the central government had for special reasons appointed a governor: this was the case at Tlatelolco, for example, which became an integral part of the capital.

Nothing would have seemed more incomprehensible to the ancient Mexicans, nor more atrocious, than the characteristic features of our modern war: huge destruction, the systematic extermination of whole nations, the annihilation of states or their overthrow.

The only native rulers who ever attempted to do away with any states, as, for example, to destroy the dynasty of Texcoco and to wipe the kingdom off the map, were Tezozomoc, the old tyrant of Atzcapotzalco, and his son Maxtlaton; they were therefore remembered, in the sixteenth century, with universal execration. They are the outcasts of Mexican historical writing. When the rulers of Tenochtitlan and Texcoco had succeeded in defeating the tyrant in 1428, they certainly took care that the tyranny should not arise again; but they also took care to invite Tlacopan, a city belonging to the vanquished tribe, to share the supremacy with them. This was the foundation of the triple alliance.[30]

Whether it was sacred or political, war in Mexico was always surrounded by a network of conventions. If it were sacred, it could be reduced to a kind of duel arranged for the service of the gods; if it were political, to a crisis or a passing tumult, in which the gods would be able to make their decisions known. The campaign might be long, because of the very great distances and the absence of any kind of transport; but the battles themselves were short.

All these considerations explain, to some degree, why the last war that ever Tenochtitlan was to wage ended so disastrously for the empire and the civilisation of the Aztecs. The Spaniards and the Mexicans were not really fighting the same kind of war. On the material plane, they fought with different weapons: on the social and moral, they had totally different concepts of war. Faced with an unforeseen attack from another world, the Mexicans were no more capable of an adequate response than would be the men of today faced with an invasion from Mars.

With their guns, their helmets and their armour, their steel swords, their horses and their sailing ships, the Europeans had a decisive superiority over the warriors of Tenochtitlan and their wooden and stone weapons, their canoes and their troops of infantry and nothing more. Would a Macedonian phalanx or one of Caesar's legions have been able to withstand artillery? The accounts of the siege of Mexico show how effective the fast-sailing Spanish brigantines were, as they swept the lake with their fire, isolating the surrounded city, cutting its lines of communication and discouraging all idea of reinforcement. They also show how the guns, by battering down walls and houses, helped the attacks of the conquistadores in the very heart of the embattled city.

And above all, as one studies these accounts,[31] one cannot

213

but see that all the traditional rules of war, which the Mexicans instinctively obeyed, were violated equally instinctively by the invaders. Far from negotiating before the battle, they got into Mexico with peaceable words and then suddenly fell upon the Indian nobles massed upon the dancing place in the courtyard of Uitzilopochtli's temple, and massacred them. Instead of trying to make prisoners, they killed as many warriors as they could, while the Aztecs wasted their time capturing Spaniards or their native auxiliaries to sacrifice them. At last, when all was over, the Mexican rulers could have expected a bitter bargaining that would fix the amount of the tribute to be paid to the conquerors; they were physically incapable of imagining what was to come, the overthrow of their entire civilisation, the destruction of their gods and their beliefs, the abolition of their political institutions, the torture of the kings for their treasure, and the red-hot iron of slavery.[32]

For the Spaniards, for their part, were making 'total' war; there was only one possible state for them, the monarchy of Charles V, and only one possible religion. The clash of arms was nothing to the clash of ideologies. The Mexicans were beaten because their thought, based upon a tradition of pluralism in both the political and the religious aspects of life, was not adapted to contend with the dogmatism of the monolithic state and religion.

It is also possible to assert that the institution of the 'war of flowers' itself may have been an important factor on the downfall of Tenochtitlan, for it had preserved Tlaxcala, an inimical state, almost at the gates of the capital, 'so that there might be captives to sacrifice to the gods'.[33] If the Mexicans had really wished to destroy Tlaxcala and do away with the danger, it is very probable that they could have done so, by concentrating the whole strength of their empire upon it. They did not do so, no doubt because in the last resort they felt bound by the necessity for perpetuating the *xochiyaoyotl*, the flowery war.

Without knowing it, they had thus provided the as yet unknown invader with the ally who was to supply him with his infantry and the retreat in which he could take refuge after his setback. As for the republic of Tlaxcala, it certainly thought that it was using these powerful strangers for its own ends – that it would profit by them to finish an ordinary war between Mexican cities to its own advantage. Tlaxcala no more saw the real nature of the peril than Tenochtitlan; or if they did, only when it was too late.[34]

In so far as war is not merely Clausewitz's continuation of politics, but a glass which reflects a civilisation in its critical moments, when its most fundamental tendencies are visible, the war-time behaviour of the Mexicans is extremely revealing. Here are clearly to be seen the promise and the shortcomings of the civilisation – a civilisation which, isolated from the rest of the world, could not withstand an attack from the outside.

By reason of its material inadequacy or the rigidity of its mind, the civilisation was defeated; and it perished before it had shown its full potentialities. It went down above all because its religious and legal conception of war paralysed it before the attack of an invader who acted in accordance with a totally different set of ideas. However paradoxical it may seem at first, one is led to believe that the Aztecs, although they were so warlike, were not warlike enough when they were confronted with sixteenth-century European Christians; or rather, that they were, but in another fashion, and that their heroism was as inadequate and as unavailing as would have been that of the soldiers of the Marne faced with today's atomic bomb.[35]

CHAPTER SEVEN

CIVILISED LIFE

Barbarism and civilisation. The Chichimecs and the Toltecs: how the barbarians became civilised—Self-control, good breeding, social order. The civilised man and his attitude: the 'precepts of the elders': the duties of the sovereign—The arts as a setting for life. Sculpture, frescoes, painting and manuscripts: the minor arts—The arts of language, music and dancing. The Nahuatl language: the system of writing: rhetorical and poetical styles: religious and profane poems: the rôle of music and dancing.

BARBARISM AND CIVILISATION

All highly developed cultures have a tendency to set themselves apart from those which surround them. The Greeks, the Romans and the Chinese always contrasted their *civilisation* with the *barbarism* of the other nations they knew: sometimes this was a justifiable contrast, as in the case of the Romans and the Germanic tribes, or the Chinese and the Huns; and sometimes highly questionable, as, for example, in the case of the Greeks and the Persians. Further more, the members of a civilised community have an inclin ation when, at a given moment, they look back into the past, to prize some ancestors – those of the 'golden age' – and to look upon others with a certain degree of pity, as having been vulgar and countrified. These two characteristics of the civilised man are both to be found in the Mexican of the classical period, or, as one may put it, between 1430 and 1520.

The central Mexicans were very much aware of the value of their culture and of its superiority to that of other Indian peoples. They did not think that they alone possessed it, but rightly considered that some other tribes, particularly those of the Gulf coast, were their equals. On the other hand, they held that certain tribes were backward and barbarous. They knew perfectly well that their own nation, which had only recently settled in the central valley, had also lived a barbarian kind of life until not long ago: but they thought of themselves as the heirs of the civilised men who had colonised the plateau and built their great towns there long before them.

They had no hesitation in thinking of themselves as former barbarians who derived their warlike qualities from their nomadic ancestors and the high civilisation that they were so proud of from their settled ancestors. To take another parallel from our Mediterranean antiquity, it may be said that their attitude was not unlike that of the Romans in the time of the Scipios, when they were still close to their unpolished beginnings and yet were already imbued with a highly-developed culture that had been evolved by others before them.

To these two extremes, the barbarian and the civilised man, answer two conceptions made up of combined history and myth – the *Chichimeca* and the *Tolteca*. The Chichimecs were the nomadic hunters and warriors of the plains and mountains of the north: in the mythical past they lived on the flesh of wild animals alone, 'which they ate raw, for they did not yet understand the use of fire. . . (They dressed in the skins of beasts and) did not know how to make houses, but lived in caves which they found already made, or they made a few little houses with the branches of trees and covered them with grass.'[1]

At the beginning of the sixteenth century the Aztecs and the other tribes that belonged to the empire, such as the Otomí of Xilotepec, came into contact with the northern barbarians in the regions of Timilpan, Tecozauhtla, Huichapan and Nopallan, and traded with them – keeping them, however, at arm's length.[2] 'Those who were called *teochichimeca*, that is to say, complete barbarians,[3] or *zacachichimeca*, which is to say, wild men of the woods,[4] were they who lived deep in the country, far away from the villages, in huts, caves and the woods; and they had no fixed abode but wandered as nomads from one part to another: when night surprised them on the road, they slept in grottoes, if they found any. They had a lord, or chief . . . and this chief had only one wife, in the same way that all the other *chichimeca* had only one wife each. None might have two wives, and each lived on his own with his mate, seeking to find his livelihood. . .'[5]

The same account, which was dictated to Father Sahagún by his Aztec informants, goes on to describe these barbarians dressed in skins, carrying bows and arrows, clever at using plants and roots – 'and it was they who first discovered and used the root which is called *peyotl*; they who eat it take it in the place of wine. In the same way they use the evil fungus called *nanacatl* which, like wine, causes drunkenness . . . Their food was herbs and the fruit of the prickly pear, the root which is called *cimatl*, and others which are found by digging in the ground . . . *mizquitl* (an acacia whose fruit is edible) and the fruit and the flowers of a palm called *izcotl*. They knew how to get honey from palm-trees, agaves and (wild) bees . . . They ate rabbits, hares, deer, snakes and a great many birds. And, as they ate victuals that were neither prepared nor mixed with others they lived healthy and strong and for a long time. On rare occasions one might die; but he would be so old and his hair so white that it would be of old age that he died.'[6]

The value of this picture of barbarian life is not only that it gives exact information on the habitat, the clothing and the food of the savages, but also that it reflects the state of mind of its authors, that is to say, the settled, town-dwelling Indians. In their eyes, the barbarian was the 'man of nature': he was stronger and healthier than the man of the town; he possessed that *manuum mira virtus pedumque* which, in the *De Natura Rerum*, the poet attributes to the earliest men.[7]

The Aztecs were quite aware that four or five centuries before they had lived in the same manner. At that remote period they called themselves 'the barbarians of Aztlán', *chichimeca azteca*, and they had been leading that kind of primitive life for a very long time, 'twice four hundred years and ten times twenty years and fourteen years', when their migration began.[8] It was not by mere chance that their former dwelling-place, after Aztlán, was called Chicomoztoc, 'the seven caves'. It may be asked what they lived upon. 'With their arrows they killed deer, rabbits, wild beasts, snakes, birds. They went dressed in skins, and they ate what they could find.'[9] They were therefore true collecting and hunting nomads, living as the Indians of northern Mexico continued to live until long after the Spanish conquest.[10]

The process of acculturation by which the barbarians who had penetrated the central valley soon came to adopt the customs, the language, the laws and the manners of the settled civilised people is known to us through the chronicles of the house of Texcoco. This dynasty, as it happened, prized itself upon its direct descent from Xolotl,[11] the Chichimec chieftain who led the barbarous hordes when they came to establish themselves after the fall of the Toltec empire.

Xolotl and his two successors still lived in caves and in the woods. The fourth ruler, Quinatzin, took to urban life at Texcoco and compelled his tribe to cultivate the ground: some of his people rebelled, and fled into the mountains. The fifth, Techotlalatzin, was taught the Toltec language by a woman from Colhuacán and he welcomed civilised men at Texcoco, his capital, and incorporated them into his tribe. At last came Ixtlilxochitl, who adopted all the 'Toltec' ways – that is to say, the ways of the civilised Nahuatl-speaking people whose culture had reached its peak before the coming of the nomads – and then his son Nezaualcoyotl, who appears as the most typical and the most refined representative of classical Mexican culture.[12] This whole transformation had taken no more than two hundred years.

For when they reached the central plateau the barbarians had come into contact not only with the remains of the high Toltec civilisation, but also with people who had stayed there and still practised these civilised ways.[13] No doubt Tula had been abandoned and the Toltec state had fallen; but the language, the religion and the manners of the Toltecs persisted at Colhuacán, Cholula, Xochimilco, Chalco and many other places. Still other little towns, such as Xaltocan, were populated by Otomí, settled peasants with rustic ways, who had nevertheless lived for a long time under Toltec influence.

The city-states of the newcomers were built up around those of the Toltecs or of the nations much subject to Toltec influence; and the same applied to the city-states of the tribes who continued to come in from the northern steppes, of whom the most recent were the Aztecs. All these tribes adopted the political and social structures of their predecessors, their gods and their arts: they took the city-state, with its council and its dynasty, dignities and knightly orders, worship of agrarian deities, calendar and systems of writing, polygamy and ball-games. All that which Theodoric, Boethius and Cassiodorus were unable to do in Italy after the fall of the Western Empire, the Mexicans achieved after the fall of Tula; and it must be admitted that in the history of human civilisations this is a most unusual success.

The Aztecs and their neighbours therefore knew that they were at the junction of two lines of descent, the one coming from the barbarians, who in no way shamed them and whose warlike virtues they cultivated, and the other from the Toltecs, the civilised people whose symbol was Quetzalcoatl, the inventor of the arts and of science, the protector of knowledge.

As the heirs of the Toltecs they classed themselves with those nations who had not been barbarians, the 'people of the rubber and the salt water (*Olmeca-Uixtotin*) who live towards those parts where the sun is born and who are never called Chichimecs'.[14] These were particularly the tribes who lived in the province of Xicalanco (in the south of the present state of Campeche) and who, lying between the Mexican and the Mayan worlds, were in friendly relations with the Aztec empire without being subject to it.

We have, therefore, in ancient Mexico a very clear case of cultural solidarity overlying political division, a markedly conscious unity, which took the traditional form of the Toltec myth – a myth which, it may be added, was rich in historical elements mixed with its symbolic figures. The Indian of Tenochtitlan or Texcoco, of Uexotla or Cuauhtitlán did not regard himself solely as a member of a given tribe, or a citizen of a given city, but as a civilised man who shared a higher culture. By this he contrasted himself not only with the Chichimecs who had remained in the nomadic, savage state, but also with the rustic Otomí,[15] the *Popoloca*, 'who speak a barbarous language',[16] and the *Tenime*, 'a barbarous people, very unskilful, stupid and rude'.[17] Implicit in this notion of superior culture was the possession of certain kinds of knowledge, the practice of certain arts, a prescribed manner of life and a behaviour that matched certain given rules.

SELF-CONTROL; GOOD BREEDING; SOCIAL ORDER

A civilised man is primarily one who can master himself, who does not display his feelings, except when this is the accepted thing to do, and then only in the accepted manner, who preserves a proper bearing in all circumstances, and a reserved and correct demeanour. What we now call good breeding had a very great importance in the eyes of the ancient Mexicans, both as a mark of each man's quality and as a necessary factor in the social order.

In the upper classes continual attention to dignity was closely linked with taking care to appear grave, untroubled and even humble; it was most important to keep in one's proper place. The young warriors were blamed because they 'spoke vainly, boasted, talked too loud and boorishly' – *ahuiltlatoa, totoquauhtlatoa, tlatlaquauhtlatoa, quauquauhtlatoa*, as the *Codex Florentino* says so prettily.[18]

'No vainglorious, presumptuous or noisy man has ever been chosen as a dignitary; no impolite, ill-bred man, vulgar in his speaking, impudent in his speech and inclined to say whatever comes into his head, has ever sat upon the *petltal* or upon the *icpalli*. And if it should happen that a dignitary makes unsuitable jokes or speaks with levity, then he is called a *tecucuecuechtli*, which means a buffoon. No important office of state has ever been entrusted to a vain man, overfree in his speaking, nor to a man that plays the fool.'[19]

The upper-class ideal was an entirely Roman *gravitas* in private life, words and bearing, together with a particularly high degree of politeness. It was allowed that some men, such as veterans, for example, did not have to live up to this, and their extravagances of language and conduct were tolerated; but they were kept out of high office. 'Those who were called *quaquachictin*, men who were slightly mad but very brave in war, or *otomí atlaotzonxintin* (slightly mad Otomí with a shaved head), were great killers, but they were unadapted for the tasks of government.'[20] A true gentleman should show himself to be 'humble and not overweening, very wise and prudent, peaceable and calm.'[21] And that, said a father to his son, 'must be the truth in your heart, before our god (Tezcatlipoca). Let not your humility be feigned, or otherwise you will be called *titoloxochton* (hypocrite) or *titlanixiquipile* (feigner); for our lord god sees what is in the heart and he knows all secret things.'[22]

This 'humility', which might perhaps be more truthfully described as pride restrained by self-control, showed itself by moderation in pleasure – 'Do not throw yourself upon women like a dog upon its food'[23] – by a measured way of speaking – 'One must speak calmly, not too fast, nor heatedly, nor loud . . . keep to a moderate pitch, neither high nor low; and let your words be mild and serene' – by discretion – 'If you hear and see something, particularly something wrong, pretend not to have done so and be quiet' – by willing readiness in obeying – 'Do not wait to be called twice: answer at once the first time' – by good taste and restraint in dress – 'Do not be too curious in your clothes, nor freakish . . . on the other hand, do not wear poor, torn garments' – and finally, by a man's whole bearing.

In the street, 'Walk quietly, neither too fast nor too slow . . . those who do not observe this rule are called *ixtotomac cuecuetz*, people who go looking in every direction like idiots, without nobility or gravity; do not walk with your head down or leaning on one side or looking to right and to left, or else it will be said that you are an ill-bred, undisciplined fool.'

At meals, 'Do not eat too quickly or in a careless manner;

do not take great mouthfuls of maize-cake, nor stuff your mouth, nor swallow like a dog, nor tear the cakes to pieces, nor hurl yourself upon what is in the plate. Eat calmly, or you will be mocked. Before the meal, wash your hands and mouth; and do the same after you have eaten.'[24]

These 'precepts of the elders', *ueuetlatolli*, made up a distinct section of literature, with its own manner and style. They show what the Aztecs thought of as conduct suitable in a well-bred man of their day. The *ueuetlatolli* preserved in its Nahuatl form by Father Olmos[25] recites at length and in great detail all the ways in which a young Mexican of the better sort was expected to conduct himself: how he was to behave to his superiors, his equals and his inferiors; how he was to revere his elders, show compassion for the unfortunate, refrain from light words and in all circumstances be most scrupulously polite.

These, for example, are the directions that must be followed if one were invited to have a meal at a great man's house. 'Take care how you go in (to the lord's house), for without your noticing it you will be watched. Come respectfully, bow and make your greeting. Do not make faces when you eat; do not eat noisily and without care, like a glutton; do not swallow too quickly, but little by little . . . If you drink water, do not make a noise, sucking it in: you are not a little dog. Do not use all your fingers when you eat, but only the three fingers of your right hand . . . Do not cough and do not spit; and take care not to dirty the clothes of any of the other guests.'[26]

This courtesy, which was formerly so firmly inculcated that even now the Indians are exquisitely polite, was not only shown in gestures, attitudes and the meaning of the words, but even in the form of the language. Nahuatl, a subtle language, rich in resources, had respectful particles and even respectful conjugations. The suffix *-tzin* was added to the names of persons one wished to honour, to their titles and to any word at all to which one wished to give a shade of respect or tenderness: *Motecuhzomatzin*, the revered Motecuhzoma; *totatzin*, our honoured father; *ixpopoyotzin*, a blind person worthy of compassion.[27]

When an honoured or beloved person was addressed, the verbs were conjugated with special suffixes. *Tiyola* means 'thou seest', but *timoyolotia* may be translated as 'your lordship sees'; *timomati* means 'thou thinkest', but *timomatia* 'thou art so kind as to think', 'thou condescendest to think'. *Miqui* is 'to die': *miquilia* 'to die honourably'.[28]

While it was generally thought suitable to retain a dignified, simple attitude, there were circumstances when, on the contrary, etiquette insisted upon a display of emotion. The bride who was about to leave her parents' home answered the speeches of the representatives of her husband's family 'with tears'.[29] Young traders beginning their career listened respectfully to the homilies of the old *pochteca*, and when they replied they wept copiously by way of showing their gratitude and humility.[30]

May not this cult of moderation in deeds and words, this dislike of excess and what the Greeks termed hubris, and the extreme importance of good breeding and civility be explained as a reaction against brutishness of manners and violence of passions? For this delicate flower of chivalry bloomed in a world which had, in the sixteenth century, barely emerged from a long period of wars, *coups d'état*, plots interspersed with assassinations, and treason.

The generation for which the 'precepts of the elders' were meant was too young to have known these troubled times; but the vicissitudes, the insecurity and the bloody outbreaks which were characteristic of the days of Atzcapotzalco's hegemony and the beginning of the triple alliance were not forgotten. The great men of those times seemed to have been in the grip of savage, uncontrollable passions, shocking rages and lusts whose violence did not stop short of crime.

The first Motecuhzoma (whose name 'he who grows angry [like a] lord' is revealing) had his own brother killed, the *tlacateccatl* Ueue Zacatzin,[31] in an access of rage over some trivial thing. The tyrant Tezozomoc and his son Maxtlaton sent their assassins to murder anyone who offended them, including Chimalpopoca, the unfortunate king of Tenochtitlan, and the king of Texcoco.[32] And even the wise king Nezaualcoyotl of Texcoco himself committed a crime that was to shame his decendants, when, distracted by his love for the young Azcaxochitzin, he had her fiancé treacherously killed on the battlefield.[33]

These fifteenth-century Mexicans, as we see them reflected in their chronicles, were passionate, scheming and unscrupulous; they would stop at nothing to satisfy their desires or their lust for power. The survivors of this troubled time seem to have grown better behaved in their old age: the philosophic poems of the king Nezaualcoyotl, the expression of a serene and disillusioned mind and of an epicureanism whose wisdom was founded upon a knowledge of the vanity of the passing show, are perfectly characteristic of the period of reaction that follows one of upheaval and disruption.

This attitude triumphed at the end of the fifteenth century and the beginning of the sixteenth, and the ideal of the civilised man succeeded that of the adventurer ready for anything; these violent beings were repressed, and a barrier was set up against the free play of instinct. After the cruellest trials, Mexico had succeeded in creating a pattern; and in this pattern, under the reign of the second Motecuhzoma, courtesy was an essential part.

As the dynasties – and particularly that of Tenochtitlan – grew stronger and chaos receded, this pattern or order took the form of monarchy and came to depend primarily on the person of the sovereign. However wide his powers, modified by those of the supreme council, they were never so great as his obligations. The kings of the allied cities, the lords of the self-ruling towns and of course above all the emperor of Mexico, were heavily burdened with duties. They were not only responsible for the conduct of the civil and military administration, but also for the welfare and even the life of the nation, for 'the abundance of fruits of the earth'.[34] They first had to ensure this by serving the gods devoutly; then they had to take all the necessary measures, such as preventing disasters or diminishing their effects, building up reserves, giving out victuals and clothing and 'showing their good-will to the common people'.[35] If they did not do

225

these things the people would murmur against them, and the emperor would feel his throne tremble.[36]

The official doctrine, which was expressed at length in the speeches at the time of the emperor's election, was that the ruler was chosen by the gods, that the burden of his office was terribly heavy, and that his primary function, after the service of the gods, was the defence of the people.

'Lord,' they said to him, 'it is you who will now carry the weight and the burden of this state. The burden of government will be upon your back. It is upon your shoulders, in your lap and between your arms that our god has set the task of governing the people; and they are fickle and prompt to anger. It is you, lord, who for certain years are going to sustain this nation and care for it as if it were a child in a cradle ... Consider, lord, that from now on you are to walk upon a very high place along a narrow path that has great precipices to the right and the left ... Be mild in the use of your power; show neither teeth nor claws ... Please the people and make them happy with games and decent amusements, for in doing this you will be famous and beloved ... Your people are protected by your shade, for you are like the *pochotl* or the *ahuehuetl* which gives a great round shadow; and the multitudes are protected by your branches.'[37]

All the contemporary documents strongly emphasise this aspect of the ruler as protector. The pattern depends upon him; and in order that this pattern may be good, humane and in conformity with the needs of the people, the emperor must control his passions – they left him in no doubt upon this point on the day of his election.

'Say nothing, do nothing with too much haste; listen to those who complain to you or bring you news calmly and to the end ... do not be partial; do not punish anybody without reason ... upon the mats and the *icpalli* of lords and judges there should be neither passion nor haste in words or deeds; nothing should be done in the haste of anger ... Never speak angrily to a man, nor terrify anyone with your ferocity. Lord, you must also take care never to speak lightly, for that would make your person despised ...

you must now make your heart the heart of an old man, grave and severe . . . Do not give yourself up to women . . . Do not suppose, lord, that the mat and the *icpalli* of kings is a place of pleasure and delight; for on the contrary, it is one of great labour, sorrow and penance.'[38]

It was the sovereign who was to be the first to obey this law of moderation and to subdue his passions, for everything depended upon him. The enlightened despot was the ideal of the time, the philosopher-emperor able to command himself in order to govern for the good of all. The more or less historical or legendary anecdotes related in the chronicles are significant: they often concern Nezaualcoyotl who, having given up the adventures and the violent ways of his youth towards the end of his reign, appears as a kind of Haroun al Raschid: there are stories of him disguised as a simple hunter, listening to the grievances and complaints of the common peasants and then sending for them to the palace to give them splendid gifts.

Or again he is shown overhearing from a balcony the words of a woodman who, sweating under his load, cried, 'The man who lives in this palace has everything he needs, while as for us, we are worn out, and we die of hunger.' The king had the woodman brought in, and having first advised him to take care of what he said, 'because walls have ears', he bade him 'think of the weight and the burden of business that he had to bear so as to protect, defend and justly maintain so great a realm', and at last he sent him away loaded with presents.

'This king was so full of compassion for the poor that he commonly went up into a *mirador* which overlooked the market-place to watch the poor people who sold salt, wood and vegetables – scarcely enough to make a living. And if he saw that these poor people did not sell their wares, he would not sit down to his meal until his major-domos had gone to buy all these things themselves to make presents of them to others. He was particularly careful to give food and clothing to the old, to the sick, to those wounded in war, to widows and to orphans, and in this way he spent a great part of the tribute he received.'[39]

In the same spirit, it was related of Motecuhzoma II, that hunting in the gardens outside the city he made the mistake of plucking an ear of maize that had already formed, without asking the peasant's leave. 'Lord, you who are so powerful,' said the peasant, 'how can you steal an ear from me? Does not your own law condemn a man to death for stealing an ear of maize or its value?'

'That is true,' replied Motecuhzoma.

'Well then,' said the gardener, 'why have you broken your own law?'

The emperor then offered to give him back his ear, but the peasant refused. Motecuhzoma gave him his own cloak, the imperial *xiuhayatl*, and said to his dignitaries, 'This poor man has shown more courage than anybody here, for he has dared to reproach me to my face with having broken my own laws.' And he raised the peasant to the rank of *tecuhtli*, entrusting him with the government of Xochimilco.[40]

What is interesting about these improving little tales is not that they do or do not describe real facts, but that they show the feelings of the time. This was what a good sovereign *ought* to be – one who would listen to complaints and remonstrances, merciful, master of himself. He was the culminating point of the community and the state, and he was to incarnate all those virtues which his time thought the most valuable and which the people expected to maintain the rightful order in the common interest.

THE ARTS AS A SETTING FOR LIFE

The arts provided the setting of civilised life, which was pre-eminently that of the upper classes, with a quality and a refinement which call to mind the golden age of the Toltecs. Mexican culture had no notion of art for art's sake, and sculpture, painting, jewellery, mosaic, feather-work and the art of the miniaturist all combined to express the beliefs of the time and its deepest tendencies, to mark the degrees of rank and to surround everyday activities with forms that had always been appreciated.[41]

Architecture has already been treated in Chapter I, and we will not speak of it again in this place; but the great buildings were filled with statues and covered with bas-reliefs,[42] a very great proportion of which were based upon religion. Profane sculpture was not wanting, however: it existed, and sometimes one finds the vigorously carved head of a man of the people, sometimes the familiar plants and animals of the country, sometimes, formalised and hieratic, the great deeds of the emperors or historic scenes, such as the conquests of Tizoc or the dedication of the great temple by his successor.

The emperors liked to leave their stone or golden likenesses behind them, and one of the very few gold figurines that escaped the Spanish melting-pot represents Tizoc.[43] Fourteen sculptors carved the statue of Motecuhzoma II at Chapultepec, and they were rewarded with immense quantities of cloth, cocoa and victuals as well as receiving two slaves each.[44]

Some monuments were decorated with frescoes. In central Mexico the tradition of fresco painting goes back as far as the civilisation of Teotihuacán, and it was particularly full of life in the region between Mexico and the Mixtec mountains. Aztec mural painting vanished with the buildings of Tenochtitlan; but in places far from the centre, such as Malinalco, traces of it are still to be seen.[45]

But although the frescoes that adorned the walls of the temples and the palaces were destroyed when the walls themselves collapsed before the attack of guns or pickaxes, Mexican painting has survived in the form of the pictographic manuscripts, some of which have come down to us. It is an art somewhere between writing and miniature-painting, with its delicate, scrupulously-worked glyphs and its representation of historic or mythical scenes.[46]

The *tlacuilo* or *tlacuiloani*, the painter-scribe, was very much respected, whether he worked for the temples, the law or the administration. The ancient Mexicans loved their books, and when the fanatical hands of Zumárraga hurled thousands upon thousands of precious manuscripts into the fire, the flames destroyed a very great part of their culture.

It was above all the minor arts that made life **more**

decorative, for they were applied, with great success, to everything from the humblest earthenware dish to jewels of gold: nothing was vulgar; nothing showed the signs of hasty workmanship or the naked pursuit of effect and profit. The conquerors were astonished by the extraordinary and luxurious productions of the craftsmen of Tenochtitlan, the goldsmiths, lapidaries and feather-workers.

These *tolteca* – for as we have seen, they were called by this honourable title, by way of showing that they were in the direct tradition of the golden age – knew how to smelt and model gold and silver, carve the hardest stones, make the scrupulously-formed mosaics of dazzling feathers which decorated the shields, the flags and the cloaks of the chiefs and the gods. The means at their disposal for the creation of all these delicate wonders were a few tools made of stone, copper and wood, moistened sand for wearing down jade or crystal, and above all an infinite patience and an astonishing sureness of taste.

The goldsmiths used the *cire perdue* method for making statuettes of Indians of foreign tribes, animals (tortoises, birds, fishes, crustaceans, lizards) and necklaces decorated with little bells and metal flowers: these are examples mentioned by Aztec informants. They were acquainted with the enhancing of the colour of gold by an alum-bath, and they hammered and chiselled it in sheets and leaves.

The lapidaries worked rock-crystal, amethyst, jade, turquoise, obsidian, mother of pearl, etc., with instruments made of reed, and sand and emery. They also set out little pieces of stone in beautiful mosaics upon a background of bone, stucco or wood.

The *amanteca*, the feather-workers, either fixed their precious tropical feathers on light reed frameworks by tying each one with cotton, or stuck them on to cloth or paper so as to form mosaics in which certain effects of colour were obtained by transparency. This was a typically and exclusively Mexican art, which lingered in the form of little feather pictures after the conquest, and then disappeared entirely.[47] Almost nothing has survived of these fragile masterpieces.

The imperial official who entered into contact with the Spaniards after their landing in the region of Vera Cruz 'took several excellently-worked, very rich golden objects out of a chest and caused to be brought ten loads of white cloth made of cotton and feathers, things very well worth seeing'.[48] According to native sources, Motecuhzoma sent Cortés the following presents: first, a costume of Quetzalcoatl, which included a turquoise mask, a plume of *quetzal* feathers, a great jade disk with a gold round in the middle of it, a shield made of gold and mother of pearl, decorated with *quetzal* plumes, a mirror encrusted with turquoises, a bracelet of gems and golden bells, a turquoise head-dress and sandals ornamented with obsidian.

The second present was a costume of Tezcatlipoca, which particularly included a feather crown, a gold breastplate and a looking-glass.

Then there was a costume of Tlaloc, with a crown of green plumes and jade earrings, a jade disk and a golden disk, a turquoise sceptre and golden bracelets and anklets. The list goes on with a mitre of jaguar-skin adorned with plumes and gems, turquoise and gold earrings, a jade and gold breastplate, a shield made of gold and *quetzal* plumes, a golden mitre with parrot-feathers and a mitre made of thin sheets of gold.[49]

Among the treasures that Cortés received from Motecuhzoma II and which he sent to Charles V in July 1519 one finds, among other things, 2 'wheels' 10 spans (6 feet 10 inches) wide, the one made of gold to represent the sun and the other of silver for the moon; a golden necklace of eight sections with 183 small emeralds and 232 garnets set in it and 27 little golden bells hanging from it; a wooden helmet covered over with gold; a gold sceptre studded with pearls; 24 shields made of gold, feathers and mother of pearl; 5 fishes, 2 swans and other birds of cast and moulded gold; 2 large gold shells and 1 gold crocodile with filigree decorations; several head-dresses, mitres, plumes, fans and fly-whisks, all made of gold and feathers.[50]

As the Aztec empire grew, so the life of the Mexicans became more and more luxurious and sumptuous, for their boundaries reached to the tropical countries that produced the feathers, the Mixtec mountains where the gold was found as gold-dust in the streams, and those parts of the Gulf coast where the best jade came from; the statues of the gods were clothed with feather cloaks, and the dignitaries, abandoning the austerity of former times, adorned themselves with brilliant plumes, chiselled gems and jewels of gold. As we have seen, men of the highest class loved learning the lapidary's art and themselves carved jade or turquoise.

Gold and silver aroused less desire and admiration than plumes and gems – the plumes and gems that perpetually recur in the language of verse and rhetoric. Lords and poets, traders and craftsmen, they were all fascinated by the gilded green of the *quetzal* plumes, the turquoise blue-green of the feathers of the *xiuhtototl*, the splendid yellow of parrot-feathers, the translucent green of the great pieces of jade brought from Xicalanco, the red of garnets and the dark lucidity of obsidian; and the polychromatic brilliance of all these things surrounded men's lives with an aura of splendour and beauty.

THE ARTS OF LANGUAGE, MUSIC AND DANCING

The Mexicans were proud of their language, Nahuatl, which, by the beginning of the sixteenth century had become the common tongue, the *koinè*, of the whole vast country. 'The Mexican language is considered the mother-tongue, and that of Texcoco is thought the noblest and the purest.[51] All the languages other than this were held to be coarse and vulgar . . . The Mexican language spreads over the whole of New Spain . . . and the others are thought barbarous and strange . . . It is the richest and fullest language that is to be found. It is not only dignified but also soft and pleasing, lordly and of a high nobility, succinct, easy and flexible.'[52]

In fact, Nahuatl has all the qualities that are necessary in the language of a civilisation. It is easy to pronounce; it is harmonious and distinct. Its vocabulary is very rich, and the structure of the language allows the creation of all necessary words, and most particularly of abstract terms. It is excellently adapted for the expression of all shades of thought and all the aspects of the physical world. It is as well adapted to the lapidary concision of annals as to the flowery rhetoric of speeches or to poetic metaphor. As the basis or raw material of a literature it could hardly be surpassed.

At the time of which we are speaking, the Aztecs' system of writing was a compromise between ideogram, phoneticism and simple representation or pictography. The symbol for defeat – a blazing temple – the glyph for war, *atl-tlachinolli*, night, shown by a black sky and a closed eye, and the chronological signs, are ideograms. The syllables or groups of syllables *tlan* (teeth, *tlan-tli*), *te* (a stone, *tetl*), *quauh* (a tree, *quauitl*), *a* (some water, *atl*), *tzinco* (the lower part of a human body, *tzintli*), *acol* (*acolli*, the elbow), *pan* (a flag, *pantli*), *ix* (an eye, *ixtolotli*), *teo* (a sun, translated as god, *teotl*), *coyo* (a round hole, *coyoctic*), *tenan* (a wall, *tenamitl*), *tecu* (a diadem and hence a lord, *tecuhtli*), *icpa* (a ball of thread, *icpatl*), *mi* (an arrow, *mitl*), *yaca* (a nose, *yacatl*) and many others all provide examples of phoneticism: the conventional images, often highly formalised, which represent the objects that have been listed, are used to write the sounds, even if there is no reference whatever to the objects themselves. Thus the name of the village of Otlatitlan is shown by a reed, *otlatl* (an ideogram) and by teeth, *tlan*, (a phonogram).

In practice the two systems were combined, and colour was also used: the word *tecozauhtla* was represented by a stone (*tetl*) upon a yellow background (*cozauic*), the word *tlatlauhquitepec* by a formalised mountain (*tepetl*) painted red (*tlatlauhqui*).[53] And mythical or historical scenes were simply represented by the characters together with the glyphs corresponding to their names and, where it was called for, by the signs dating the event.

In its state at that time, this writing did not permit the exact notation of spoken language. It was adapted for summarising events, and by a mixture of phonograms, symbols and representations it provided a basis for memory.

Historical accounts, hymns and poems had to be learned by heart, and the books acted as prompters to the memory. This was one of the principal aspects of the education that the priests of the *calmecac* gave their young men. 'They carefully learnt the songs that were called the songs of the gods, written in the books. And they carefully learned the account of days, the book of dreams and the book of the years.'[54]

Fortunately in the period that followed the conquest, thanks to enlightened men like Sahagún, a certain number of Indians learnt to write in Latin characters, and they used this tool – infinitely better than anything they had had up to that time – to transcribe those native books that had not been destroyed or to set down what they had learnt by heart. In this way something, though no doubt a very small part, of the ancient Mexican literature was saved.

This literature was 'so varied and so wide that no other people who had reached the same degree of social development possessed anything that approached it.'[55] It covered all aspects of life, for its aim was to help the memory to retain the whole accumulated knowledge of the foregoing generations, their religious ideas, myths, ritual, divination, medicine, history, law, and in addition to all this it included a great deal of rhetoric and lyric and epic poetry.[56]

It was divided into prose and verse: prose for instructive treatises, mythical and historical narratives; verse (usually trochaic) for religious or profane poems. Many accounts or descriptions which with us would have been in prose, were learnt in Mexico in the form of poetry or rhythmic verses, as being easier to memorize. Rhetorical and poetic style made the utmost use of the language's possibilities. The richness of Nahuatl allowed the piling-up of near-synonyms, separated from one another by faint shades of meaning, for the description of the one deed; and although this may give a certain tautological air in translation, in the original it can be exquisite.

In order to say that the sorcerer Titlacahuan took on the appearance of an old man, the literal expression of the Aztec narrator is, 'He transformed himself into a little old man, he changed himself, he disguised himself, he became very much bowed, his head became quite white, his hair quite white.'[57] Another very common stylistic usage is that of expressing an idea by the juxtaposition of two words, forming a binominal term, as *mixtitlan ayauhtitlan* (in the clouds, in the mist), meaning 'mysteriously'; *noma nocxi* (my hand, my foot), 'my body'; *in chalchiuitl in quetzalli* (jade, feathers), 'richness' or 'beauty'; *itlatol ihiyo* (his word, his breath) 'his speech'; *in xochitl in cuicatl* (flower, song) 'a poem', etc.

The same tendency is to be seen in that parallelism, continually sought after in poems and treatises, which consists of setting two phrases with the same signification side by side: *choquiztli moteca, ixayotl pixahui*, 'sorrow overflows, tears fall'.[58] Phonetic parallels were also esteemed, as well as assonances and alliterations. All these figures, together with often exceedingly elaborate metaphors, were the mark of fine language, the speech of the well-bred, civilised man.

Just as the style of the annals was generally dry, succinct and reduced to the barest relation of the facts, so that of speeches was flowery and even, to our taste, turgid and bombastic. Some examples have already been given, but it is impossible to over-emphasize the extraordinary appetite of the Mexicans for this philosophico-moral rhetoric. They could make untiring speeches upon any subject whatsoever, and endlessly answer one another with commonplaces, in the Latin rhetoric sense of generally accepted ideas, upon which they would throw the cloaks of their metaphors, by way of exercise. 'They were much addicted to the art of oratory . . . During their harangues they sat upon their heels, without touching the ground; they did not look up or raise their eyes; they did not spit or make gestures, and they did not look you in the face. When a speaker had finished, he rose and withdrew with his face lowered, without turning his back, very modestly.'[59]

On all public occasions, or those of private life, there would be positive tournaments of eloquence, whether the matter in question was the election of an emperor, the birth of a baby, the departure of a merchant-caravan or a marriage.

Poetry was no less esteemed. The dignitaries and their families – and this included some most distinguished women – prided themselves upon poetic excellence. At Texcoco, where everything to do with fine language was particularly honoured, one of the four great councils of government was called 'the council of music and the sciences'. As well as the execution of the laws relating to worship and witchcraft, its functions included the encouragement of poetry: it organised competitions, and at the end of them the king presented valuable gifts to the prizewinners.[60]

There were scholarly noblemen who were occasional poets, the most illustrious of them being the king Nezaual-coyotl himself; and there were also professional poets in the service of great men; these celebrated the deeds of heroes, the grandeur of royal houses and also the delight and sadness of life. These poets taught singing and music in the 'houses of song' (*cuicacalli*) that were attached to the palaces or maintained by the districts.

The very name of the poet (*cuicani*, the singer) shows that poem and song were synonymous, for the poem was always sung or at the very least declaimed to the accompaniment of musical instruments. The text of some poems is preceded by a notation that shows the rhythm of the *teponaztli*, whose beat was to sustain the recital.[61]

Certain poems show that the poet was conscious of his high mission—

> I chisel the jade, I pour gold in the crucible:
> Here is my song!
> I inlay the emeralds:
> Here is my song.[62]

He also said—

> I, the poet, the master of song,
> I, the singer, I beat on my drum.
> Let the beating awaken
> The souls of my companions who are dead.

And—

> I, the singer, I make a poem
> That shines like an emerald
> A brilliant, precious and splendid emerald.
> I suit myself to the inflexions
> Of the tuneful voice of the *tzinitzcan* . . .
> Like the ring of little bells,
> Little golden bells . . .
> I sing my song
> A scented song like a shining jewel,
> A shining turquoise and a blazing emerald,
> My flowering hymn to the spring.[63]

The Aztecs themselves divided poetry into a certain number of kinds, of which the first included the *teocuicatl* (holy song) or hymns; and fortunately, by means of Sahagún's informants, we have the transcript of some of these – a veritable treasure for the study of the language of the ancient Mexicans and their religious thought.[64] In reading them, it must be remembered that these poems were not only sung, but 'acted'; that is to say, each of the verses (no doubt repeated a great many times) accompanied a given phase of the ritual, some set action of the priests or some specific masked dance.

These religious songs, handed down from a remote period by tradition, were often very obscure or even totally incomprehensible to the Aztecs themselves, or at least to those who were not priests. They are loaded with esoteric allusions and metaphors.

> The flower of my heart has opened,
> Here is the lord of Midnight.
> She has come, our mother, she has come,
> She, the goddess Tlazolteotl.

> The god of the maize is born
> In the paradise of Tamoanchan,
> In the place where the flowers raise their heads
> He (who is called) 'One – flower'.

237

The god of the maize is born
In the garden of rain and mist,
There where the children of men are made,
There where they fish for jade fishes.

Here is the day: dawn is coming up:
Quechol-birds are flying about from place to place
    and feeding
There where the flowers stand upright . . .[65]

In honour of Tenochtitlan's national god, they sang—
I am Uitzilopochtli, the young warrior.
There is none like me.
I have not put on my parrot-feather cloak in vain,
For thanks to me the sun is risen.[66]

And for the goddess Teteoinnan, the mother of the gods—
The yellow flower has opened.
She, our mother with the skin mask,
She has come from Tamoanchan.

The yellow flower has bloomed.
She, our mother with the skin mask,
She has come from Tamoanchan.

The white flower has opened.
She, our mother with the skin mask,
She has come from Tamoanchan.

The white flower has bloomed.
She, our mother with the skin mask,
She has come from Tamoanchan.

Ah, she has become a goddess,
Among the cactus, our mother,
The obsidian butterfly.

Ah, you have beheld the Nine Steppes!
She feeds on the hearts of stags,
Our mother, the goddess of the earth.[67]

And here is another terrestrial goddess, Ciuacoatl, in her agrarian and her warlike aspects—

> The eagle, the eagle, Quilaztli
> Her face is painted with snake's blood
> And eagles' feathers are her crown.
> It is she who is the protecting cypress of
> The Country of Chalman and Colhuacán.
>
> The maize is in the sacred field.
> The goddess leans on her stick with bells.
> The agave-thorn, the agave-thorn is in my hand,
> The agave-thorn is in my hand.
> In the sacred field
> The goddess is leaning on her stick with bells.
>
> The bundle of weeds is in my hand.
> In the sacred field
> The goddess leans on her stick with bells.
>
> 'Thirteen – eagle', that is how they name her,
> Our mother, the goddess of Chalman.
> Give me the cactus-arrow, the sacred emblem.
> Here is my son, Mixcoatl.
>
> Our mother the warrior, our mother the warrior,
> The roe-deer of Colhuacán,
> She is adorned with plumes.
>
> Here is the dawn, the order of battle is given.
> Here is the dawn, the order of battle is given.
> May we bring back some prisoners!
>
> The earth shall be ravaged!
> She, the roe of Colhuacán,
> She is adorned with plumes.[68]

Other, and much more simple, hymns are in fact little more than indefinitely repeated magical formulæ; an example is the song of Chicomecoatl, the goddess of maize.

239

In singing this, they endeavoured to stir nature into its annual re-birth—

> Oh revered goddess of the Seven Ears,
> Rise, awake!
> Oh our mother, you are leaving us today,
> You are going to your own country, Tlalocan.
>
> Rise, awake!
> Oh our mother, you are leaving us today,
> You are going to your own country, Tlalocan.[69]

The Mexicans classed poems other than hymns in several categories according to their subject, origin or nature – *yaocuicatl*, war-song; *chalcayotl*, poem after the fashion of Chalco; *xochicuicatl cuecuechtli*, flowery, bantering song; *xopancuicatl*, poem to spring; etc. Some of these poems, for example the song of Quetzalcoatl,[70] were real sagas, and others reflections upon the brevity of life or the uncertainty of fate.

In the combinations of recital, song, dance and music there were also to be found the elements of a dramatic art: in these performances there were actors dressed to represent historical or mythical heroes; they used dialogue, and at times there were exchanges between the characters and a choir. These performances, which were at once ballets and tragedies, would present the king Nezaualpilli, for example, or his father Nezaualcoyotl, or the emperor Motecuhzoma.[71] Mimed songs, some of them sung by women, were inserted into these compositions: for instance—

> My tongue is of coral,
> Of emerald my beak;
> I think much of myself, oh my parents,
> I, Quetzalchictzin.
> I open my wings,
> I weep before them:
> How shall we ever rise into the sky?

The actress who sang this was probably dressed as a bird.[72]

Flowers and death, like twin obsessions, adorn all Mexican lyric poetry with their brilliance and their shadows.

Oh, if only one lived for ever.
Oh, if only one never died.
We live with our soul torn apart,
Lightning flashes about us
We are spied upon and attacked.
We live with our soul torn apart. We have to suffer.
Oh, if only one lived for ever.
Oh, if only one never died.

And again—

Shall my heart go
As flowers that wither?
Some day shall my name be nothing?
My fame nothing, anywhere upon the earth?
At least let us have flowers! At least let us have some
singing!
How shall my heart manage (to survive)?
We go about on the earth in vain.[74]

This poem from Chalco shows the same preoccupation—

Vainly you seize your flowered *teponaztli*,
You throw handfuls of flowers; but in vain.
They wither.

We too, we are here singing our new song,
And there are new flowers too
In our hands.
May our friends delight in the flowers,
May the sadness fade out of our hearts.

Let no one be overwhelmed by sadness,
Let no one's thoughts wander about over the earth.
Here are our precious flowers and songs.
May our friends delight in them,
May the sadness fade out of our hearts.

Oh friends, this earth is only lent to us.
We shall have to leave our fine poems,
We shall have to leave our beautiful flowers.
That is why I am sad as I sing for the sun,
We shall have to leave our fine poems,
We shall have to leave our beautiful flowers.[75]

And from here we pass on to the expression of that epicurean philosophy which seems to have been so general among the more educated people—

> Oh you do not come twice on to the earth,
> Chichimec lords!
> Let us be happy. Does one take flowers along to the
>   land of the dead?
> They are only lent to us.
> The truth is that we go;
> We leave flowers and singing and the earth.
> The truth is that we go . . .
> If it is only here on the earth
> That there are flowers and singing,
> Let them be our wealth,
> Let them be our adornment,
> Let us be happy with them.[76]

The magnificent landscape of the country is also to be seen in Mexican poetry. One of the ambassadors sent by Uexotzinco to ask help from Motecuhzoma, sees, from the mountains, the whole of the valley of Mexico spread out—

> I climb; I reach the height.
> The huge blue-green lake
> Now quiet, now angry,
> Foams and sings among the rocks . . .
> Flowery water, green-stone water,
> Where the splendid swan
> With its rippling feathers
> Calling swims to and fro.

And when the sun sets—

> Our father, the Sun,
> Dressed in rich feathers, thrusts himself
> Down into a vase of gems,
> Decked with a turquoise necklace
> Among many-coloured flowers
> Which fall in a perpetual rain.[77]

Short extracts like these can scarcely give an idea of the wealth of this literature – for it is rich, although only fragments have come down to us. The ancient Mexicans' passionate love of oratory and poetry, music and dancing, had free rein at the feasts, the banquets and the innumerable ceremonies at which one might see the young men, splendidly adorned, dancing with the courtesans in all their glory, and the dignitaries and the emperor himself taking part in the traditional balls. Dancing was not only an amusement; it was not even only a rite: it was a way of deserving the favour of the gods 'by serving them and calling upon them with one's whole body'.[78]

Aztec music, of which nothing is left to us because it was not written, was not rich in resources; it had but a few wind-instruments, the conch, the trumpet, the flute, the whistle; and – most important – some percussion, the upright drum (*ueuetl*) and the two-toned wooden gong (*teponaztli*).

The music primarily gave rhythm for singing and dancing; and in the cool nights of the high plateau, by the light of resinous torches, a collective ecstasy would seize upon the crowd as it sang and danced, every movement and attitude obeying the law of ritual, at the foot of the pyramids whose heads rose into the darkness. There, in the communion of song and rhythmic movement to the beat of gongs, the crowd found release for the passions of its violent soul; and this without overstepping the boundaries of social duty. This self-controlled civilisation, which imposed such a continual discipline upon all, and particularly upon its upper classes, had the wisdom to provide a permitted relaxation under the eyes of the gods for the repressed forces. Poems and music, rhythm and dance hour after hour in the red glare of the torches in the great square of the holy city – this was the liberation that the system offered for a while to the impassive men of whom it asked so much.

Such as they were, with their greatness and their weaknesses, their ideal of order and their cruelty, their obsession with the mystery of blood and death, their sensitivity to the beauty of flowers, birds and gems, their strength of religious feeling – strong to the point of suicide – their excellent practical organisation of the state, their attachment to their land and their maize, which still did not keep their eyes from turning continually to the stars – with all this, these ancient Mexicans were civilised men.

Their culture, so suddenly destroyed, is one of those that humanity can be proud of having created. In the hearts and minds of those who believe that our common inheritance is made up of all the values that our species has conceived in all times and all places, it must take its place among our precious treasures – precious because they are so rare. At long intervals, in the immensity of the world's life and in the midst of its vast indifference, men joined together in a community bring something into existence that is greater than themselves – a civilisation. These are the creators of cultures; and the Indians of Anahuac, at the foot of their volcanoes, on the shores of their lake, may be counted among them.

APPENDIX ONE

THE PRONUNCIATION OF AZTEC WORDS

The traditional orthography used in this book is based upon the following principles:

1 All the vowels are pronounced as they are in Spanish: e is always pronounced, even when it is at the end of a word, and its sound is roughly that of the French é.

2 The consonants are pronounced as they are in English with the exception of

x which is pronounced sh. For example, xicotl = shicotl.

z which is pronounced s. For example, zan = san.

qu which is pronounced k before e and i, but kw before a. For example, calpixque = calpishké; quimichin = kimichin; quauitl = kwawitl.

H is breathed; ll has the English value; u and y are semi-vowels, u being pronounced like the w in well and y like the y in yet. The stress is usually upon the penultimate syllable.

APPENDIX TWO

These are the names of the eighteen months of the Mexican year, with a short account of the rites that were proper to each of them.

1   *Atl caualo* (stopping of the water) or *Quiauitl eua* (the tree rises). Sacrifice of children to Tlaloc, the rain-god, and to the *Tlaloque*.

2   *Tlacaxipeualiztli* (flaying of men). Feast of Xipe Totec. Sacrifice of prisoners, who were then flayed. The priests put on their skins.

3   *Tozoztontli* (lesser vigil). Offering of flowers; worship of Coatlicue.

4   *Uey tozoztli* (great vigil). Feasts in honour of Centeotl, god of maize, and of Chicomecoatl, goddess of maize. Offerings of flowers and food in local temples and private chapels. Procession of girls carrying ears of maize to the temple of Chicomecoatl. Songs and dances.

5   *Toxcatl* (? drought). Feast of Tezcatlipoca. Sacrifice of a young man personifying Tezcatlipoca, he having lived like a lord for a year.

6   *Etzalqualiztli* (*etzalli*, a dish made of boiled maize and beans; *qualiztli*, the act of eating). Feast of Tlaloc. Ceremonial baths in the lake. Dances and the eating of *etzalli*. Priestly fasts and penances. Sacrifice of victims personifying the gods of water and rain.

7   *Tecuilhuitontli* (lesser feast of the lords). Rites celebrated by the salters. Sacrifice of a woman representing Uixtociuatl, goddess of salt-water.

8   *Uey tecuilhuitl* (great feast of the lords). Distribution of victuals to the populace. Dances. Sacrifice of a woman personifying Xilonen, goddess of the young maize.

9   *Tlaxochimaco* (offering of flowers). The people went into the country to gather flowers and decorated the temple of Uitzilopochtli. Rejoicings, banquets, important dances.

10   *Xocotl uetzi* (the fruit falls). Feast of the god of fire. Sacrifice of prisoners at Xiuhtecuhtli or Ueueteotl. The

young men climbed a maypole with an image made of *huauhtli*-paste on top of it and fought for the pieces.

11 *Ochpaniztli* (sweeping). Feast of the goddesses of the earth and of vegetation, who are always shown holding a grass broom in their hands, with which they were supposed to sweep the path of the gods (that is, of the maize, vegetation, etc.). Dances. Mock battles between women, female healers and courtesans. Sacrifice of a woman incarnating Toci or Teteoinnan, the mother of the gods. Parade of warriors before the emperor, who gave them badges of honour or weapons.

12 *Teotleco* (return of the gods). The gods were held to come back to the earth: first Tezcatlipoca and finally the old god of the fire, to whom human sacrifices were offered.

13 *Tepeilhuitl* (feast of the mountains). Little images of *huauhtli*-paste were made in the shape of mountains (gods of the rain) and eaten. Sacrifice of five women and one man, representing the agrarian deities.

14 *Quecholli* (name of a bird). Feast of Mixcoatl, the god of hunting. Arrows were made. Great hunt upon Zacatepetl. Sacrifices to Mixcoatl.

15 *Panquetzaliztli* (raising of the *quetzal*-plume banners). Great feast of Uitzilopochtli: mock battles. Procession of the god Paynal, Uitzilopochtli's assistant, going through many places in the neighbourhood of Mexico. Sacrifices.

16 *Atemoztli* (coming down of the water). Feast of the gods of rain. Fast. Making of amaranth-paste images of the rain-gods which were then 'killed' with a *tzotzopaztli* (a long flat piece of a loom). Offerings of food and drink.

17 *Tititl* (?). Sacrifice of a woman entirely clothed in white, personifying the old goddess Ilamatecuhtli. Carnival battles in which the youths attacked the women with bolsters.

18 *Izcalli* (growth). Feast in honour of the god of fire. Children were presented to the fire and their ears were pierced. Every four years victims dressed and decorated to represent the god were sacrificed.

And in the last place came the five *nemontemi* days, thought to be so baneful that nothing was done while they lasted.

NOTES

1 *Mexica* is the plural of *Mexicatl*, 'a Mexican'. It is pronounced meshícatl, with the stress on the i. (See Appendix I on the pronunciation of Aztec words.)

2 'I have heard tell of a great lord called Muteczoma' writes Cortés to Charles V (*Cartes de Relación*, [New York, 1828] p. 48). It was on the shore of the Gulf of Mexico, at San Juan de Ulúa, during Holy Week, 1519, that the Spaniards had their first contact with, officials of the Mexican empire; these were Pinotl, governor of the province of Cuetlaxtlan, with two accompanying administrators of towns, and two dignitaries, Tentlitl and Cuitlalpitoc, called by Bernal Díaz Tendil and Pitalpitoque (Bernal Díaz del Castillo, *Historia verdadera de la Conquista de la Nueva España*, [Mexico 1950] vol. I, p. 160). The Aztec version of the events, collected by Sahagún (*Historia general de las Cosas de Nueva España*, [Mexico 1938] vol. IV pp. 134 ff.) describes this first encounter; the Mexican dignitaries having arrived by boat and having been received on board, 'the Spaniards asked them, "Who are you? Where do you come from?" They answered, "We come from Mexico." The Spaniards said, "If it is true that you are Mexicans, what is the name of the king of Mexico?" They answered, "Lords, his name is Motecuhzoma."' Then followed an exchange of presents (the Mexicans gave splendid embroidered cloth and the Spaniards some glass baubles) and the Mexicans regained the shore, and 'day after day, night after night, they travelled to tell Motecuhzoma and to be the first to bring him the truth.' To confirm what they had to say, they brought the emperor not only the presents of Cortés, but drawings of the Spaniards' ships, guns, horses and armour.

As the Spaniards thrust deeper into the country, they heard more and more of Motecuhzoma and his power. 'When they speak of the Mexicans in this country it is as who should say the Romans' (Díaz, p. 179). The lord Olintecutli spent an evening telling the Spaniards of the greatness of Mexico, the wealth and the military power of the emperor. 'Cortés and all the rest of us were astonished when we heard of it.' (Ibid. p. 230).

The fame of Motecuhzoma stretched beyond the limits of the empire, into the country of the northern 'savages'. Father Soriano, in an unpublished manuscript (see Jacques Soustelle, *La Famille otomí-pame du Mexique central*, [Paris 1937] and *Documents sur les Langues pame et jonaz du Mexique central* in the *Journal de la Société des Américanistes*, [Paris 1951] vol. XL pp. 1–10) states that the Pames worshipped Motecuhzoma. Even now, throughout the region formerly inhabited by the Chichimecs of the Sierra Gorda the word 'moctezuma' means the ruins of ancient cities. Motecuhzoma is also still to be seen in native stories, in which he appears both as a great king and as a benevolent magician, the possessor of magical powers, such as that of changing himself into an eagle, of flying, etc. (Nahuatl *Tale of Motecuhzoma and of the Snake*, collected in 1942. R. and I. Weitlaner, *Acatlán y Hueycantenango, Guerrero*, in *México Antiguo* [Mexico 1943] vol. VI p. 174).

3 See p. 233.

4 This is the expression used by Mendieta in his *Historia eclesiástica indiana*, book V, 1st part, ch. XLI.

5 This is the case, for example, with the documents numbered 108 to 118 in the Aubin-Goupil collection in the Bibliothèque Nationale at Paris. See E. Boban, *Documents pour servir à l'histoire du Mexique* (Paris 1891) vol. II, pp. 287 ff.

6 Sahagún, vol. IV p. 163.

7 The list of provinces, with the account of the taxes paid by each, is given in the *Codex Mendoza*, edited by J. C. Clark, (London 1938). See also R. H. Barlow,

The Extent of the Empire of the Culhua Mexica (University of California Press, Berkeley, 1949).

8 Now Tuxpan, State of Veracruz, and Tuxtepec, State of Oaxaca.

9 Michoacán (in Nahuatl 'the country of the owners of fish', or 'of fishermen') had as its capital Tzintzuntzan, on the shore of the great lake of Pátzcuaro. The Mexicans had tried in vain to conquer it: the emperor Axayacatl was heavily defeated at Taximaroa. (Tezozomoc, edited by Ternaux-Compans, [Paris 1853] pp. 279–283).

10 It was thus for example that the province of Cuetlaxtlan, on the Gulf of Mexico, rebelled against Axayacatl in the year *chicnaui acatl*, 'nine – reed', or 1475. (*Codex Telleriano-Remensis* ed. Hamy, [Paris 1899] p. 37). The Cuetlaxtecs shut the Mexican tax-gatherers into a house and set fire to it (Tezozomoc, vol. I p. 176).

11 The *coa* (Aztec *uictli*) was the Indians' ploughing implement: it was a digging-stick that broadened, above its point, into a kind of spade. It is still used in some parts.

12 'For, said they (the Mexicans), their calling was not to work, but to fight and to make weapons.' (Tezozomoc, vol. II p. 67).

13 Tolocan, now Toluca, capital of the State of Mexico. Tlachco, now Taxco, in the State of Guerrero.

14 Ornaments which the Mexicans fixed to the lower lip.

15 This feast was called *Atamalqualiztli* '(feast at which) boiled *tamales* are eaten'. In the course of this ceremony, '*manca in atl, uncan temia in cocoa ihuan in cueyame ihuan in yehuantin moteneua mazateca uncan quintoloaya in cocoa zan yoyoltiuia*' – a vessel was set down full of water containing snakes and frogs, and the people called Mazatecs swallowed them alive. (*Codex Florentino*, ed. Anderson and Dibble [Santa Fe, New Mexico, 1951] vol. II p. 163).

16 Tepoztlán, in the present State of Morelos, was a little town conquered by the Mexicans under Auitzotl. Its inhabitants, who spoke Nahuatl, worshipped the

god Tepoztecatl, 'he of Tepoztlán', whose temple still exists. (cf. R. H. K. Marett, *Archaeological Tours from Mexico City* [Oxford University Press, 1933] p. 90). This god is set down as one of the gods of drunkenness (*Codex Florentino*, vol. I p. 24).

17 For example, the *Mimixcoa icuic*, 'song of the *Mimixcoa*' (the cloud-snakes), *Codex Florentino* vol. II p. 209, and the song of Amimitl, ibid. p. 210. These texts are both, the one partially and the other wholly, drawn up in the Chichimec language.

18 See the admirable statue of a *maceualli* in Salvador Toscano, *Arte precolumbino de México y de la América Central*, (Mexico 1952) p. 284.

CHAPTER ONE

THE CITY

1 Glyph is the usual term for the 'characters' of Aztec or Mayan writing.

2 Hermann Beyer, *The original meaning of the Mexican coat of arms*, in *México Antiguo*, vol. II (Mexico 1929) pp. 192–193.

3 Lawrence Ecker, *Testimonio otomí sobre la etimología de 'Mexico' y 'Coyoacán'*, in *México Antigua*, vol. V (Mexico 1940) pp. 198–201. See also C. A. Castro, *Testimonio Pame Meridional sobre la etimología de 'México'*, in *Tlatoani*, No. 2 (Mexico 1952) p. 33.

4 Father Antonio del Rincón, *Arte Mexicana* (Mexico 1595). Reprinted by A. Peñafiel (Mexico 1885). P. 81 *'Mexicco: Ciudad de México, i.e. en medio de la luna'*.

5 Alfonso Caso, *El Ombligo de la Luna*, in *Tlatoani*, no. 5–6 (Mexico 1952) p. 74.

6 This is the name for Mexico in the Codex of Huichapan, a post-cortesian manuscript in the Otomí language which is preserved in the Mexican national museum of history and anthropology. This codex has been described by Alfonso Caso, *Un Códice en otomí*, in the *Proceedings of the XXIII International Congress of Americanists* (New York 1930) pp. 130–135, and by Jacques Soustelle, *La Famille otomí-pame du Mexique central*, (Paris [Institut d'Ethnologie] 1937) pp. 213–214. Even now the Otomí use the word *bondo* or *bonda* for the city of Mexico, and the word *dezânâ* for the Mexican language (Nahuatl).

7 This manuscript belongs to the Bibliothèque Nationale (Aubin-Goupil collection). It was published in Paris under the title *Histoire mexicaine*. The picture mentioned here is on p. 48.

8 The *Codex Mendoza* is a historical document of the very first importance; it was drawn up by native scribes at the command of the viceroy don Antonio de Mendoza (1535–1550) to be sent to Charles V.

The ship which was carrying it to Spain was seized by French privateers, and the codex came into the possession of André Thévet, the king's cosmographer, whose name is to be seen upon the page that is quoted here. The codex is now in the Bodleian library at Oxford, and it was edited in 1938 by James Cooper Clark (London, Waterlow and Sons).

9 According to tradition, the Mexicans came from a mythical place, an island in the middle of a lake, whose name Aztlán (whence *Azteca*, the Aztecs) evokes an idea of whiteness.

10 This account is taken from pp. 62–66 of the *Crónica Mexicayotl*, a collection of chronicles written in Nahuatl after the conquest, published in Mexico (*Imprenta Universitaria*) in 1949.

11 A pictographic manuscript with Nahuatl captions, belonging to the Bibliothèque Nationale (Aubin-Goupil collection). It has been published by the *Journal des Américanistes* (Paris 1949). The scene mentioned here is on p. 13.

12 This is the expression used by the emperor Cuauhtemotzin. See *Ordenanza del Señor Çuauhtémoc*, published by Silvia Rendon (Tulane University of Louisiana, New Orleans, 1952).

13 In 1925, Hermann Beyer described the spear-thrower which was still in use at that time for wildfowling in the region of Texcoco, in the magazine *México Antiguo*, vol. II.

On the subject of the god Atlaua, see the hymn *Atlahoa icuic*, which was sung in his honour (*Codex Florentino*, in Nahuatl with English translation, edited by Anderson and Dibble [Santa Fé, New Mexico, 1951] vol. II p. 213) and Seler's remarks in Sahagún, *Historia general de las Cosas de Nueva España*, (Mexico 1938) vol. V p. 170.

On Amimitl, see the hymn to this god (*Codex Florentino*, the same edition, p. 211) and Seler's remarks on p. 104 of the same edition of Sahagún. Amimitl and Atlaua were the gods of the lake-dwellers of Cuitlahuac, a village on the sweet-water lake, whose inhabitants lived primarily upon fish and wildfowl. The *Historia de los Mexicanos por sus pinturas*, a document based upon precortesian native manuscripts and drawn up after the conquest (published by Joaquín García Icazbalceta, *Nueva Colección de documentos para la historia de México*, vol. III [Mexico 1891] pp. 228-263) states that Amimitl was the chief god of the men of Cuitlahuac, and that he was identified with an arrow of the Chichimec hunting-god Mixcoatl.

The hymn to Amimitl is in a dialect of Nahuatl that the Mexicans scarcely understood any more and which they described as 'Chichimec', as may be seen by the Aztec note to the text in the Madrid manuscript – 'This song of Amimitl is completely Chichimec (barbarous) and it is not really known what it means in our Nahuatl language.'

As to Opochtli, he was the god of a small coastal town, Uichilat, whose people were Chichimecs; and he was a water-god. His particular weapons were the darts meant for duck-hunting and the thrower. The *Historia de los Mexicanos por sus pinturas*, which gives these details, adds that this water-god was, like Uitzilopochtli, left-handed (*opochtli*, 'left' or 'left-handed man'; *uitzilopochtli*, 'the left-handed humming-bird' or 'humming-bird from the left') and that the two gods *fueron muy amigos*, were great friends. Still according to the same source, the village where this water-god was worshipped took the name of Uitzilo-pochco, 'Uitzilopochtli's place', after the coming of the Mexicans. It is the present town of Churubusco.

In each of these three cases, we have to do with the deities of 'lake-dwelling savages', deities whose chief rôle was the protection of wildfowling on the lake.

14 Tezozomoc, *Histoire du Mexique*. Translation by H. Ternaux-Compans (Paris 1853) vol. I p. 15.

15 *Crónica Mexicayotl*, pp. 71-73.

16 *Codex Florentino*, Anderson and Dibble, vol. II p. 77.

17 On the fall of Tlatelolco, see particularly Tezozomoc, op. cit., pp. 221–247; Ixtlilxochitl, *Historia Chichimeca,* (Mexico 1892) pp. 251–252; *Crónica Mexicayotl,* pp. 117–120; *Codex Azcatitlan,* p. 19. This last manuscript shows the great temple of Tlatelolco, with the body of Moquiuixtli lying broken on its steps.

18 See particularly A. F. Bandelier, *On the social organisation and mode of government of the ancient Mexicans* in the *XII Annual Report of the Peabody Museum* pp. 557–699, and George C. Vaillant, *Aztecs of Mexico* (Garden City, New York, 1947) pp. 111 ff. Bandelier's ideas are based upon a very debatable assimilation of the Mexicans with the North American Indians, and they are now quite out of date; Vaillant, one of the best American archæologists, has nevertheless a tendency to follow the same errors, though in a much attenuated form.

19 Tezozomoc, p. 10.

20 On the *calpulli,* see particularly Manuel M. Moreno, *La Organización política y social de los Aztecas* (Mexico 1931).

21 This map is in the Bibliothèque Nationale (Aubin-Goupil collection). See E. Boban, *Documents pour servir à l'histoire du Mexique. Catalogue raisonné de la collection de M. E. Eugène Goupil* (Paris 1891) vol. II pp. 318–321.

22 In the *Crónica Mexicayotl,* pp. 74–75, Uitzilopochtli speaks of fourteen *calpulli* and gives the order to divide them into four sections, Moyotlan, Teopan, Tzaqualco [*sic*] and Cuepopan.

23 On this point, see Vaillant, p. 134, who adopts the figure of 60,000 homes and allows them five persons on the average, or 300,000 inhabitants. The 'anonymous conqueror' (*Narrative of some things of New Spain, translated into English by M. H. Saville* [New York 1917]) is the source of this estimate. Torquemada, *Veinte i un Libros rituales i Monarchia indiana,* (Madrid 1723) vol. I p. 295. It must also be remembered that

whole families lived on boats, as is the case now in some Asiatic countries. See Sahagún, vol. IV p. 220.

24 The conquerors reached the edge of the lake at Mizquic and spent their last night on the coast at Iztapalapan. 'And seeing so many towns and villages built in the water and other great towns on the dry land . . . we were struck with astonishment, and we said that these were enchantments, like those that the book of Amadis speaks of, because of the great towers, the temples and the pyramids which rose from the water; and some soldiers even wondered whether it were not a dream,' writes a witness (Bernal Díaz del Castillo, *Historia verdadera de la Conquista de la Nueva España* [Mexico 1950] vol. I p. 330).

25 Hernan Cortés, *Cartas de Relación* (New York 1828) p. 109.

26 Ibid. p. 158.

27 This is the famous 'sad night' of June 30, 1520, during which the invaders were expelled from the city by the emperor Cuitlahuac.

28 Díaz del Castillo, pp. 355–356.

29 Hernan Cortés, pp. 146–147.

30 *Relation abrégée sur la Nouvelle Espagne et sur la grande ville de Temixtitan [sic] Mexico, écrite par un gentilhomme de la suite de Fernand Cortés*, published by H. Ternaux-Compans, *Voyages, relations et mémoires originaux pour servir à l'histoire de la découverte de l'Amérique* (Paris 1838) vol. X p. 93.

31 Cortés, p. 108.

32 Díaz del Castillo, vol. I p. 332.

33 See the reproduction of this map in Ignacio Marquina, *Arquitectura prehispánica* (Mexico 1951) p. 182.

34 On this important monument some six miles from Mexico, see Marquina, p. 164, and the very complete work published by the department of monuments in the ministry of public education: *Tenayuca*, (Mexico, 1935).

35 See the plan of the central square and the buildings which surrounded it in Marquina, plate 54.

36 'Could we make a better choice than our beloved son Uitziliuitl? Although he is still young, he will be able to govern us and defend the temple of Uitzilopochtli,' Tezozomoc, vol. I p. 18. 'Do not forget that all your ancestors . . . thought it their duty to govern and to judge impartially, and to defend the temple of Uitzilopochtli.' Speech addressed to Itzcoatl, ibid. p. 46.

37 Chimalpopoca, 'the smoking shield', reigned from 1414 to 1428 over a city that was still dependent upon Atzcapotzalco. He was murdered upon the orders of the ruler of Atzcapotzalco.

38 Motecuhzoma, 'he who grows angry (like a) lord', had the appellation of Ilhuicamina, 'he who shoots arrows against the sky'. He is sometimes called *Ueue*, 'the elder', to distinguish him from the second emperor of the name. He reigned from 1440 to 1469.

39 Tezozomoc, pp. 151–153.

40 Tizoc, 1481–1486. Auitzotl, 1486–1503.

41 *Codex Telleriano-Remensis*, a pictographic manuscript with Spanish annotations which belongs to the Bibliothèque Nationale. Reproduced with an introduction by E. T. Hamy (Paris 1899) pp. 38 and 39.

42 See particularly Marquina, p. 186.

43 Many of these details can be restored by comparison with the pyramid of Tenayuca, which has already been mentioned, and with the Aztec temple of Huatusco, State of Veracruz, whose sanctuary has survived almost untouched. See Vaillant, *Aztecs of Mexico*, pl. 51, and Marquina, photo 60.

Another Aztec temple in good condition is that of Teopanzalco (Cuernavaca): cf. George C. Vaillant, *Enlivening the Past*, in *Natural History* vol. XXXI (New York 1931) p. 531.

For the Mayan monuments, see Sylvanus G. Morley, *The Ancient Maya*, (Stanford, California, 1946) p. 348.

The *Codex Ixtlilxochitl* in the Bibliothèque Nationale in Paris shows the two sanctuaries at the top of the pyramid of the great temple, with their distinctive ornamentation. Boban, atlas, pl. 71. The great temple of Texcoco was also crowned with two sanctuaries: Ixtlilxochitl, *Historia Chichimeca*, p. 184.

44 The fifteenth month, which was consecrated particularly to Uitzilopochtli, was called *Panquetzaliztli*, 'the feast of the banners of *quetzal*-plumes'.

45 On the Toltec monuments of Tula, see Marquina, op. cit., p. 145, and Alberto Ruz Lhuillier, *Guía arqueológica de Tula*, (Mexico 1945). On the Tolteco-Maya monuments of Yucatán, see Morley, pp. 325 ff.

46 Ruz Lhuillier, p. 36.

47 Tezozomoc, p. 193. Díaz (pp. 359–360) concurs: he states that there were even law-suits between the conquerors and the representatives of the Spanish crown to decide how the treasure should be divided.

48 *Relation abrégée sur la Nouvelle Espagne . . .* p. 98.

49 Sahagún, vol. I pp. 218 ff. Nahuatl text in *Codex Florentino* vol. II pp. 165–180. Cortés (p. 152) writes that the chief 'mosque' (temple) had no less than 'forty very high and well-built towers'.

50 Díaz del Castillo, pp. 360–361.

51 See José García Payón, *La Zona arqueológica de Tecaxic-Calixtlahuaca y los Matlatzincas* (Mexico 1936). In the State of Veracruz, the same author has studied the temple of the wind-god at Cempoala, which has the same circular shape. See Marquina, pp. 472–473.

52 Marquina, photo 78.

53 *Codex Florentino*, vol. II p. 168.

54 Díaz del Castillo, p. 361, 'And not far from there (the temple of Quetzalcoatl) there was a large reservoir which received the water by a covered channel from the aqueduct which came into the town from Chapultepec.' On the various springs and the priests' baths. see the *Codex Florentino*, vol. II pp. 167, 171, 174, 178,

55 *Codex Florentino*, vol. II p. 177. These two houses were called Yopicalco and Euacalco.

56 *Relation abrégée . . .* p. 100.

57 Sahagún, vol. II, pp. 308 ff.

58 Cortés, p. 160.
59 Díaz del Castillo, vol. I pp. 346 ff.
60 On the great market of Tlatelolco, see Cortés, pp. 147–151; Díaz del Castillo, pp. 352–354; *Relation abrégée ...* pp. 95–96; Sahagún, vol. I pp. 325–327.
61 No doubt the drying-up of the valley had been going on for a long time through natural causes, but it has been considerably hastened by human agency. In order to avoid any more floods, the draining canal of Nochistongo was opened in 1609, and then, in 1900, the great Desagüe canal and the Tequixquiac tunnel. An unforeseen and catastrophic result of these works has been not only the disappearance of the surface-water, which has transformed the lakes into dusty wastes, but the drying-out of the subsoil. In formerly water-logged parts the water made up four fifths of the soil: this being removed – a condition made worse by the sinking of many artesian wells – the ground shrinks and subsides. Thus the sites upon which the city of Mexico stands, being for the most part alluvial *jaboncillo*, regularly contract: the average level of the town sinks by about a foot and a half in a year, which is ten times faster than it did in 1910. The bottom of the lake of Texcoco is now nearly ten feet above the level of Mexico, as well as the canal and the tunnel for drainage; and therefore, to prevent the floods, which were starting again worse than ever, pumps have had to be installed at great expense to deal with seepage and sewage.
62 Sahagún, vol. IV (account of the siege of Mexico by Aztec witnesses), p. 206.
63 *Codex of 1576*, pp. 35 and 36; *Codex Axcatitlan*, pp. 10 and 11.
64 On the aqueduct of Chapultepec, see Sahagún, vol. III p. 293; Cortés, p. 157; *Relation abrégée*, p. 93.
65 Of the various accounts that have come down to us, that of Tezozomoc (vol. II pp. 55–58) is the most complete, and it goes into all the magical and religious aspect of the matter. Ixtlilxochitl (p. 291) devotes a

short chapter to the history of the spring of Acuecuexatl, principally to emphasize the benevolent rôle of
Nezaualpilli, the king of Texcoco. The flood is
mentioned in the *Codex of* 1576, p. 76, which states
that it destroyed the maize-fields: at the side of the
year *chicome acatl*, 'seven – reed', 1499, a stream of
water is to be seen, carrying away ears of corn.
Sahagún (vol. III p. 293) briefly relates the tradition
and adds that the viceroy, don Gastón de Peralta,
tried to make use of Acuecuexatl, but without success,
and that he had to give up the idea.

66   On the latrines, see Díaz del Castillo, p. 353; Sahagún,
vol. III p. 295, 'the land which has been thus manured
is called *tlalauic, quiere decir tierra suave, porque la
han adobado con estiércol.*' On the cleaning of the
streets, Toribio, quoted by Prescott, vol. II p. 114.

67   Vaillant, p. 225.

68   Spengler, *Le Déclin de l'Occident* (Paris 1948) vol. II
pp. 88 and 93.

CHAPTER TWO

SOCIETY AND THE STATE AT THE BEGINNING OF THE SIXTEENTH CENTURY

1   On the migration of the Mexicans, see particularly *Codex of* 1576, a pictographic manuscript in the Bibliothèque Nationale, Paris, and published under the title *Histoire de la Nation mexicaine* (Paris [Lerous] 1893); and *Codex Azcatitlan,* published in the *Journal de la Société des Américanistes,* vol. XXXVIII (Paris 1949).

2   This refers to the capture and execution of 'king' Uitziliuitl the elder by the men of Colhuacán. *Codex Azcatitlan,* pl. XI; and all the old sources concur on these events.

3   Alonso de Zurita, *Breve y sumaria relación* . . . p. 96.

4   Ibid. p. 93.

5   Ibid. p. 95.

6   Torquemada, *Veinte i un libros rituales i Monarchía indiana,* book XIV, ch. V. Cf. Manuel M. Moreno, *La Organización política y social de los Aztecas,* (Mexico 1931) p. 46.

7   Diego Durán, *Historia de la Nueva España y islas de Tierra Firme,* (Mexico 1867) vol. I pp. 323–324.

8   Sahagún, vol. I p. 144.

9   Ibid. vol. II pp. 212–214.

10   See *Uitznauac yaotl icuic,* 2nd strophe, in which the archaic *ihiiaquetl* is the equivalent of *iyac. Codex Florentino,* edition cited, vol. II p. 207.

11   *Quachic,* 'he who has his hair cut on the top of his head (*quaitl*)'. *Quachichictli,* 'corona de clérigo', Molina, *Vocabulario en lengua castellana y mexicana* (Mexico 1571: facsimile edition, Leipzig 1880) p. 84 of the Mexican section.

12 The jaguar was a symbol of Tezcatlipoca. See Jacques Soustelle, *La Pensée cosmologique des ancients Mexicains* (Paris 1940) p. 15.

13 The eagle was a symbol of the sun. Ibid. p. 8. In the national museum of Mexico there is an admirable head of an eagle-knight in carved stone. This sculpture is reproduced in André Malraux, *Le Musée imaginaire de la Sculpture mondiale* (Paris 1952) pl. 354.

14 *Codex Florentino*, vol. II pp. 114 and 115. The traditional expression *atl-tlachinolli*, 'water and conflagration', means war, and more particularly sacred war; it is written with a special hieroglyphic in which there are the signs for water and for fire. See Alfonso Caso, *El Teocalli de la Guerra Sagrada*, (Mexico 1927) pp. 30 and 31.

15 Tezozomoc, vol. II pp. 164–166.

16 Ibid. vol. I pp. 70–71.

17 Sahagún, vol. I p. 138.

18 Ibid. vol. I pp. 159–162. Aztec text in *Codex Florentino* vol. II pp. 93–95.

19 *Quaquachictin*, plural of *quachic*. *Otomi*, plural of *Otomitl*. *Tequiuaque*, plural of *tequiua*.

20 Sahagún, vol. I p. 168.

21 On the *pilli* (or rather *pipiltin*, plural) see Zurita, p. 98.

22 The *Codex Mendoza* gives the following exact details—
    at Oztoman, a *tlacochtecuhtli* and a *tlacateccatl*
    at Quetcholtenanco, a *tlacatecuhtli*
    at Atlán and at Tezapotitlán, a *tlacochtecuhtli*
    at Xoconochco, a *tezcacoacatl* and a *tlillancalqui*
    at Zozolan and at Uaxyacac (Oaxaca), a *tlacatecuhtli* and a *tlacochtecuhtli*.

23 On the *calpixque*, see Zurita, p. 165.

24 Díaz del Castillo, vol. I p. 187.

25 Pomar, *Relación de Texcoco* (1582) (Mexico 1891) p. 31.

26 Sahagún, vol. II p. 317.

27 Zurita, p. 112.

28 Ibid.

29 Torquemada, vol. I p. 185.

30 Sahagún, vol. I pp. 298–299.

31 *Anales de Cuauhtitlán. Códice Chimalpopoca: Anales de Cuauhtitlán y Leyenda de los Soles. Traducción directa del nahuatl por el lic. don Primo Feliciano Velázquez*, (Mexico 1945) p. 7.

32 Cf. for example, *tlallocan tlamacazqui*, *quiaui teteu*, 'priests of Tlalocan, gods of the rain', *Codex Florentino* vol. II p. 210. Piltzintecuhtli, god of youth and the dance, is termed *tlamacazecatla*, an archaic form of *tlamacazqui* (ibid.).

33 Sahagún, vol. I p. 299. *Quequetzalcoa* is the plural of *quetzalcoatl*.

34 Alfonso Caso, *La Religión de los Aztecas* (Mexico 1936) pp. 45 ff. Sahagún, vol. I p. 237.

35 This word comes from *tlaquimilolli* 'a thing wrapped up (in cloth)', in Spanish *lío* or *envoltorio*. During the migration, the images of the gods or the sacred objects that stood in their stead were carried swathed in this way. In historical times, certain temples preserved *tlaquimilolli* that contained, for example, a mirror (Tezcatlipoca) or agave-thorns (Uitzilopochtli): Pomar, op. cit., p. 13.

36 Zurita, p. 217.

37 Torquemada, vol. II p. 104.

38 *'Intla ie itlano, in iehoatl in cihoatlamacazqui, auh intla uel omotlali in tlatolli intla ocezque, in tetahoan, in tenanhoan in tlaxillacaleque in pipilti(n).'* *Codex Florentino*, vol. II p. 215.

39 The sweeping of the temples was not merely an act of cleanliness. It had a ritual meaning; for in sweeping, one opened the way for the gods. One of the months of the year was called *Ochpaniztli*, 'sweeping'.

40 These delicacies were *tzopelic tamalli*, 'sugared tamales'. *Codex Florentino*, vol. II p. 126.

41 *'Tlazoltilmatica'*, *Codex Florentino*, vol. II p. 116. The goddess of maize had the name of Chicomecoatl, 'seven-serpent', or again of Chicomollotzin, 'the venerable (goddess of) seven ears of maize'.

42 Torquemada, vol. II p. 189.

43 Sahagún, vol. II p. 211.

44 Ibid. vol. I pp. 324 and 350.

45 Fr. Andrés de Alcobiz, *Estas son las leyes que tenían los Indios de la Nueva España* ... (1543) (Mexico 1891) p. 310.

46 *Historia de los Mexicanos por sus pinturas*, p. 259.

47 This idea continually recurs throughout the literature. See *Codex Telleriano-Remensis* (Paris 1899) p. II (verso), where a stream of water is shown carrying away men and wealth.

48 Tezozomoc, vol. II pp. 78–79.

49 *Codex Mendoza*, pp. 40, 45 and 48.

50 An excellent description of mercantile life is to be found in Sahagún, vol. II pp. 339 ff.

51 Chimalpahin Quauhtlehuanitzin, *Anales* (R. Siméon, Paris 1889) p. 174.

52 Sahagún, vol. II p. 339.

53 This refers to a province that had only recently been subjugated. It was inhabited by Tzotzil, a Mayan-speaking tribe, and it now forms part of the Mexican state of Chiapas. Tzinacantlan, 'place of the bats' in Aztec, is a translation of Tzotzil, which comes from the Mayan *tzotz*, a bat.

54 Sahagún, vol. II p. 343.

55 Ibid. p. 364.

56 Ibid. p. 364.

57 This was the *Yiacatecuhtli icuic*, published with a Spanish translation in Sahagún, vol. V p. 185, and with an English translation in *Codex Florentino*, edition cited, vol. II p. 214.

58 Sahagún, vol. II p. 367. During these festivities the dignitaries danced in front of the merchants, who did not take part in the dancing, but offered presents afterwards.

59 Ixtlilxochitl, *Historia Chichimeca*, p. 268. He adds, 'She was so cultured that she could give points to the king and the most cultivated men, and she was poetically gifted. And with these gifts and graces she held the king very much under her domination ... She lived apart, in great pomp and majesty, in a

palace that the king had built for her.' Might not this
be a portrait of a favourite of Louis XV?

60 *Anales de Cuauhtitlán*, edition cited, p. 8.
61 Sahagún, vol. III pp. 109 ff.
62 *Codex Florentino*, vol. III p. 13. A poetical translation
    of this text is to be found in J. H. Cornyn, *The Song
    of Quetzalcoatl*, in *Mexican Folkways*, vol. IV No. 2
    (Mexico 1928) pp. 78 ff.
63 Ixtlilxochitl, *Relaciones*, p. 59 (Colhuacán) and p. 454
    (Xochimilco).
64 Sahagún vol. II p. 389.
65 *Codex Florentino*, vol. II p. 207. The text of the
    commentaries in Aztec is given by Eduard Seler,
    Die religiösen Gesänge der alten Mexikaner, in *Gesam-
    melte Abhandlungen* . . . vol. II (Berlin 1904) pp. 959–
    1107: Spanish translation in Sahagún, edition cited,
    vol. V, *Los cantares a los Dioses*.
66 *Anauatl iteouh: tzapoteca in uel inteouh catca*, in *Codex
    Florentino*, vol. I p. 16.
67 Sahagún, vol. II p. 386.
68 Ibid. vol. III p. 133.
69 The 'golden mantle', *teocuitlaquemitl*, distinguishes the
    god Xipe Totec. See *Codex Florentino*, vol. II p. 213.
70 Díaz del Castillo, vol. I p. 349.
71 Pomar, p. 41. The *Crónica Mexicayotl*, p. 113, says
    that the sons of Motecuhzoma I who were not able to
    reign gave themselves up to the practice of the minor
    arts.
72 Tezozomoc, vol. II pp. 206 and 209.
73 Motolinía, *Memoriales*, p. 344.
74 Molina, p. 50 verso.
75 Tezozomoc, vol. II pp. 81–82.
76 Chimalpahin Quauhtlehuanitzin, p. 108.
77 'Labrador, gañán.' Molina, p. 124.
78 On the landless peasants, see Zurita, p. 157.
79 Motolinía, p. 319.
80 Ibid. All the details given in this paragraph come from
    the same source.

81 Sahagún, vol. II p. 308 (Motecuhzoma). Motolinía, p. 323 (Nezaualpilli).
82 Sahagún, vol. I p. 321.
83 Alcobiz, pp. 308 and 313.
84 Motolinía, p. 320, '*En esta tierra, de balde daban su cuerpo las más veces.*'
85 Sahagún, vol. II pp. 371 ff and p. 379.
86 Ibid. vol. I pp. 321–322.
87 *Codex Telleriano-Remensis*, p. 11 verso.
88 Zurita, p. 93.
89 Alcobiz, pp. 309, 314.
90 Zurita, p. 221.
91 For example, Tezozomoc, vol. I pp. 45 and 45, 71 and 72; Ixtlilxochitl, *Historia Chichimeca*, p. 170.
92 The Spaniards' cupidity was much disappointed when they found that the copper axes which they had taken to Cuba, believing them to be gold, became covered with verdigris. (Díaz del Castillo, vol. I p. 49).
93 Zurita, p. 159.
94 Tezozomoc, vol. I pp. 67–68, 128, 135, 179.
95 Ibid. p. 183.
96 Díaz del Castillo, vol. I p. 184.
97 Zurita, p. 161.
98 Ixtlilxochitl, *Historia Chichimeca*, p. 168.
99 Sahagún, vol. I pp. 158–159.
100 Ixtlilxochitl, *Historia Chichimeca*, p. 206. Tezozomoc, vol. II p. 67.
101 Zurita, p. 158.
102 Particularly Bandelier, *On the social organization and mode of government of the ancient Mexicans*, in the *XII Annual Report of the Peabody Museum*, pp. 557–699.
103 *Relación de la genealogía y linaje de los señores que han señoreado en esta tierra de la Nueva España* . . . *Escribimos por mandado de nuestro Prelado, a ruego é intercesión de Juan Cano, Español, marido de doña Isabel, hija de Montezuma, el segundo de este nombre, señor que era de la Ciudad de México*, published by J. García Icazbalceta, *Nueva Colección de documentos para la historia de México*, (Mexico 1891) pp. 263–281.

104 *Historia de los Mexicanos por sus pinturas*, p. 249.

105 See the discussion of this question in Marshall H. Saville, *Tizoc, great lord of the Aztecs* (1481-1486), in *Contributions from the Museum of American Indian, Heye Foundation*, vol. III no. 4 (New York 1929) p. 23.

106 Ixtlilxochitl, *Historia Chichimeca*, p. 213; Oviedo, *Diálogo del Alcayde de la Fortaleza de la Cibdad é Puerto de Santo Domingo de la Isla Espanola* . . . (con) *un caballero vecino de la gran cibdad de México, llamado Thoan Cano*, published by William H. Prescott in *History of the Conquest of Mexico* (Philadelphia 1864) vol. III, appendix, pp. 452 ff. See also Pomar, p. 25.

107 Zurita, p. 80.

108 Ixtlilxochitl, p. 241.

109 Torquemada, vol. I p. 101.

110 Tezozomoc, vol. I pp. 332–333.

111 Sahagún, vol. II p. 321.

112 See Tezozomoc, vol. I pp. 306 and 335; vol. II p. 73.

113 Sahagún, vol. II p. 322. Models for speeches are given, ibid., pp. 77, 82, 91, 93 and 97. For descriptions of the imperial vestments see Tezozomoc, passages quoted, note 112, and Saville, *op. cit.*, p. 40.

114 Pomar, p. 35.

115 In the *Codex Mendoza*, p. 2, Acamapichtli is shown before his election as emperor together with the glyph *Ciuacoatl*. On the title of *Ciuacoatl* at Xochimilco, cf. *Historia de los Mexicanos por sus pinturas*, p. 262; at Colhuacán, *Codex Azcatitlan*, p. XI; and at Texcoco, Ixtlilxochitl, *Relaciones*, pp. 178 and 193, and Pomar, p. 19.

116 Tezozomoc, vol. I p. 100.

117 Chimalpahin Quauhtlehuanitzin, p. 126.

118 Torquemada, vol. II pp. 351–352.

119 Tezozomoc, vol. I p. 129.

120 Ibid. p. 195.

121 Ibid. pp. 212, 305, 333; vol. II p. 68.

122 Ibid. vol. II p. 107.

123 Ibid. vol. I p. 188.

124 *Crónica Mexicayotl*, p. 129.
125 Chimalpahin Quauhtlehuanitzin, p. 107.
126 Torquemada, vol. II p. 352.
127 *Crónica Mexicayotl*, p. 115.
128 Ibid. p. 149.
129 A remarkable fact was that at Texcoco the traders had access to one of the four great councils, that of finance, together with the dignitaries. Ixtlilxochitl, *Relaciones*, p. 326; Torquemada, vol. I p. 147.

CHAPTER THREE

THE WORLD, MAN AND TIME

1 There is an immense literature upon the subject. The chief native pictographic manuscripts to be consulted are the following:

Codex Borbonicus (Paris 1899)

Codex Borgia (Kingsborough, London 1831–1848, vol. III)

Codex Cospiano di Bologna (Rome 1898)

Codex Fejérváry-Mayer (Paris 1901)

Codex Magliabecchiano (Rome 1904)

Codex Ríos (Vaticanus A) (Rome 1900)

Codex Telleriano-Remensis (Paris 1899)

Tonalamatl Aubin (Paris 1900)

Codex Vaticanus B (Rome 1896).

Some texts are paraphrases of pre-cortesian pictographic manuscripts: chief among these are the *Anales de Cuauhtitlán* and the *Historia de los Mexicanos por sus pinturas.* Of the Spanish chroniclers, Sahagún contains the essential; but the following may also be consulted with profit:

Durán, *Historia de las Indias de Nueva España y las Islas de Tierra firme,* (Mexico 1867–1880) (2 volumes)

Motolinía, *Memoriales,* (Mexico 1903)

Torquemada, *Veinte i un libros rituales i Monarchía indiana* (Madrid 1723) (3 volumes).

On towns other than Mexico, see:

Muñoz Camargo, *Historia de Tlaxcala* (Mexico 1892)

Pomar, *Relación de Texcoco* (Mexico 1891).

Modern authors:

Alfonso Caso, *La Religión de los Aztecas* (Mexico 1936)

Alfonso Caso, *El Pueblo del Sol* (Mexico 1953)

Eduard Seler, *Gesammelte Abhandlungen zur Amerikanischen Sprach- und Alterthumskunde* (particularly vol. I [Berlin 1903] pp. 417–503, and vol. II [104] pp. 959–1107) Jacques Soustelle, *La Pensée cosmologique des anciens Mexicains* (Paris 1940).

2 On the Maya-Quiché, see the *Popol-Vuh*. C. J. Villacorta and Flavio Rodas, *El Manuscrito de Chichicastenango* (*Popol Buj*) (Guatemala 1927). Leonhard Schultze-Jena, *Popol Vuh, das heilige Buch der Quiché-Indianer von Guatemala* (Stuttgart 1944).

3 *Leyenda de los Soles, Codex Chimalpopoca*, (Mexico 1945) pp. 119 ff.

4 A. Caso, *La Religión de los Aztecas*, figures 1, 2, 3 and 4.

5 Muñoz Camargo, *Historia de Tlaxcala*, p. 155.

6 Sahagún, vol. II, pp. 256 ff. The Aztec text, after the Madrid manuscript, is to be found in Garibay, *Llave del Náhuatl* (Otumba 1940) pp. 125–130.

7 *Quauhxicalli*, from *quauhtli*, an eagle, and *xicalli*, a calabash or vessel, means 'the vessel of the eagle, of the sun'.

8 *Anales de Cuauhtitlán, Codex Chimalpopoca*, p. 8.

9 See, for example, *Codex Telleriano-Remensis*, pp. 32 verso, 38 verso, 39, 40 etc.

10 On Xipe Totec, see the representation of this god dressed in the skin of a victim in Caso, *El Pueblo del Sol*, pl. IX. On the rites celebrated in honour of the god, *Codex Florentino*, vol. II pp. 46 ff.

11 Jacques Soustelle, *Respect aux dieux morts*, in *Cahiers de la Compagnie Madeleine Renaud—J.-L. Barrault* no. 1 (Paris [Julliard] 1954) pp. 93 ff.

12 For example, Cortés had the feet of the pilot Gonzalo de Umbría cut off, two Spaniards hanged and others given two hundred strokes of the whip (Díaz del Castillo, vol. I p. 220). He had Indian prisoners' hands cut off (ibid. p. 265). On the massacres of Cholula and Mexico, see Díaz del Castillo, p. 309, and Sahagún, vol. IV pp. 169–171. On the torture and the execution of Cuauhtemotzin, see Héctor Pérez Martínez, *Cuauhtémoc, vida y muerte de una cultura*

(Mexico) (French translation [Laffont] Paris 1952).

13 The passage referring to the mutual feelings of captive and captor is to be found in the *Codex Florentino* vol. II pp. 52–53. For the words of the emperor to a prisoner of war, see Tezozomoc, vol. II p. 177.

14 Tezozomoc, vol. I p. 116.

15 Muñoz Camargo, pp. 125–128. Another version, less favourable to the Tlaxcaltec warrior, is given by Tezozomoc, vol. II p. 175. See also Torquemada, vol. I p. 220.

16 It was Cortés who had Quauhpopoca and four other dignitaries burnt alive in front of the imperial palace: see Díaz del Castillo, vol. I p. 375, and Prescott, *History of the Conquest of Mexico*, (Philadelphia 1864) vol. II pp. 171–173.

17 Ixtlilxochitl, *Historia Chichimeca*, pp. 205–208.

18 See Alfonso Caso, *El Teocalli de la Guerra Sagrada* (Mexico 1927).

19 Alfonso Caso, *El Pueblo del Sol* (Mexico 1953).

20 Sahagún, vol. I p. 259 ff.

21 *Codex Florentino,* vol. I p. 1.

22 Ibid. vol. II p. 207.

23 Ibid. vol. III p. 208.

24 See the statues of Coatlicue in Malraux, *Le Musée imaginaire de la Sculpture mondiale* (Paris [Gallimard] 1952) pl. 352 and 355. Comments by J. Soustelle, ibid., pp. 740–741.

25 *Teteo innan icuic* (Song of the mother of the gods), *Codex Florentino*, vol. III p. 208. *Ciuacoatl icuic*, ibid. p. 211.

26 Pp. 49 and 59 of the *Codex Magliabecchiano* are devoted to the representation of the gods of drunkenness and to that of the goddess of the agave and of *octli*, Mayauel.

27 Sahagún, vol. V p. 150 (hymn to Xipe Totec).

28 Ibid. pp. 90–91 (song of Xochipilli), 98 (song of Xochiquetzal), 158 (song of Chicomecoatl) and 178 (song of Macuilxochitl).

29 Paul Westheim, *Arte antiguo de México*, (Mexico 1950) fig. 55.

30 Jacques Soustelle, *La Pensée cosmologique* ... pp. 80–81.
31 The literal meaning of *tonalpoualli* is 'the account of the days'. See Alfonso Caso, *¿Tenían los Teotihuacanos conocimiento del Tonalpohualli?* in *México Antiguo*, vol. IV no. 3–4 (Mexico 1937) pp. 131–143. *Tonalamatl* means 'the book of the days', and is used for the manuscript which the soothsayers employed.
32 The representation of these groups of thirteen is particularly to be found in the codices *Borbonicus, Telleriano-Remensis and Ríos*. There are detailed explanations in Sahagún, vol. I pp. 305–361.
33 *Codex Fejérváry-Mayer*, p. 1.
34 *Codex Cospiano*, pp. 12–13; *Borgia*, p. 72.
35 The fall of Mexico and its capture by Cortés (August 13, 1521) happened on a day 1 *coatl* considered generally favourable, but in a year *calli*, whose sign brings to mind decline, the setting of the sun, decadence, death. The last Mexican emperor was called Cuauhtemotzin, 'the descending eagle', that is to say, 'the setting sun'.
36 Sahagún, vol. II pp. 11–26.
37 Ibid. p. 23.
38 Tezozomoc, vol. I pp. 229–231. Another prodigy took place at Tlatelolco, according to the same author, when the king's wife, taking her bath, began talking in the manner of the characters in Diderot's *Les Bijoux indiscrets*.
39 Sahagún, vol. IV p. 25.
40 Ixtlilxochitl, *Historia Chichimeca*, p. 313.
41 Sahagún, vol. IV p. 24.
42 Jacques Soustelle, *La Famille otomi-pame du Mexique central*, (Paris 1937) pp. 532–533.
43 On this question see A. Casa, *El Pueblo del Sol*, pp. 20–21.
44 Ixtlilxochitl, *Historia Chichimeca*, p. 227. Pomar (*Relación de Texcoco*, p. 24) confirms Ixtlilxochitl's version. The same belief was to be found at Tlaxcala (Muñoz Camargo, *Historia de Tlaxcala*, p. 130).

A MEXICAN'S DAY

1 Sahagún, vol. II p. 364.
2 Díaz del Castillo, vol. I p. 335.
3 *Codex Telleriano-Remensis*, pp. 29–30.
4 R. H. Barlow, *The Extent of the Empire of the Culhua Mexica* (Berkeley 1949) p. 42.
5 Díaz del Castillo, vol. I p. 336.
6 From *petlatl*, mat, and *calli*, house: literally 'a mat house' and thus 'wickerwork chest'. The Spanish word *petaca*, which is derived from *petlacalli*, means a cigarette-holder in Europe, but in Mexico it has retained its sense of 'valise'.
7 Díaz del Castillo, vol. I p. 335. The secret room in which the treasure was hidden was opened in the end by the Spaniards, who were then Motecuhzoma's guests (ibid. p. 364). It contained such vast wealth, especially in gold, that Díaz 'held it for certain that in the whole world there was not its like.'
8 Díaz del Castillo, vol. I p. 344.
9 Sahagún, vol. I p. 95.
10 Ibid. vol. II p. 31.
11 Ibid. vol. II pp. 347–349 and 361. They were sparing, as tradesmen ought to be, and they only gave the fire-god the heads of the birds served at the banquet.
12 Ixtlilxochitl, *Historia Chichimeca*, pp. 174 ff.
13 Ixtlilxochitl here employs the Arabic word *alcázar*: this must no doubt be understood as summer-houses or little rural châteaux.
14 Ixtlilxochitl, *Historia Chichimeca*, pp. 208–212.
15 R. H. K. Marett, *Archaeological Tours from Mexico City*, (Oxford University Press 1933) pp. 76–77.
16 Díaz del Castillo, vol. I pp. 330–331.
17 Cortés, pp. 160–162.
18 Andrés de Tapia, *Relación sobre la conquista de México*, published by J. García Icazbalceta in *Documentos para la historia de México* (Mexico 1866) pp. 581–582.
19 Díaz del Castillo, vol. I pp. 348–349.
20 Tezozomoc, vol. I pp. 211–212.

21 *Relation anonyme* . . . published by Ternaux-Compans: *Voyages, relations et mémoires* . . . vol. X (Paris 1838) p. 100.

22 Rafael García Granados, *Filias y Fobias* (Mexico 1937)· pp. 111–112.

23 Zurita, *Breve y sumaria relación* . . . p. 111. Motolinía, *Memoriales*, p. 305.

24 Tapia, p. 581.

25 Clavigero, *Historia antigua de México*, vol. II p. 349.

26 Ibid. p. 368.

27 Sahagún, vol. II p. 346. *Codex Florentino*, vol. II p. 139.

28 *Codex Florentino*, vol. II pp. 130–131. Uitzilopochco (now Churubusco) means 'the place of Uitzilopochtli'. Uitzilatl means 'the water (*atl*) of the humming-bird (*uitzilin*)'.

29 *Codex Florentino*, vol. II p. 77.

30 A good description and drawings are to be found in Clavigero, vol. II pp. 349 ff.

31 Robert Redfield, *Tepoztlán, a Mexican Village*, (University of Chicago 1930) p. 137.

32 *Codex of* 1576, p. 45.

33 A very fine obsidian mirror with a frame of carved wood is to be found in the Museum of the American Indian, Heye Foundation, New York. It is illustrated in C. A. Burland, *Art and Life in ancient Mexico* (Oxford 1948) p. 43. The Musée de l'Homme in Paris has a marcasite mirror whose back is engraved with a representation of the wind-god Eecatl. See E. T. Hamy, *La Galerie américaine du Musée d'Ethnographie du Trocadéro* (Paris, n.d.) vol. I pl. XI no. 34.

34 *Codex Telleriano-Remensis*, p. 17.

35 On the Huaxtecs, see Sahagún, vol. III p. 132. On the Otomí, ibid. p. 124.

36 *Codex Azcatitlan*, pl. V, XI etc.

37 Sahagún, vol. III p. 123.

38 Ibid., vol. II pp. 128–130.

39 The Aztec word *tzictli*, which has been corrupted into *chicle*, means the gum that comes from the

coagulated sap of the *chicozapote* (*Achras sapota L.*), a tree of the tropical regions. It is the raw material of chewing-gum. Cf. Maximino Martínez, *Plantas útiles de la República Mexicana* (Mexico 1928), pp. 142–145.

40 Sahagún, vol. III pp. 47–48.

41 Among the Olmecs: see, for example, the statue called The Wrestler in the *Catalogue de l'Exposition d'Art mexicain* (Paris, *Musée d'Art modern*, 1952) pl. IV and V. Among the Mayas, see particularly Agustín Villagra Caleti, *Bonampak, la ciudad de los muros pintados* (Mexico 1949), and Gilbert Medioni, *Art maya du Mexique et du Guatemala* (Paris 1950).

42 Sahagún, vol. III p. 132, '*Los hombres* (Huaxtec) *no traen maxtles con que cubrir sus vergüenzas.*' On the clothing of the Tarascas, see Muñoz Camargo, *Historia de Tlaxcala*, p. 9. The *Codex Telleriano-Remensis*, p. 33 verso, shows a warrior of Xiquipilco (valley of Toluca) wearing a *maxtlatl*, in the act of fighting with a Tarasca dressed in a short white tunic.

43 *Relation anonyme* . . . Ternaux-Compans, vol. X p. 64.

44 *Codex Telleriano-Remensis*, pp. 29 verso, 30, 32 etc.

45 '*Liberales de su cuerpo*', according to Sahagún, vol. I pp. 317–318.

46 *Codex Magliabecchiano*, the first eight leaves.

47 See the illustrated album of Wilfrido du Solier, *Indumentaria antigua mexicana* (Mexico 1950).

48 Sahagún, vol. II pp. 293–295.

49 Boban, pl. 66, 68, 69.

50 Marquina, *Arquitectura prehispánica*, fig. 49.

51 Marquina, fig. 69.

52 *Codex Telleriano-Remensis*, pp. 31, 34, 37, 42 etc.

53 *Codex Azcatitlan*, pl. V, X, XI. *Codex Telleriano-Remensis*, p. 43. Boban, pl. LXX (clothing of Tlaloc).

54 du Solier, pl. X.

55 *Codex Florentino*, vol. II p. 93.

56 *Codex Telleriano-Remensis*, p. 30.

57 Sahagún, vol. III pp. 131–132.

58 Aztec text of the manuscript of Sahagún in Walter Krickeberg, *Los Totonaca* (Mexico 1933), pp. 50–51.

59 Sahagún, vol. III p. 134.
60 Ibid., p. 124.
61 Krickeberg, p. 50.
62 For example, the statue of the goddess Chalchiuhtlicue in the Mexican museum. A. Caso, *El Pueblo del Sol*, pl. V.
63 J. Soustelle, *La Famille otomí-pame du Mexique central* (Paris 1937), pp. 91–95 and 516.
64 du Solier, pl. XXV, XXVI, XXVII, XXXII. See also Keith Anderson's drawings in George C. Vaillant, *Artists and Craftsmen in ancient Central America*, (New York 1935) p. 65.
65 Especially the Otomí of the State of Mexico.
66 *Crónica Mexicayotl*, pp. 90–91.
67 See particularly Barlow, *The Extent of the Empire of the Culhua Mexica* (Berkeley 1949).
68 Gabriel Fernández Ledesma, *Calzado mexicano*, (Mexico 1930).
69 Díaz del Castillo, vol. I p. 333.
70 Tezozomoc, vol. I p. 307. The act of piercing the nasal septum is shown in various manuscripts, for example, the *Codex Nuttall*: this picture is reproduced in C. A. Burland, *Magic Books from Mexico* (Penguin edition 1953) pl. XIII.
71 *Codex Florentino*, vol. II p. 94.
72 Tezozomoc, vol. I pp. 187–188. On the ornaments and emblems, see Eduard Seler, *Altmexikanischer Schmuck und soziale und militärische Rangabzeichen*, in *Gesammelte Abhandlungen* . . . vol. II, 1904, pp. 397–419: and Hans Dietschy, *La Coiffure de plumes mexicaine du musée de Vienne*, in *Actes du XXVIIIe Congrès international des Américanistes* (Paris 1948) pp. 381–392.
73 Villagra Caleti, pl. I.
74 Sahagún, vol. II p. 119.
75 Motolinía, p. 305.
76 Ixtlilxochitl, *Historia Chichimeca*, p. 193.
77 Ibid.
78 Zurita, p. 112.

79 Motolinía, p. 306.
80 Díaz del Castillo, pp. 343-345.
81 Motolinía, pp. 306-307.
82 Ixtlilxochitl, *Relaciones*, p. 238.
83 Ibid., *Historia Chichimeca*, p. 184.
84 Andrés de Alcobiz, *Estas son las leyes que tenían los Indios de la Nueva España* . . . (1543), published by J. García Icazbalceta, *Nueva Colección de documentos para la historia de México* (Mexico 1891), p. 308.
85 For the organisation of the judiciary, see Zurita, pp. 109-113.
86 *Codex Florentino*, vol. II pp. 42 ff. See also Appendix II of this book, *The eighteen months and the rites*.
87 *Uey tecuilhuitl. Codex Florentino*, vol. II pp. 91 ff.
88 On the month *Panquetzaliztli* see *Codex Florentino*, vol. II pp. 130 ff. On *Atemoztli*, ibid., pp. 137-138. On *Tititl*, ibid., pp. 145-146.
89 Ixtlilxochitl, *Historia Chichimeca*, p. 286.
90 A list and description of all these little trades is to be found in Sahagún, vol. III pp. 52 ff.
91 *Crónica Mexicayotl*, pp. 132-133.
92 Tezozomoc, vol. II pp. 56-57.
93 *Huauhtli* is *Amaranthus paniculatus var. leucocarpus:* Maximino Martínez, *Plantas útiles de la República Mexicana* (Mexico 1928), pp. 22-27. *Chian is Salvia hispanica L.* (ibid., pp. 134-138).
94 Clavigero, vol. II, p. 366.
95 Ignacio Alcocer, *Las Comidas de los antiguos Mexicanos*, an essay added as a supplement to vol. III of Sahagún, p. 367.
96 Díaz del Castillo, vol. I p. 344.
97 Ibid., p. 345.
98 Sahagún, vol. II pp. 306-307.
99 Alcocer, pp. 367 ff.; Sahagún, vol. II pp. 305-307.
100 On the different kinds of water-birds on the lake of Mexico, see Sahagún, vol. III pp. 172 ff.
101 Sahagún, vol. III pp. 193-195; Alcocer, *loc. cit.*
102 Sahagún, vol. II p. 372.
103 Muñoz Camargo, p. 155. He says himself, on p. 156,

that dogs were still sacrificed to Tlaloc in his day, and that he had taken it up with the authorities in order to have 'this error extirpated'.

104 Martínez, *Plantas útiles* . . . p. 25.
105 *Codex Florentino*, vol. II p. 92.
106 Sahagún, vol. III p. 125.
107 Ibid., pp. 233–237.
108 Chimalpahin Quauhtlehuanitzin, p. 106.
109 Ixtlilxochitl, *Historia Chichimeca*, p. 206.
110 Sahagún, vol. II pp. 372–374.
111 Muriel N. Porter, *Pipas precortesianas*, in *Acta Anthropologica*, III, 2, (Mexico 1943).
112 Muñoz Camargo, p. 134; Sahagún, vol. II p. 367 and vol. III pp. 229–231.
113 On *peyotl* (*Lophophora williamsii*) see particularly Léon Diguet, *Le Peyotl et son usage rituel chez les Indiens du Nayarit* in *Journal de la Société des Américanistes* (Paris 1907); A. Rouhier, *Le Peyotl la plante qui fait les yeux émerveillés* (Paris 1927); Richard Evan Schultes, *Peyote, an American Indian heritage from Mexico*, in *México Antiguo*, vol. IV. no. 5–6 (Mexico 1938) pp. 199–208; Maximino Martínez, *Plantas medicinales de México*, pp. 215 ff.
114 Sahagún, vol. II p. 367.
115 On the gods of drunkenness, see particularly A. Caso, *El Pueblo del Sol*, pp. 68–69. The *Codex Magliabecchiano* devotes ten pages (49–59) to representations of these gods. Mayauel is shown in the *Codex Borbonicus*, p. 8. In Sahagún, vol. I p. 237, it may be seen how great an importance the priests of the *Centzon Totochtin* had in the Aztec clergy. A religious song proper to these deities is reproduced in the *Codex Florentino*, vol. II p. 213.
116 Sahagún, vol. II pp. 99 ff.
117 Sahagún, vol. I p. 293.
118 Ixtlilxochitl, *Relaciones*, p. 238.
119 Ixtlilxochitl, *Historia Chichimeca*, pp. 188–189.
120 Sahagún, vol. I p. 357.
121 Tezozomoc, vol. II p. 80.

122 *Popol-Vuh:* cf. Ch. III, note 2. The decorated vase from Teotihuacán belongs to the Musée de l'Homme at Paris: a reproduction is to be found in J. Soustelle, *La Culture matérielle des Indiens Lacandons,* in the *Journal de la Société des Américanistes,* vol. XXIX, (Paris 1937) pl. II C.

123 *Codex Florentino,* vol. II pp. 126–127.

124 Motolinía, p. 320.

125 *Codex Magliabecchiano,* p. 80; J. Cooper Clark, *The Story of Eight Deer,* (London 1912) p. 14.

126 On *tlachtli,* see particularly
Muñoz Camargo, p. 136
Frans Blom, *The Maya ball-game Pok-ta-pok,* (Publication no. 4, Middle American Papers, Tulane University of Louisiana, New Orleans 1932)
T. A. Joyce, *The pottery whistle-figurines of Labaantun,* in the *Journal of the Royal Anthropological Institute,* vol. LXIII, 1933, pp. XV–XXV.

127 Symbolic nature of the ball-game: A. Caso, *El Pueblo del Sol,* pp. 103–104.
Death of the lord of Xochimilco: Ixtlilxochitl, *Historia Chichimeca,* p. 255.

128 Alfonso Caso, *Un antiguo juego mexicano, el Patolli,* in *México Antiguo,* vol. II, no. 9 (Mexico 1925) pp. 203–211. See also A. Caso, *Notas sobre juegos antiguos* in *Mexican Folkways,* vol. VII, no. 2 (Mexico 1932) pp. 56–60; Muñoz Camargo, p. 136; and *Codex Magliabecchiano,* p. 60.

129 Sahagún, vol. I p. 346.

130 Muñoz Camargo, p. 159.

131 Sahagún, vol. I pp. 241–242.

CHAPTER FIVE

FROM BIRTH TO DEATH

1 Sahagún, vol. II pp. 186 ff.
2 Ibid., pp. 189–190.
3 Muñoz Camargo, p. 149. This author insists upon the obligation upon the parents to make known the birth of the child to their relatives and friends, who would be vexed if they were not told. See also Sahagún, vol. II pp. 196 ff.
4 Sahagún, vol. I p. 323; vol. II p. 211.
5 Sahagún, vol. II pp. 212–217. The *Codex Mendoza* depicts these rites, and in the picture the midwife is shown with the wrinkles of an old woman.
6 Sahagún, vol. I p. 321.
7 A. Caso, *Explicación del reverso del Codex Vindobonensis*, (Mexico 1951).
8 For example, see *Codex of* 1576, p. 5 (glyphs corresponding to the proper names Quauhcoatl, Apanecatl, Tezcacoatl and Chimalman), pp. 28 (Tezozomoctli), 32 (Tenochtli); *Codex Azcatitlan*, pp. XI (Uitziliuitl, Chimalaxochitl, Tozpanxochitl), XIII (Tezozomoc and Quaquauhpitzauac), XIV ff. (names of the Mexican emperors); *Codex Telleriano-Remensis*, pp. 30 (Uitziliuitl), 31 (Chimalpopoca and Itzcoatl), 32 (Nezaualcoyotl), 33 verso (Quauhtlatoa), 36 (Nezaualpilli), etc.
9 Torquemada, vol. II pp. 186–187.
10 Ibid.
11 Sahagún, vol. I p. 195, 'If (the boy who was going to enter the *calmecac*) were the son of poor people. . .'
12 Ibid., p. 299.
13 Torquemada, vol. II. p. 179.
14 Sahagún, vol. I pp. 288 ff.; Torquemada, vol. II p. 221; Zurita, p. 121.
15 Sahagún, vol. II p. 222.
16 Ibid., vol. I p. 298.
17 Torquemada, vol. II p. 189.

18 Sahagún, vol. I pp. 291–293.
19 Ibid., p. 293.
20 *Codex Florentino*, vol. II pp. 137–138.
21 Torquemada, vol. II pp. 220–221.
22 Ibid., p. 187.
23 Ixtlilxochitl, *Historia Chichimeca*, p. 213.
24 Sahagún, vol. II p. 151.
25 Motolinía, p. 255.
26 Sahagún, vol. II p. 152.
27 For a description of the preparations and of the wedding itself, see Sahagún, vol. II pp. 152 ff., and Motolinía, pp. 260 ff.
28 This scene is shown in the *Codex Mendoza*, p. 61.
29 Motolinía, p. 263.
30 Oviedo, *Diálogo del Alcayde de la Fortaleza de la Cibdad é Puerto de Santo Domingo . . . de la una parte, é de la otra, un caballero vecino de la gran Cibdad de México, llamado Thoan (sic) Cano*, published by Prescott, *History of the Conquest of Mexico*, Appendix (Original Documents), vol. III, pp. 453–454.
31 Pomar, *Relación de Texcoco*, p. 25.
32 Ixtlilxochitl, *Historia Chichimeca*, p. 213.
33 *Relation anonyme . . .* Ternaux-Compans, *Voyages, relations et mémoires*, vol. X (Paris 1838), p. 103.
34 Muñoz Camargo, p. 137.
35 Ixtlilxochitl, *Historia Chichimeca*, p. 267.
36 Ibid., pp. 219–222.
37 Ibid., p. 294.
38 Ibid., p. 268.
39 Ibid., p. 267.
40 *Crónica Mexicayotl*, pp. 137–139, 143–146, 150–157.
41 Ibid., pp. 125–127
42 Motolinía, p. 325.
43 Muñoz Camargo, p. 138.
44 *Crónica Mexicayotl*, pp. 117–119.
45 Ixtlilxochitl, *Historia Chichimeca*, p. 29.
46 *Historia de los Mexicanos por sus pinturas*, published by Icazbalceta, *Nueva Colección de documentos para la historia de México*, vol. III (Mexico 1891) p. 249.

47 *Relación de la genealogía y linaje de los señores* . . .
published by Icazbalceta, ibid., pp. 273-275. On the
Toltec character of Colhuacán, see Ixtlilxochitl,
Relaciones, p. 59.

48 Chimalpahin Quauhtlehuanitzin, p. 108.

49 Sahagún, vol. II p. 351.

50 Motolinía, p. 320.

51 *Codex Florentino*, vol. II p. 93.

52 Ibid., pp. 61-62.

53 *Codex Telleriano-Remensis*, p. 17.

54 Alcobiz, *Estas son las leyes* . . . published by Icazbalceta, *Nueva colección de documentos* . . . vol. III
(Mexico 1891) p. 311.

55 Ixtlilxochitl, *Historia Chichimeca*, pp. 285-287.

56 See George C. Vaillant, *Aztecs of Mexico*, (Garden-
City, N.Y., 1947) p. 112, and Ixtlilxochitl, *Relaciones*,
p. 239.

57 Zurita, p. 112.

58 Seler, in Sahagún, vol. V p. 118.

59 Sahagún, vol. II pp. 158-159.

60 The Aztec text of the prayer to Ayopechcatl is to be
found in Sahagún, vol. V pp. 116-117 (with translation
and commentary by Seler) and in the *Codex Florentino*,
vol. II p. 211 (with English translation).

61 Sahagún, vol. II pp. 30, 32, 33, and pp. 176-178.

62 Martínez, *Plantas medicinales de México* (Mexico
1944), pp. 331-338. Modern experiments show that
this plant does in fact possess the properties that the
ancient Mexicans attributed to it.

63 'The tail of this little animal is highly medicinal.
Women in labour who drink a small amount are
delivered at once . . . Whoever eats the bones or the tail
of the *tlaquatzin*, even a dog or a cat, instantly voids
his own bowels.' (Sahagún, vol. III p. 156). A decoc-
tion of *nopal* leaves was also used (ibid., p. 263).

64 Sahagún, vol. II p. 181.

65 Ibid., pp. 181-183. The young men were not alone in
attributing magic properties to the bodies of the
'valliant women'. Malignant wizards did their utmost

to acquire the left arm of one of these women: they used it, in their spells, to paralyse the inhabitants of a house and send them to sleep while they robbed it at their leisure. (Sahagún, vol. I pp. 350–351.)

66 *Codex Florentino*, vol. I p. 6. On the 'coming back' of the *Ciuateteo*, see *Codex Telleriano-Remensis*, p. 18 verso, and Sahagún, vol. I p. 341.

67 See Georgette Soustelle, Tequila: *Un Village Nahuatl du Mexique Oriental* (Institut d'Ethnologie, Paris, 1958).

68 *Codex Florentino*, vol. I p. 4.

69 Hernando Ruiz de Alarcón, *Tratado de las supersticiones y costumbres gentílicas que oy viuen entre los Indios naturales desta Nueva España*, (1629), published in *Anales del Museo Nacional de México*, vol. VI (Mexico 1892) pp. 123–223. '*La causa de la enfermedad del niño es faltarle su hado o fortuna o estrella, que estas tres cosas se comprehenden en la lengua mexicana debaxo deste nombre tonalli*' (p. 197).

70 Sahagún, vol. I p. 48.

71 Ibid., p. 287.

72 Ibid., p. 22.

73 Ruiz de Alarcón, pp. 182–183.

74 *Codex Florentino*, vol. I pp. 13 and 16.

75 Jacinto de La Serna, *Manual de ministros de Indios para el conocimiento de sus idolatrias y extirpación de ellas* (1656), published in *Anales del Museo Nacional de México*, vol. VI, 1892, pp. 261–480, p. 284.

76 *Codex Florentino*, vol. I p. 15. On Tzapotlatenan, ibid., p. 5.

77 Ruiz de Alarcón, pp. 193–197.

78 The *ololiuhqui* (a *Datura*?) does not appear to have been exactly identified. Cf. Martínez, *Plantas medicinales de México* (Mexico 1944) pp. 505–508, and B. P. Reko, *Das mexikanische Rauschgift 'ololiuhqui'*, in *México Antiguo* vol. III, no. 3–4 (Mexico 1934) pp. 1–7.

79 Ruiz de Alarcón, pp. 142–145: de La Serna, p. 303.

80 *Codex Florentino*, vol. I p. 4. Motolinía, p. 126, 'The magicians had bundles of thin cord like bunches of

keys, and these they threw on the ground. If the cords remained entwined, it was said to foretell death, but if one or several of them separated itself from the others, it was a sign of recovery.'

81 De La Serna, pp. 400–401.

82 Sahagún, vol. III p. 47, 'The (woman healer) pretended to draw worms from the teeth, and from the other parts of the body, paper and flint, which is used as a knife in this country; and in drawing all this from the bodies of the sick people she claimed to heal them.'

83 Ruiz de Alarcón, pp. 196, 200, 230: de La Serna, pp. 414–415.

84 Ruiz de Alarcón, p. 200. Quato and Caxoch are two deities who appear only in the invocations of doctors and midwives. Cf. de La Serna, p. 409.

85 Martínez, *Plantas medicinales* . . . pp. 378–379.

86 De La Serna, p. 416.

87 De La Serna (pp. 425–426) describes the operation: each stage was accompanied by magical formulæ addressed to the bones, the splints and the cords.

88 Clavigero, *Historia antigua de México*, vol. II p. 349.

89 Sahagún, vol. III p. 281.

90 Ibid., p. 282. The epidemic referred to is that of *matlazahuatl* (? plague) which killed at least two million people in 1576.

91 Ibid., p. 267.

92 On Francisco Hernández, see Clavigero, vol. II p. 345, and Martínez, *Plantas medicinales* . . . pp. 14–16. The first edition of Francisco Hernández's book appears to be that of Mexico in 1615 (abridged), which was followed by the best-known edition, that of Rome, in 1651.

93 On this subject, see particularly Sahagún, vol. III pp. 229–276; Ignacio Alcocer, *Consideraciones sobre la medicina azteca*, an essay published as a supplement to Sahagún, vol. III pp. 375–382; Martínez, *Plantas útiles de la República mexicana* (Mexico 1928) and *Plantas medicinales de México* (Mexico 1944); Del Paso y Troncoso, *Estudio sobre la historia de la medicina*

en México. La Botánica entre los Nahoas, in *Anales del Museo Nacional de México,* vol. III, 1896, pp. 140–235; Paul C. Standley, *Trees and Shrubs of Mexico,* in *Contributions from the U.S. National Herbarium,* vol. XXIII (Washington, 1920–1926).

94 Torquemada, vol. I p. 206.

95 *Codex Florentino,* vol. I pp. 8–11. Sahagún, vol. I p. 28, says, 'And even now, when an Indian commits murder or adultery, he takes refuge in one of our monasteries . . . He confesses . . . and asks for a certificate signed by the confessor so that he may show it to the authorities, the governor or the *alcaldes,* to prove that he has confessed and done his penance and that consequently the law has nothing further to do with him.'

96 Sahagún, vol. I p. 287.

97 Sahagún, vol. III p. 198.

98 On the tomb-pyramid of Palenque, cf. Alberto Ruz Lhuillier, *Estudio de la cripta del Templo de las Inscripciones en Palenque,* in *Tlatoani,* vol. I, no. 5–6 (Mexico 1952) pp. 3–28. By the same author, *Exploraciones en Palenque: 1950–1951,* in *Anales del Instituto Nacional de Antropología e Historia,* vol. V (Mexico 1952) pp. 25–66. Jacques Soustelle, *Une Ancienne Cité maya: Palenque,* in *Revue de Paris,* February 1954, pp. 111–121.

On the tombs of Monte Albán, cf. Alfonso Caso, *Las Tumbas de Monte Albán,* in *Anales del Museo Nacional de México,* Epoca 4a., vol. VIII, no. 4 (Mexico 1933) pp. 641–648.

On the pyre of Quetzalcoatl, see *Anales de Cuauhtitlán, Códice Chimalpopoca,* (Mexico 1945) p. 11.

99 Ixtlilxochitl, *Historia Chichimeca,* p. 97.

100 Muñoz Camargo, p. 148.

101 *Relation anonyme . . .* p. 213.

102 Letter published by Ternaux-Compans in *Voyages, relations et mémoires,* vol. X (Paris 1838) p. 213.

103 Pomar, *Relación de Texcoco,* p. 38.

104 *Codex Magliabecchiano,* pp. 66–69.

105 Pomar, *loc. cit.:* Tezozomoc, vol. I pp. 302–303.
106 *Auh in uncan chicunamictlan uncan ocempopolioa*—and
there, in the ninth dwelling-place of the dead, there
they were completely done away with. (*Codex Florentino*, vol. III p. 42.)

CHAPTER SIX

WAR

1 Alfonso Caso, *El Teocalli de la Guerra Sagrada* (Mexico 1927) pp. 30-32.
2 *Leyenda de los Soles, Códice Chimalpopoca,* (Mexico 1945) p. 123.
3 Ixtlilxochitl, *Historia Chichimeca,* p. 190.
4 Ibid.
5 Tezozomoc, vol. II p. 26.
6 Ibid., vol. I pp. 48-49.
7 Motolinía, pp. 294-295.
8 Tezozomoc, vol. I p. 26.
9 *Crónica Mexicayotl,* p. 119: Tezozomoc, vol. I pp. 216 ff., pp. 221-222.
10 This Tlacaeleltzin, a famous figure in Aztec history, was the founder of the dynasty of the *Ciuacoatl,* which, running parallel with that of the emperors, was very important in the expansion of Tenochtitlan's empire. At that time, in 1428, he had the military title of *atempanecatl,* 'he (who commands) at the water's edge'.
11 Tezozomoc, vol. I pp. 35-36.
12 Andrés de Tapia, *Relación de la conquista de México,* published by Icazbalceta in *Documentos para la historia de México* (Mexico 1866), p. 592: 'He who obeyed peaceably was not obliged to pay a definite tribute, but, so many times in the year, he sent a present at his own discretion . . . And in these cities no steward or taxgatherer was placed.'
13 Plural of *quauhnochtli,* the term for the heart of a sacrificed warrior: it was also used as a military title.
14 Motolinía, p. 295.
15 On the embassies, see Motolinía, *loc. cit.,* and Ixtlilxochitl, *Historia Chichimeca,* pp. 190-192.
16 Plural of the word *achcauhtli,* which meant officials, of varying status according to the city. At Mexico they formed a kind of police-force for the application of judicial decisions.

17 Sahagún, vol. I p. 345.
18 On the *quimichtin*, see Motolinía, p. 295: 'They were called mice because they went about by night or secretly, hiding themselves.' On the disguised merchants called *naualoztomeca*, see Sahagún, vol. II pp. 356 ff.
19 Fifth statute of Nezaualcoyotl: Ixtlilxochitl, *Relaciones* p. 237.
20 Motolinía, p. 298.
21 Tezozomoc, vol. I p. 257.
22 A scene shown in the *Codex Telleriano-Remensis*, p. 42 verso, the year 'six—reed'.
23 This scene from the *Codex Nuttall* is reproduced in Herbert J. Spinden, *Ancient Civilisations of Mexico and Central America* (New York [American Museum of Natural History] 1928) fig. 85.
24 As examples of these emblems may be quoted the *zaquanpapalotl*, butterfly made of yellow feathers; the *quetzaltotol*, *quetzal*-bird; the *zaquanpanitl*, a flag of yellow feathers; the *zaquantonatiuh*, a solar disc of feathers; the *macuilpanitl*, an ornament made of five banners; etc. These badges and some others, after the original paintings by Aztec artists, are shown in Sahagún, vol. II pl. 2, 3 and 4.
25 Motolinía, p. 297.
26 Motolinía, *loc. cit.*, gives this information speaking of the king of Texcoco. A page of a pictographic manuscript attributed to Ixtlilxochitl in the Bibliothèque Nationale at Paris, shows Nezaualcoyotl, king of Texcoco, dressed in magnificent feather-armour, his head covered with a helmet, holding in his hands a shield and a sword, while round his neck there is hung a little conical drum. Boban has published a reproduction of this page in *Catalogue raisonné . . . atlas*, pl. 67.
27 Tezozomoc, vol. I p. 257.
28 *Codex Mendoza*, p. 6: *Codex Nuttall*; reproduction in J. Cooper Clark, *The Story of 'Eight Deer'* (London 1912) pl. D.

29 Similar scenes are described in Tezozomoc, vol. I pp. 128, 135 and 179.

30 R. H. Barlow, *La Fundación de la Triple Alianza* (1427–1433) in *Anales del Instituto Nacional de Antropologia e Historia* vol. III (Mexico 1949) pp. 147–156. See particularly p. 151.

31 Sahagún, vol. IV. Díaz del Castillo, *Historia verdadera* . . . vol. II pp. 74–305. Cortés, pp. 196–456. Clavigero, vol. III pp. 165–314. Prescott, vol. II pp. 301–474 and vol. III pp. 1–214.

32 In the account given in Sahagún (vol. IV p. 220) of the Mexican defeat, this passage stands out – 'Everywhere, and in the streets, the Spaniards were robbing; they were searching for gold . . . They took, they picked out the best-looking light-brown women . . . And they also picked out men, strong men, fully grown or young . . . and they branded them with a red-hot iron at once near the mouth, on the jaw, round the lips.' The Aztec text is in Garibay, *Llave de Náhuatl* (Otumba 1940) pp. 151–152.

33 Muñoz Camargo, p. 116.

34 Muñoz Camargo, p. 104, describes the Tlaxcaltecs of the sixteenth century, disappointed and bitter, reduced to the same condition as the other Indians, yet boasting with much 'braggadocio and foolishness' of the decisive rôle that they had played in the fall of Tenochtitlan.

35 There are few subjects as interesting as the causes for the defeat of the Mexicans in 1521. Unlike Arnold J. Toynbee, who thinks that the Mexican civilisation practically fell of itself, I maintain that it was in point of fact murdered. (*Note sur la meurtre des civilisations*, in *Liberté de l'Esprit*, no. 22, Paris 1951 pp. 166–167.) At this point, one may repeat the observation of Spengler, 'This culture is a unique example of death by violence. It did not languish; it was neither oppressed nor frustrated; but it was assassinated in its prime, cut off as a flower might be cut off by a passer-

by.' (*Déclin de l'Occident*, Paris 1948 [Gallimard], vol. II p. 46.)

The success of the Spaniards may be assigned to four sets of causes:

1 Military causes, which have been treated here.
2 Biological causes. Smallpox was brought in by a Negro from Cuba, and the epidemic claimed thousands of victims in this population which knew nothing of the disease. The emperor Cuitlahuac died of it after reigning only eighty days.
3 Religious causes. At the outset, the Spaniards were very much helped by the belief (apparently shared by Motecuhzoma) that Cortés and his soldiers were the god Quetzalcoatl and his suite.
4 Political causes. The conquerors would never have attained their ends if they had not been so greatly helped by the Tlaxcaltecs and other Indians, particularly the followers of the pretender Ixtlilxochitl at Texcoco. All these Indians, whose thought and reasoning worked only within the frame of reference of the autonomous city-state, saw this war as nothing more than an ordinary struggle between cities: apart from a few far-sighted men like the younger Xicotencatl (killed by Cortés) none of them suspected that they were in the presence of an enemy who was determined to annihilate their political autonomy, their religion and their civilisation. Their eyes were opened only when they found themselves plunged into the same slavery as that which had first been imposed upon the defeated Aztecs. But then it was too late.

CHAPTER SEVEN

CIVILISED LIFE

1 André Thevet, *Histoyre du Méchique*, an unpublished sixteenth-century French manuscript printed by E. de Jonghe in *Journal de la Société des Americanistes*, vol. II (Paris 1905) pp. 8 ff.

2 Francisco Ramos de Cárdenas, *Descripción de Querétaro* (1582) published by Primo F. Velázquez, *Colección de documentos para la historia de San Luis Potosí* (San Luis Potosí 1897) pp. 12–13. This author particularly mentions an Otomí *pochtecatl* from Nopallan who 'went to sell his goods among the Chichimec Indians who were in a state of war with the province (of Xilotepec) and would not submit to any authority. He took them clothes made from the thread which is obtained from a tree or plant called *magey* [*sic*] and he took salt, which is a thing much sought after by them . . . and they gave him in exchange the skins of deer, lions, jaguars, hares . . . and bows and arrows.'

3 In the Spanish text of Sahagún, vol. III p. 117, the word *teochichimeca* is translated by the expression *del todo barbados*, an obvious error for *del todo bárbaros*, 'completely barbarous'. The prefix *teo-*, literally 'divine', often has the sense of 'to the highest degree' or 'pre-eminently'.

4 The exact meaning of *Zacachichimeca* is prairie-savages. (*Zacatl* = grass, prairie.)

5 Sahagún, vol. III p. 117.

6 Ibid., pp. 118–119.

7 *De Natura Rerum*, V. 967.

8 *Crónica Mexicayotl*, p. 14, '*Auh inicompa cenca huecahuaque inicompa catca onoco Chichimeca Azteca in Aztlán ontzon xihuitl ipan matlacpohual xihuitl ipan matlactli onnahui xihuitl iniuh neztica intlapohual huehuetque, inic nican yehual nemi* – for a very long time they stayed there, they lived there at Aztlán, the Aztec Chichimecs, for twice four hundred years, and

ten times twenty years, and fourteen years, according
to the account of the ancients, and then they began
their march hither.'

9 Ibid., p. 18.

10 Paul Kirchhoff, *Los recolectores-cazadores del Norte de
México*, in *El Norte de México y el Sur de Estados
Unidos*, (Mexico 1943) pp. 133–144.

11 Xolotl is no doubt a mythical character, the symbol of
various barbarous chiefs of the period. His traditional
name is that of the dog-god which is one of the forms
of Quetzalcoatl. When Quetzalcoatl vanished underground, into the world of death, to reappear, it was in
the shape of Xolotl that he did so: and as we know,
the dog was also the companion of the dead. On the
plane of history, the Toltec civilisation (Quetzalcoatl)
vanished to be reborn in a new form (Xolotl).

12 See Ixtlilxochitl, *Historia Chichimeca*, particularly
pp. 57 ff. and pp. 73 ff.

13 See *Mapa Tlotzin*, a pictographic manuscript which
shows the old Chichimecs and their first contacts with
the settled people, *Anales del Museo Nacional de
México*, vol. III (Mexico 1886) pp. 304–320 (with a
reproduction of the manuscript).

14 Sahagún, vol. III p. 144. On these civilised nations
of the east, see particularly Walter Krickeberg, *Los
Totonaca* (Mexico 1933) pp. 119, 125; and Paul
Kirchhoff, *Los Pueblos de la historia Tolteca-Chichimeca:
sus migraciones y parentescos*, in *Revista mexicana de
estudios antropológicos*, vol. IV, no. 1–2, (Mexico
1940) pp. 77–104.

15 The contempt of the Aztecs for the Otomí showed
in everyday phrases: ' "Are you an Otomí, that you
do not understand what you are told? Are you not
perhaps a real Otomí?" Awkward and clumsy people
were insulted thus.' Sahagún, vol. III pp. 124, 132.

16 This term was applied to various tribes, particularly
those between Tehuacán and the coast of the Gulf.
Popoloca, verb, means 'to speak a barbaric language':
Molina, *Vocabulario de la lengua Mexicana* (1571),

(facsimile edition, Leipzig 1880) p. 83 verso, Mexican part.

17 Sahagún, vol. III p. 133. This refers to the Yopi or Tlappanecs of the mountainous region on the borders of the present states of Guerrero and Oaxaca.

18 *Codex Florentino*, vol. III p. 58.

19 Sahagún, vol. II p. 137.

20 Ibid., p. 137.

21 Ibid., p. 138.

22 Ibid., pp. 138–139.

23 Ibid., p. 143.

24 Ibid., pp. 146–149.

25 Angel María K. Garibay, *Historia de la Literatura náhuatl*, (Mexico 1953), pp. 415 ff.

26 Ibid., pp. 442–443.

27 Ignacio Dávila Garibi, *Epítome de raíces nahuas*, in *Investigaciones lingüísticas*, vol. V, no. 1–2 (Mexico 1938), p. 187.

28 Rémi Siméon, *Estudios gramaticales del idioma náhuatl* (Mexico 1902) p. 26: Garibay, *Llave del Náhuatl* (Otumba 1940) p. 44.

29 Sahagún, vol. II p. 154.

30 Ibid., pp. 363, 375.

31 *Crónica Mexicayotl*, pp. 132–133. By command of Motecuhzoma I the great dike was built to protect the city from the waters of the lake. While the masons worked, the emperor's brother ostentatiously sang and beat his drum. 'Who is it that is singing and playing like that?' asked the emperor. 'It is your brother, the *tlacateccatl*,' they answered. 'What will the men of the shore and the men of the dry land say, since they have all come to work here, and they see this idler (literally 'dead hand' – *mamiqui*) covering us with shame?' cried Motecuhzoma; and he gave orders to kill Ueue Zacatzin.

32 Ixtlilxochitl, *Historia Chichimeca*, pp. 96, 105, 119–120, etc. Tezozomoc, vol. I p. 23. The *Anales de Cuauhtitlán, Codex Chimalpopoca* (Mexico 1945) pp. 44–45, give a list of the crimes ordered by Tezozomoc and his son.

33 Ixtlilxochitl, *Historia Chichimeca*, p. 215.

34 Pomar, Relación de Texcoco, p. 35.

35 *Codex Florentino*, vol. II p. 92.

36 Tezozomoc, vol. II p. 64, 'Everything was in such disorder that Auitzotl feared that he would be killed by his own subjects.'

37 Sahagún, vol. II pp. 83–92.

38 Ibid.

39 Ixtlilxochitl, *Historia Chichimeca*, pp. 231–234.

40 Tezozomoc, vol. II pp. 81–82.

41 There is no question here of treating Mexican art in general, nor of giving its history. The reader is referred to the work of Salvador Toscano, *Arte precolombino de México y de la América Central* (Mexico 1952). See also Paul Westheim, *Arte antiguo de México* (Mexico 1950) and *México en el Arte* (special French edition, Mexico [National Institute of Fine Arts] 1952).

42 As well as the preceding works, see André Malraux, *Le Musée imaginaire de la Sculpture mondiale* (commentary upon the Mexican sculptures by Jacques Soustelle) (Paris 1952, [Gallimard]); Ignacio Marquina, *Arquitectura prehispánica* (Mexica 1951); Alfonso Caso, *Arte prehispánico*, in *Veinte Siglos de Arte mexicano* (Mexico 1940), pp. 26–70; C. A. Burland, *Art and Life in ancient Mexico*, (Oxford 1948); Franz Feutchtwanger and Irmgard Groth Kimball, *L'Art ancien du Mexique* (Paris 1954 [Braun]); Paul Rivet and Gisèle Freund, *Mexique précolombien* (Neuchâtel 1954). The reader is also referred to the illustrated catalogue of the exhibition of Mexican art (*Musée d'Art Modern*, Paris 1952).

43 Marshall H. Saville, *Tizoc, great lord of the Aztecs* (1481–1486), in *Contributions from the Museum of the American Indian, Heye Foundation*, vol. VII, no. 4, (New York 1924). Description of the statuette, p. 40. Reproduction, pl. LIV and LVIII.

44 Tezozomoc, vol. II pp. 209–210.

45 On the paintings of Teotihuacán, see Agustín Villagra, *Teotihuacán, sus pinturas murales*, in *Anales del*

Instituto Nacional de Antropología e Historia, vol. V (Mexico 1952) pp. 67–74. On the frescoes of Tizatlán, Alfonso Caso, *Nota arqueológica sobre las ruinas de Tizatlán, Tlaxcala,* in *México Antiguo,* vol. II, no. 11–12 (Mexico 1927) pp. 279–280. On Malinalco, José García Payón, *Los Monumentos arqueológicos de Malinalco, Estado de México,* in *Revista mexicana de Estudios antropológicos,* vol. VIII, no. 1–2–3 (Mexico 1946) pp. 5–64.

46 Cf. C. A. Burland, *Magic Books from Mexico* (Penguin edition, 1953).

47 The craftsmen's methods are described in Seler's translation of the Aztec text in Sahagún, vol. V pp. 195–239. Cf. Vaillant, Artists and *Craftsmen in ancient Central America,* (New York, National Museum of Natural History, 1935).

48 Díaz del Castillo, vol. I p. 161.

49 Sahagún, vol. IV pp. 138–139.

50 Clavigero, vol. II pp. 341–343.

51 It should be clearly understood that Nahuatl was the language common to Texcoco and Mexico, but that it was spoken more elegantly at Texcoco.

52 Muñoz Camargo, p. 25.

53 Antonio Peñafiel, *Nombres geográficos de Mexico,* vol. II (atlas), pl. XX and XXXI. This work also contains a large number of examples of the joint use of ideograms and phonograms.

54 '*Uel nemachtiloia in cuicatl in quilhuia teocuicatl, amoxxotoca. Ioan uel nemachtiloia in tonalpoalli, in temicamatl, ioan in xiuhamatl.*' (*Codex Florentino,* vol. III p. 65.) The ancient Mexicans attached great importance to warning dreams. The tyrant Tezozomoc caused Nezaualcoyotl to be murdered after he had dreamt that he was being attacked by an eagle, a tiger, a snake and a coyote, which made him fear the young prince's vengeance.

55 John H. Cornyn, *Aztec Literature,* in *XXVIIe Congrès international des Américanistes* (Mexico 1939) vol. II p. 324.

56 On this subject see:
   Angel María K. Garibay, *Historia de la Literatura náhuatl* (Mexico 1953); *La Poesía lírica azteca* (Mexico 1937); *Poema de travesuras (xochicuicatl cuecuechtli)*, in *Tlalocan*, vol. III, no. 2, (Mexico 1952) pp. 142–167.
   Daniel G. Brinton, *Ancient Nahuatl Poetry* (Philadelphia 1890).
   John H. Cornyn, op. cit. and *The Song of Quetzalcoatl*, in *Mexican Folkways*, vol. IV, no. 2 (Mexico 1928), pp. 78–90.

57 Garibay, *Llave del Náhuatl* (Otumba 1940) p. 111.

58 Ibid., p. 113.

59 Muñoz Camargo, p. 143.

60 Ixtlilxochitl, *Relaciones*, p. 326: Torquemada, vol. I pp. 146–147.

61 See for example the poem published by Brinton as no. XVIII in *Ancient Nahuatl Poetry*, p. 104.

62 Garibay, *Historia de la Literatura náhuatl*, p. 66.

63 Cornyn, *Aztec Literature*, pp. 328–331.

64 The Aztec religious poems, published without translation in the original text by Sahagún (vol. I pp. 244–252) have been edited and translated
   in English (very faulty translation) by Daniel G. Brinton, *Rig-Veda americanus*, (Philadelphia 1890):
   in German by Eduard Seler, *Die religiösen Gesänge der alten Mexikaner*, in *Gesammelte Abhandlungen*, vol. II, 1904, pp. 959–1107:
   in English, by Anderson and Dibble, *Codex Florentino*, vol. II pp. 207–214.
   There is a Spanish version in Sahagún, vol. V pp. 13–192.

65 Hymn sung every eight years, at the feast of Atamalqualiztli. Sahagún, vol. V pp. 134 ff.: *Codex Florentino*, vol. II p. 212.

66 Song of Uitzilopochtli. Sahagún, vol. V p. 13: *Codex Florentino*, vol. II p. 207.

67 Song of the mother of the gods. Sahagún, vol. V p. 52: *Codex Florentino* vol. II p. 208.

68 Song of Ciuacoatl. Sahagún, vol. V p. 119: *Codex Florentino*, vol. II p. 211.
69 Song of Chicomecoatl. Sahagún, vol. V p. 158: *Codex Florentino*, vol. II p. 213.
70 *Codex Florentino*, vol. III pp. 13–36. Cornyn, *The Song of Quetzalcoatl*. It is obvious that an epico-mythic cycle about the Plumed Serpent existed: fragments of it are to be found in Brinton, *Ancient Nahuatl Poetry*, p. 104, and in the *Anales de Cuauhtitlán, Codex Chimalpopoca* (Mexico 1945) pp. 7–11.
71 Garibay, *Historia de la Literatura náhuatl*, pp. 331 ff.
72 Ibid., p. 377.
73 Garibay, *Poesía lírica azteca*, p. 34.
74 Garibay, *Historia de la Literatura náhuatl*, p. 176.
75 Ibid., pp. 184–185.
76 Ibid., p. 187.
77 Garibay, *Poesía lírica azteca*, pp. 39–40.
78 Motolinía, p. 344.

BIBLIOGRAPHY

BIBLIOGRAPHY

Many references are given in the Notes: here we refer only
to the most frequently-quoted works or to those which treat
some of the chief subjects of the book in a general manner.

Anales de Cuauhtitlán: facsimile of the Aztec text, with
Spanish translation, in *Códice Chimalpopoca* (Mexico
1945).

Anonymous Conqueror, *Relation abrégée sur la Nouvelle
Espagne*: published by H. Ternaux-Compans in *Voyages,
relations et mémoires* . . . vol. X (Paris 1838) pp. 49-105.

Barlow, R. H., *The Extent of the Empire of the Culhua
Mexica* (University of California Press, Berkeley, 1949).

Boban, Eugène, *Documents pour servir à l'histoire du Mexique.
Catalogue raisonné de la collection de M. Eugène Goupil
(ancienne collection J. M. A. Aubin)* (Paris 1891) 2 vols.,
1 atlas.

Caso, Alfonso, *La Religión de los Aztecas* (Mexico 1936).

Caso, Alfonso, *El Pueblo del Sol* (Mexico 1953).

Chimalpahin Quauhtlehuanitzin (Domingo Francisco de
San Anton Muñon), *Anales* (6th and 7th accounts translated by Rémi Siméon) (Paris 1889).

Clavigero, Francisco Javier, *Historia antigua de México.
Primera edición del original escrito en castellano por el
autor* (Mexico [Porrua] 1945) 4 vols.

Codex Azcatitlan. A pictorial manuscript reproduced in
facsimile by the *Journal de la Société des Américanistes,
nouvelle série*, vol. XXXVIII (Paris 1949). Commentary
in Spanish by R. H. Barlow, pp. 101-135.

*Codex Borbonicus. Manuscrit mexicain de la Bibliothèque du
Palais-Bourbon . . . avec un commentaire explicatif par
E. T. Hamy* (Paris 1899).

*Codex Florentino. Florentine Codex, General History of the
Things of New Spain (by) Fray Bernardino de Sahagún.*
Translated from the Aztec into English by Arthur J. O.
Anderson and Charles E. Dibble. Book I, *The Gods*
(Santa Fe, New Mexico, 1950): Book II, *The Ceremonies*
(1951): Book III, *The Origin of the Gods* (1952).

Codex of 1576, published under the title of *Histoire de la*

Nation mexicaine . . . A pictorial manuscript with Nahuatl text. (Paris [Leroux] 1893).

Codex Magliabecchiano. Il codice Magliabecchiano XIII.3 della R. Biblioteca Nazionale di Firenze riprodotto in fotocromografia . . . (Rome [Stabilimento Danesi] 1904).

Codex Mendoza. Edited by J. Cooper Clark (London 1938) 3 vol.

Codex Telleriano-Remensis. Manuscrit mexicain du cabinet de Ch.-M. Le Tellier, archeveque de Reims à la Bibliothèque Nationale (*MS mexicain no.* 385). *Reproduit en photochromographie. Introduction par le Dr. E. T. Hamy* (Paris 1899).

Cortés, Hernán, *Cartas de Relación.* Published by Francisco Antonio Lorenzana under the title of *Historia de Méjico* (New York 1828).

Crónica Mexicayotl. (A chronicle attributed to Tezozomoc). Text in Aztec: Spanish translation by Adrián León (Mexico 1949).

Díaz del Castillo, Bernal, *Historia verdadera de la Conquista de la Nueva España* (Mexico 1950) 3 vols.

Durán, Fr. Diego, *Historia de las Indias de Nueva España y Islas de Terra firme* (Mexico 1867) 2 vols., 1 atlas.

Garibay, Angel María K., *Historia de la Literatura náhuatl, Primera parte (etapa autónoma: de c.* 1430 *a* 1521) (Mexico [Porrúa] 1953).

Historia de los Mexicanos por sus pinturas. MS published by Joaquín García Icazbalceta in *Nueva Colección de documentos para la historia de México,* vol. III (Mexico 1891) pp. 228–263.

Ixtlilxochitl (don Fernando de Alva), *Obras históricas, publicadas y anotadas por Alfredo Chavero:* vol. I, *Relaciones* (Mexico 1891), vol. II, *Historia Chichimeca* (Mexico 1892).

Mapa Tlotzin. A pictorial MS published in *Anales del Museo Nacional de México,* vol. III (Mexico 1886) pp. 304–320.

Marquina, Ignacio, *Arquitectura prehispánica* (Mexico 1951).

Molina, Fr. Alonso de, *Vocabulario de la lengua mexicana* (Mexico 1571). Facsimile edition, Leipzig 1880.

Motolinía, Fr. Toribio, *Memoriales* (Mexico 1903).

Muñoz Camargo, Diego, *Historia de Tlaxcala* (Mexico 1892).

Pomar, Juan Bautista, *Relación de Texcoco* (1582): published by Joaquín García Icazbalceta in *Nueva Colección de documentos para la historia de México*, vol. III (Mexico 1891).

Prescott, William H., *History of the Conquest of Mexico* (Philadelphia 1864), 3 vols.

Sahagún, Fr. Bernardino de, *Historia general de las Cosas de Nueva España* (Mexico [Pedro Robredo] 1938) 5 vols.

Seler, Eduard, *Gesammelte Abhandlungen zur Amerikanischen Sprach- und Alterthumskunde* (Berlin 1903–1923) 5 vols.

Soustelle, Jacques, *La Pensée cosmologique des anciens Mexicains* (Paris [Hermann] 1840).

Tapia, Andrés de, *Relación hecha por el Sr. Andrés de Tapia sobre la Conquista de México:* published by Joaquín García Icazbalceta in *Colección de documentos para la historia de México*, vol. II (Mexico 1866) pp. 554–594.

Tezozomoc, Alvaro, *Histoire du Mexique*, translated from an unpublished manuscript by H. Ternaux-Compans (Paris 1853) 2 vols.

Torquemada, Fr. Juan de, *Veinte i un libros rituales i Monarchia indiana* (Madrid 1723) 3 vols.

Toscano, Salvador, *Arte precolombino de México y de la América central* (Mexico [Universidad Nacional Autónoma] 1952).

Zurita, Alonso de, *Breve y sumaria relación de los señores y maneras y diferencias que había de ellos en la Nueva España . . . por el Dr Alonso de Corita, oidor que fué de la Real Audiencia que reside en la muy insigne y gran ciudad de México de la Nueva España:* published by Joaquín García Icazbalceta in *Nueva Colección de documentos para la historia de México*, vol. III (Mexico 1891) pp. 73–228.

INDEX

INDEX